# 100 THINGS
# VIKINGS FANS
## SHOULD KNOW & DO
## BEFORE THEY DIE

# 100 THINGS VIKINGS FANS SHOULD KNOW & DO BEFORE THEY DIE

Mark Craig

TRIUMPH
BOOKS

Library of Congress Cataloging-in-Publication Data

Names: Craig, Mark, author.
Title: 100 things Vikings fans should know & do before they die / Mark Craig.
Other titles: One hundred things Vikings fans should know and do before they die
Description: Chicago, Illinois : Triumph Books LLC, [2016]
Identifiers: LCCN 2016016923 | ISBN 9781629371955
Subjects: LCSH: Minnesota Vikings (Football team)—History. | Minnesota Vikings (Football team)—Miscellanea.
Classification: LCC GV956.M5 C73 2016 | DDC 796.332/6409776579—dc23
LC record available at https://lccn.loc.gov/2016016923

This book is available in quantity at special discounts for your group or organization. For further information, contact:

**Triumph Books LLC**
814 North Franklin Street
Chicago, Illinois 60610
(312) 337-0747
www.triumphbooks.com

Printed in U.S.A.
ISBN: 978-1-62937-195-5
Design by Patricia Frey
Photos courtesy of USA TODAY Sports Images unless otherwise indicated

*To my wife, Tammy; daughters, Jessica and Caleigh; and mom, Iona; thanks for helping me in so many ways—once it finally hit me that 100 chapters is a lot of chapters. Caleigh, you no longer have to help me count them down. To my readers over the many years, thanks, and I hope you enjoy the book.*

# Contents

# Foreword

The Minnesota Vikings have a rich and storied history. Since 1961 they have fielded some of the most talented players, have been led by extraordinary coaches, and have been cheered on by the most amazing fans. From the cold, snowy days at Met Stadium to the thunderous noise of the Metrodome and now—onto a *new* era in a *new* stadium—the Vikings are built on the blood, sweat, and tears of all those who have ever worn the purple and gold.

In 1988, when I was drafted by the Vikings, I didn't know what to expect. As a kid growing up in Arizona, I knew about the Purple People Eaters—as well as Bud Grant and Fran Tarkenton—but I had no idea how that rich history would impact my NFL experience.

When I arrived as a rookie, the amount of talent in the Vikings locker room was insane. It was a team shaped by the Bud Grant legacy of honor, discipline, toughness, and a team-first attitude. From the moment I stepped on the practice field, the message from every coach and veteran player was crystal clear. You had to prove yourself worthy of wearing the Vikings jersey—and you had to do it every day. They demanded excellence. They demanded respect for the team, the game, and for the opportunity you were being given.

I was lucky to be surrounded with a talented group of veteran linemen to learn from. With Gary Zimmerman, Kirk Lowdermilk, Tim Irwin, and Dave Huffman in your face, you learned and learned quickly. You definitely did not want to let them down. I spent hours watching film of Zim and Chris Doleman go at it in practice and was amazed. Then I had to face Keith Millard every day. He was outstanding and was even named the Defensive Player of the Year in 1989.

In 1990 John Randle arrived, and we had some epic battles. He went just as hard in practice as he did in games. He barked and screamed and did all his crazy stuff. The o-line always looked at me and said, "Randall, you've got to shut him up." In the back of my mind, I was thinking, *What if I lose?* But I *hate* losing, so I would dig deep and find a way to stop him. During our playing days, I never let him know how hard he made me work, but I tell him now that he helped put me into the Hall of Fame. After dealing with guys like Millard, Doleman, and Randle in practice, gameday seemed easy! There's no doubt that we made each other better.

I was also fortunate to be drafted by a team with one of the best o-line coaches in the business: Johnny Michels. Tough and demanding, he was chiseled out of the same stone as Bud Grant. The first time I met him, he told me no rookie would ever play on his offensive line. Even as a first-round draft pick, I thought he was going to cut me every day of training camp.

Johnny gave you that tough love, but he was an incredible teacher. I think he knew more about offensive line play than any other human being in the world. The proof of his coaching excellence can be found in Canton. I think he may be one of the only position coaches with four Hall of Fame players: Ron Yary, Zimmerman, me, and Mick Tingelhoff.

Being selected to the Hall of Fame was beyond my wildest dreams. My favorite part of the Hall of Fame experience has been getting to know many of the greats who came before me, the guys who built the league into what it is today. I love hearing their stories. I just sit back and soak it all up. The opportunity to share in the living history of the NFL is priceless. It's also given me the chance to build friendships with some of the Vikings greats. I feel honored to spend time with guys like Paul Krause, Yary, Tingelhoff, Carl Eller, Alan Page, Fran Tarkenton, and Coach Grant. It's still hard to believe that I'm a part of that club.

In addition to these legends, thanks to Mark Craig of the *Minneapolis Star Tribune* and author of this book, the Vikings have been on a roll with recent Hall of Fame enshrinees. I first met Mark in 2009. He was tasked with presenting my case to the Hall of Fame Selection Committee. As you might imagine, it's not easy to successfully garner 80 percent of the vote for any one finalist. But I've heard from others in the selection room that Mark is relentless. They say he's a master of Vikings history and is well-versed in all things NFL. He does his homework—meticulously researching every detail and carefully crafting his position. He skillfully presents each case and is well-prepared for any challenges and passionately defends his position.

Thanks in no small part to Mark's efforts, I was selected for the Hall of Fame in 2009. Randle was selected in 2010, followed by Doleman (2012), Cris Carter (2013), and Tingelhoff (2015). I'm sure glad Mark Craig is on our team! As long as he's in that room fighting for us, I think there will be more Vikings who get the "Call to the Hall."

While there were many magical moments in my 14-year career, the thing I'm asked about the most is our 1998 season. It was an amazing year with the highest of highs and the lowest of lows. To go 15–1 in this league is no easy task, but we had a special group of guys. As players, we felt we could do anything. It started with Brad Johnson at quarterback. We had a great o-line, Robert Smith was on fire, Jake Reed and Cris Carter were invincible, and Randy Moss was lethal in his rookie season. When Brad went down to injury, Randall Cunningham stepped in, and we didn't skip a beat. We felt that our offense was unstoppable. On the other side of the ball, our defense could shut down anyone it wanted. The stars were all aligned. That's why the overtime loss to the Atlanta Falcons was so devastating. It was there for our taking, and we didn't find a way to finish it. That season was truly amazing. It was by far the most fun I ever had as a Viking, but at the same time, it was the most disappointing. I would've loved to bring a Super Bowl title to Minnesota. The fans deserved it, the Vikings organization deserved it. I still believe it will happen and, like all Minnesotans, I hope I'm there to help celebrate the moment.

The second most popular question I get is why a kid from the deserts of Arizona has made his home in the cold of Minnesota. It's the people. The quality of life is amazing. The people who fill the stadium every week to cheer on the Vikings are some of the greatest fans there are. I always tried to earn their respect with my play on the field and through my actions off the field. During my playing career, I started working in the elementary school classroom. I wanted kids to know the importance of education. When I retired I took a full-time job as an elementary school basic skills instructor. I feel like the luckiest man in the world because I've been blessed to have two careers I love. I have the people of Minnesota to thank for that.

So, to all the Vikings fans out there, I salute you. It was an honor and privilege to wear the purple and gold. The passion, support, and belief you give this team is what makes Minnesota a special place to play and live. I hope this book brings you great joy and allows you to celebrate many old traditions as well as build new ones.

Skol Vikings!

—Randall McDaniel
Hall of Fame offensive lineman
12-year Vikings veteran

# Introduction

The typical Vikings fan is Charlie Brown barreling toward the perfectly placed football with passion, persistence, and renewed trust that Lucy absolutely will not pull it away in the final seconds. Not this time. No way.

And then, well, you know, as Chuck takes his mighty swing, he senses that familiar feeling of impending doom. He knows he'll be flat on his back with another tale of missed opportunity. But he also knows he'll get back up and try again. The list includes four Super Bowl losses in eight seasons—including Super Bowl IV as a 12-point favorite—Drew Pearson's push-off in '75, Darrin Nelson's drop in '88, Brett Favre's interception in '09, Gary Anderson's Wide Left I in '99, and Blair Walsh's Wide Left II in '16. Sorry, I'll stop there.

I didn't grow up a Vikings fan. I was born in northeast Ohio, in 1965, a year after the Browns won their last major championship. So don't feel too jinxed, Vikings fans. In my world the sentence: "I just hope the Browns reach the Super Bowl in my lifetime" went from punch line to serious query as 50 Super Bowls have come and gone.

As a kid soaking up NFL football in the '70s, I always was fascinated by the Vikings. John Wayne could have formed any posse he wanted and not been any tougher than Bud Grant and his Purple People Eaters. The Minnesotans were ice-breathing monsters who stalked their prey in a perpetual cloud of frozen breath. And when they weren't hunting their opponent's offense, their own quarterback, Fran Tarkenton, was a must-see magician with tricks no one had ever seen before.

Naturally, my desire to move *south* from Cleveland instead led my wife, Tammy, and me to the Twin Cities with our four-year-old daughter, Jessica, in 1999. A second daughter, Caleigh, was born in 2004 with an oddly inherent love of anything purple and no hint of liking orange and brown. We're Minnesotans now, though Ahmad Rashad's "Miracle at the Met" catch still stings some 36 years later. Shhh, don't tell anyone.

My first experience covering the Vikings for the *Minneapolis Star Tribune* was the 2003 season. Mike Tice's team jumped out to a 6–0 start and faltered but still clung to first place in the NFC North until the final play of the season at Sun Devil Stadium against a 3–12 Arizona Cardinals team. As time expired that afternoon, Cardinals receiver Nate Poole knocked the Vikings from the playoff race with a sucker punch touchdown catch. Considering the Vikings had led the division for all but the final play that season, Poole's catch was an instant classic in the snakebite section of Minnesota's proud franchise. Lucy had pulled the ball away again. But a year later, the Vikings and their fans were back in the scrum with fists flying, competing as hard as always. They made the playoffs at 8–8, were given no shot of winning a playoff game in Green Bay, and then upset the Packers as Randy Moss pretended to moon the crowd at Lambeau Field.

No, the Vikings haven't won a Super Bowl. But they've been a consistently competitive force ever since Grant said yes to general manager Jim Finks and joined the team on March 10, 1967. Since the 1970 merger, the Vikings rank third in playoff appearances (26), fourth in division titles (17), and seventh in victories (397). So Grant's arrival was, to me, the easy choice when I ranked the order of chapters of *100 Things Vikings Fans Should Know & Do Before They Die*.

In ranking the other 99, I wanted to intermingle the many different eras since the team's inception in 1961. This is a franchise that has had some amazing characters from Marshall to Moss, Page to Peterson, Carl Eller to Cris Carter. Along the way there have been many stories, highlights, Hall of Famers, and, yes, painful moments to remember.

You'll find some stories familiar and hopefully some that you'll be reading for the first time. I want to thank Hall of Fame guard Randall McDaniel for taking the time to write the foreword for this book. Randall is one of my favorite former players because of his perfect blend of greatness and humility. He went to 12 Pro Bowls in 14 seasons but would rather talk about the difference he's trying to make now as a basic skills instructor for K-5 students in the Twin Cities.

Typically, Randall's students don't even know he played for the Vikings. But most of them are in the next wave of young fans who will be going to games at U.S. Bank Stadium for decades to come. As Randall tells them and others, the future looks bright, and eventually the Vikings will return to the Super Bowl and win one. Just line up and try again.

# 1 Bud Grant Arrives

Harry Peter "Bud" Grant Jr. didn't blast in from Canada as much as he eased across the border, like a new marshall swaggering through swinging doors to an unruly saloon as the chorus stops and heads turn to face those steely blue eyes of authority. "What made Bud such a great coach was his unique style of saying nothing," Vikings defensive end Bob Lurtsema told the *Minneapolis Star Tribune*. "Just one look from Bud would maintain your 110 percent effort."

On March 9, 1967, the Vikings were 84 games old. They were 29–51–4 with no playoff appearances and no head coach. Legendary players with names like Marshall, Tingelhoff, and Eller were starving for Grant's organized vision and calm confidence. Six seasons of Norm Van Brocklin's mood swings, volatile temper, and shoot-from-the-lip belittlement had taken a toll and created the kind of toxicity that led quarterback Fran Tarkenton to demand a trade before Van Brocklin resigned and then stick to it afterward because he "didn't want Van Brocklin's blood on my hands."

March 10, 1967 was a new day, and it would become the most important one in the history of a Vikings franchise that was born on January 28, 1960. Owner Max Winter had tried unsuccessfully to hire Grant away from the Winnipeg Blue Bombers before the Vikings began play in 1961. But this time on March 10, with four CFL Grey Cup titles to his credit, Grant said yes to Winter and general manager Jim Finks, who had been an adversary of Grant's in the CFL.

Four games into his Vikings career, Grant was 0–4 overall and 0–3 at home. He had lost to the San Francisco 49ers, Los Angeles Rams, Chicago Bears, and St. Louis Cardinals by a combined score of 117–55. And on deck were Vince Lombardi's Green Bay Packers. They hadn't lost in 11 games, including a win over the Kansas City Chiefs in Super Bowl I. But in a cold October drizzle at Milwaukee County Stadium, Grant beat Lombardi 10–7 with quarterback Joe Kapp completing only two passes and the defense setting up 10 fourth-quarter points with a pair of interceptions. The Packers, of course, would go on to win Super Bowl II. "It didn't make any difference if it was the Packers or the Little Sisters of the Poor," Grant said after the game. "It was important that we win today. It was the timing. We're not that bad…Now, we should start moving forward a little."

And they did. They reached the playoffs in Grant's second season and the Super Bowl in his third season. Grant coached from 1967 to 1983, retired, and came back for one season in 1985 after Les Steckel posted a then-franchise-record 13 losses. In 18 seasons Grant went 168–108–5 (.609). From 1969 to 1976, he went

## Grant, the Athlete

Born May 20, 1927 in Superior, Wisconsin, Grant was stricken with polio at age eight but turned to athletics and became a three-sport star in football, basketball, and baseball at Superior Central High. He went to the University of Minnesota, starring in basketball and football while picking up extra cash pitching for baseball teams in the local town-ball leagues. In 1950 the Philadelphia Eagles drafted him 14th overall as an end, while the Minneapolis Lakers selected him as a 6'3" forward in the fourth round of the NBA draft. Always the financial pragmatist, Grant turned down the Eagles' offer of $7,500 because he knew he could make more money in Minneapolis as a backup with the Lakers and hired gun as a pitcher in summer town ballgames.

Grant played two seasons with the Lakers and won an NBA championship in 1950. Then he played two seasons for the Eagles, leading them in sacks one year and 56 catches (second most in the NFL) as a receiver for 997 yards and seven touchdowns. When the Eagles wouldn't pay Grant the $9,000 he sought for a third season, he bolted to Canada for $10,000.

95–31–1 while earning seven of his 11 division titles, the last NFL title before the AFL-NFL merger, three post-merger NFC championships, and four Super Bowl appearances. "Bud Grant has more leadership ability, more common sense than any person I have ever known or been around in my life," Tarkenton told the *Minneapolis Star Tribune* as Grant was preparing to enter the Pro Football Hall of Fame in 1994.

Grant didn't win a Super Bowl, but he forever set the standard for one of the NFL's most consistently competitive franchises. Heading into the 2016 season, the Vikings had reached the playoffs 28 times. Since the 1970 merger, the Vikings ranked third in playoff appearances (26), fourth in division titles (17), and seventh in victories (397).

In 1957, at age 29, with no head coaching experience, Grant went from player to coach in Winnipeg. In 10 seasons, he went 118–64–3 with four championships. Grant, of course, would fall short on the NFL's big stage. His playoff record of 10–12 included lopsided losses to the Chiefs in Super Bowl IV, the Miami Dolphins in Super Bowl VIII, the Pittsburgh Steelers in Super Bowl IX, and the Oakland Raiders in Super Bowl XI. In those four losses, the Vikings were outscored 95–34 while being outrushed by an average margin of 216–57.

As the painful losses have piled up over the years, fans have become more guarded and suspicious of the inevitable trap door. They still cheer like mad and hope for the best, but they definitely expect the worst. "I probably wouldn't say this if I was living in Minnesota," former Vikings left tackle Todd Steussie said. "But Vikings fans enjoy griping about a loss as much as they do celebrating a win. There's a level of mistrust that's been built in for generations. They still want to be fans. But at the same time, they're saying, 'I'm not going to let you guys get my hopes up just to have you burn me again.'"

# 2 Super Bowl IV

The hot-air balloon race scheduled as part of the pregame festivities for Super Bowl IV never went off as planned. On a dreary day in New Orleans, the balloon representing the NFL and carrying a Vikings mascot barely got off the ground before crashing into the stands inside Tulane Stadium. Things went downhill from there.

Favored by 12 points, the Vikings were dominated by a Kansas City Chiefs team that made the most out of coach Hank Stram's astute gameplans. The Vikings threw three interceptions, lost two fumbles, and were a step slow throughout a 23–7 loss in their first of four Super Bowl appearances. "We made more mental mistakes in one game than we did in one season," safety Karl Kassulke told reporters after the game.

It wasn't supposed to be this way.

Bud Grant's Vikings had dominated the NFL. They went 12–2, winning 12 straight after a season-opening loss. They led the league in points scored (379) and fewest points allowed (133). They crushed the Cleveland Browns 27–7 at Metropolitan Stadium in the final NFL championship game before the AFL-NFL merger. In that game rough-and-tumble quarterback Joe Kapp, who was nicknamed "Indestructible," ran over Browns linebacker Jim Houston, sending the woozy Houston to the sideline.

Meanwhile, Stram's Chiefs had finished runner-up in the AFL's Western Division. Quarterback Len Dawson, the losing quarterback in Super Bowl I and a former five-year backup in the NFL, was underappreciated in spite of Joe Namath and the New York Jets famously upsetting the Baltimore Colts in Super Bowl III the year before.

History, of course, would be much kinder to the Chiefs. A team with seven Hall of Fame players, including five on defense, would take their Hall of Fame coach's innovative gameplans and attack the Vikings, who many sportswriters were regaling as one of the most physical teams the NFL had ever seen.

The night before the game, NFL Films convinced Stram to be miked for sound during the game, something that had never been done before. It cost NFL Films founder Ed Sabol $1,000, but it was money well spent because Stram's strutting, wisecracking chatter became part of NFL lore, much to the chagrin of Vikings fans expecting a blowout back on January 11, 1970.

One of the most famous scenes is Stram yelling, "C'mon Lenny! Pump it in there, baby! Just keep matriculating the ball down the field, boys!" He also took excessive joy in the Vikings' confusion, once yelling, "Kassulke was running around there like it was a Chinese fire drill. They don't know where [running back] Mike [Garrett] was, didn't know where he was! They look like they're flat as hell."

Stram knew the Vikings liked to use smaller, quicker center Mick Tingelhoff to take out linebackers. Stram countered with something the Vikings weren't expecting: he put 265-pound tackle Curley Culp directly over Tingelhoff in a five-man line. Culp's performance that day would help limit the Vikings' vaunted running game to 67 yards and play a significant role in helping Culp enter the Hall of Fame as a senior candidate and pioneering nose tackle decades later. "No one really cared for Hank Stram, but he had a pretty good strategy," Vikings running back Dave Osborn said in 2015. "Everybody played a 4-3 defense. Stram looked at us and knew he couldn't beat us that way. So he came out with a five-man line and two linebackers. They had someone in every crack. It was too many men. Every time Bill Brown and I got the ball in the backfield before we even made two steps, they got to us."

The Chiefs led 9–0 when Vikings kick returner Charlie West fumbled, and Kansas City recovered at the Minnesota 19. Six plays later, Garrett scored on a five-yard run on a trap draw play that Stram's cackling sideline footage captured forever. "Was it there, boys?" he yelled to his players on the sideline. "Was that there, rats? Nice going, baby! The mentor! 65 Toss Power Trap!"

Stram also was the team's offensive coordinator. He knew the Chiefs couldn't block ends Carl Eller and Jim Marshall one-on-one while throwing deep passes. He also knew their tendency to bat down shorter passes. So Stram double-teamed the ends and used shorter passes while sliding the pocket. Meanwhile, "65 Toss Power Trap" was designed to counter the aggressive pass rush of the famed Purple People Eaters' defensive front.

Grant made halftime adjustments, and the Vikings marched 69 yards in 10 plays to make it 16–7 on Osborn's four-yard run. But Dawson came right back with a 46-yard touchdown pass to Otis Taylor. "The second half, our coaches made the adjustments, and we blocked them," Osborn said. "But we were too far gone. They had us beat."

# 3 Randy and Red Resurrect a Franchise

Coach Dennis Green walked down the hall and into offensive coordinator Brian Billick's office in Winter Park, Minnesota. It was April 18, 1998, and the NFL draft was starting in less than an hour. "I think we're going to get Randy Moss," Green told Billick. For months the Vikings had talked about selecting Moss. But every conversation ended with someone saying, "Yeah, but we'll never get him, so let's move on," Billick said.

But this time Green was hearing that concerns about Moss' character would cause him to slide past 20 teams and into the Vikings' lap at No. 21. Billick looked up and this was his first thought: *What are you smoking, Denny?* But Green was clear-headed and sober. Moss, the enigmatic superstar with the rebellious attitude and checkered legal past going back to high school in West Virginia, was considered too toxic for many NFL teams. "Once we got Randy, that's when the excitement and the magic around the Vikings began," Billick said. "I don't think I even paid that much attention to the rest of the draft that year."

Like Billick, the fans knew the 6'4", 215-pound Moss was the deep threat the team needed to complete the puzzle on a team that had made the playoffs in five of Green's first six seasons but had never made it past the divisional round. The Moss pick would be remembered as the spark that resurrected interest in the Vikings. For the next 14 years, the Vikings would sell out every game at the Metrodome. "Growing up in St. Paul, I remember when the games weren't selling out," said center Matt Birk, a rookie backup in 1998. "But in 1998 it was like almost everything came together. Not only did we win, we were the sexy, exciting team. I think that appealed to more people. We got a lot of younger fans that year. The Metrodome became the hip place to be."

The Vikings set the NFL scoring record of 556 points while going 15–1 that season. The way that season ended—with a 30–27 overtime loss to the Atlanta Falcons in the NFC Championship Game—is the memory most associated with 1998. But the excitement generated that season was lasting and just plain fun. And it all started with a lanky kid from Rand, West Virginia, who was so gifted and so incredibly fast for his size that his nickname, "SuperFreak," was spot on.

Left tackle Todd Steussie remembers Moss turning heads in the huddle during a scrimmage against the New Orleans Saints in training camp. Brad Johnson, who would get hurt and be replaced by Randall Cunningham early that season, was the starting quarterback at the time. "Randy obviously had this incredible speed, and he was saying, 'Trust me, Brad, you can't overthrow me,'" Steussie said. "He said, 'I might not be there when you see me, but I'll be there when the ball gets there.' Sure enough, next play, boom, Randy goes the distance for a touchdown."

Moss would score 156 regular-season touchdowns during a 14-year career with five NFL teams, including seven years in his first stint with the Vikings and a month in his disastrous second stint in 2010. He led the league in touchdown receptions five times, including an NFL-record 23 with the 16–0 New England Patriots in 2007. His national breakout game came on a rainy October night at Lambeau Field in 1998, when he had five catches for 190 yards and two touchdowns. On Thanksgiving Day in Dallas, where Cowboys owner Jerry Jones had passed on Moss in the draft, the SuperFreak caught three balls for 163 yards and three touchdowns. Moss caught 69 passes for 1,313 yards and a league-high 17 touchdowns that season. A year later, season-ticket sales at the Metrodome increased from 43,472 to 60,025.

Moss wasn't the only larger-than-life presence that arrived in 1998. Shortly before training camp, ownership changed hands, introducing a suspicious band of Upper Midwestern fans to San Antonio businessman Red McCombs, whose Texas-sized personality and deep southern drawl blew into town serving optimism with a Purple Pride chaser. Although Minnesotans would come to distrust the out of towner because of his threats to move the team if he didn't get a new stadium, 1998 was one of the greatest honeymoons between an owner and his fanbase. "When we would do a radio show from a bar or a restaurant back in 1998 and Red would show up, he was like the Pied Piper," said Dan Barreiro, a KFAN talk show host and former *Minneapolis Star Tribune* sports columnist. "It was like the emperor has arrived."

*Vikings wide receiver Randy Moss warms up prior to a game during the 1998 season, when the rookie exploded on to the scene with 1,313 yards and 17 touchdowns.*

Steussie said it was McCombs who got the fans more involved at the Metrodome. "Everything was tied into Red showing up in '98," Steussie said. "I played there for like five years before 1998 and I didn't even know the names of the 10 co-owners we had. Then here comes this gregarious, dynamic owner running around yelling, 'Purple Pride! Purple Pride!' The fans bought into Red."

Early in the 1998 season, McCombs taped a message that was shown on the Jumbotron at the Metrodome. It was his invitation to "come on out and meet the players in the parking lot after the ballgame." "I remember looking up and seeing that," Steussie said. "I was like, 'Oh, my God, he did not just say that, did he?'" Before 1998 players would hang out in the parking lot after games, and the fans would be long gone. "I don't want to get anybody in trouble, but a couple of guys had coolers in their cars," Steussie said. "Unless it was 20 below, we'd sit out there and drink beer."

That ended in 1998. "We were like a rock band coming out of that place after games," wide receiver Jake Reed said. "People were everywhere…It wasn't, 'Are we going to win?' It was, 'How much are we going to win by?'"

With each victory, the fans got louder and more willing to trust that the Vikings wouldn't stomp on their hearts like the old days. "People thoroughly believed because of the team's history and losing four Super Bowls that this was going to be the year they won their Super Bowl," Billick said. "No environment got louder or was tougher to play in for the opposing team than the Metrodome was that year. We were good, we were exciting, we could score a lot of points, and we had Randy, the most exciting player in the league. That was going to be the year."

# The 1998 NFC Championship Game

There's a popular phrase in Minnesota that starts something like, "Only the Vikings could…" Boy, was that phrase ever in play on January 17, 1999. Only the Vikings could be this good and have it all end so badly. Only the Vikings could have a perfect kicker fail with such soul-crushing imperfection. Only the Vikings could set a league record for points in a season and be remembered for taking a knee. Only the Vikings could have such a sweet, sweet season leave such an eternally bitter taste. "We thought it was our year," cornerback Jimmy Hitchcock told the *Minneapolis Star Tribune* after the Vikings lost to the Atlanta Falcons 30–27 in overtime in the NFC Championship Game at the Metrodome. "It just didn't turn out that way. I never saw it coming like this, never. I just feel empty."

The 1998 season was supposed to be an exorcism for a snake-bitten franchise. A 4–0 preseason was followed by a 15–1 regular season that came within a three-point loss at Tampa Bay of being perfect. A record 556 points was followed by a 41–21 playoff-opening win against the Arizona Cardinals. Next up was Atlanta, which was 15–2 but still an 11-point underdog heading to the Metrodome. What could possibly go wrong in Minnesota's first home NFC title game since 1976?

For most of the first half, the answer was nothing. The Vikings led 20–7 and were going full-throttle, facing third and 10 from their 18-yard line with 1:08 left in the first half. Quarterback Randall Cunningham dropped deep to throw behind a superb line, but defensive end Chuck Smith beat left tackle Todd Steussie for a strip sack that was recovered by defensive tackle Travis Hall. "It's like anything; if it works, the thinking was good, and if it didn't, you've got a second-guess," Vikings offensive coordinator

Brian Billick said. "Would you have done it knowing it would be a fumble? No."

One snap later, the Falcons trailed only 20–14. Chris Chandler's 14-yard touchdown pass to Terance Mathis changed the game and woke the purple demons.

The Vikings' high-powered offense of Cunningham, Cris Carter, rookie phenom Randy Moss, Robert Smith, et al., would score only seven points with the season slipping away in the second half. Still, the Vikings led 27–17 when Cunningham threw a five-yard touchdown pass to Matthew Hatchette with 13:41 left in regulation. Surely, the Vikings were Miami-bound for their first Super Bowl in 22 seasons, right?

Not exactly.

Needing only a 38-yard field goal to go back up by 10 points with 2:07 left, the Vikings put their trust in kicker Gary Anderson. And why not. Anderson had swung his right leg 106 times that season and never missed. He had made 39 straight field goals that season and 44 going back to the 1997 season. But in true Vikings fashion, Anderson pulled it wide left by about a foot. "I really can't understand this," said Vikings holder Mitch Berger. "I mean, he kicks 100-plus kicks and makes them all. Then for that to be the one to miss, I can't figure that out. That's tough. And it wasn't the pressure because that never bothers Gary. It was just so unexpected. But everybody's going to miss sometime." Meanwhile, Anderson spoke like a man who might have been thinking that he was due to miss. "That's part of kicking field goals," he said. "You don't make them all."

By that point in the game, the Vikings defense was decimated by injuries. Lineman John Randle was out of the game, and defensive coordinator Foge Fazio had run out of healthy linebackers. The Falcons needed only 1:18 to score a touchdown and tie the game. But the Vikings still had 49 seconds and three timeouts when they got the ball back at their 20-yard line. They called the first timeout after Cunningham ran for seven yards. Then Cunningham threw incomplete to Moss.

What happened next is something that has become a festering sore for the past generation or so. What happened next ushered in three of the more distasteful words in a Vikings fan's vocabulary.

*Take a knee.*

With history's most explosive offense at the time, coach Dennis Green had 30 seconds and two timeouts to try and move about 38 yards into field goal range. But he took a knee.

The Vikings won the overtime coin toss but ended up punting twice. Finally, with a Metrodome playoff-record crowd of 64,060 holding its breath, Falcons kicker Morten Andersen lined up at the exact spot on which Anderson had missed from 38 yards. The kick was good. Naturally. "This one hurts," Fazio said after the game. "I'm still hurting. We're all hurting."

And the hurt still lingers. In 2010, as he was entering the Pro Football Hall of Fame, Randle was asked how often he thinks about that loss. He said every day. "If I hear someone say, 'ATL,' or 'Atlanta,' or 'Georgia,' it reminds me," Randle said. "When we go down to the Masters golf tournament, just that reminds me of it. It's just probably something that will stick in my head for the rest of my life."

# 5 Adrian Peterson, MVP or Miracle?

Cleveland Browns Hall of Famer Jim Brown was sitting in a small interview room in Berea, Ohio, years ago, trying to forearm shiver some sense into a young reporter too caught up in comparing great running backs. "Why," said the man generally considered the greatest running back of all time, "would you want to take away from one great running style by trying to compare it to another great running style. You can't make comparisons. A great running style is like a fingerprint or a voice on the phone that you know without having to look at the person's face. You should recognize it and enjoy the greatness without judging it against greatness that came before it or the greatness that will come later on."

Great running styles often can be summed up in one word. Brown was overpowering like a man among children. Barry Sanders was nimble like a ballerina in a bowling ball's body. Walter Payton was "Sweetness." Gale Sayers slashed. O.J. Simpson dashed. Earl Campbell was unbridled. Eric Dickerson was smooth.

The running back position faded as the NFL shifted to a passing league long ago. But something unusual resurfaced in Minnesota in 2012. Just when none of us thought it was possible for a running back to lead a rebuilding, quarterback-challenged throwback team to the playoffs, along came Adrian Peterson. The Vikings running back did just that while also defying the odds and the human body by rushing for 2,097 yards after tearing the anterior cruciate and medial collateral ligaments in his left knee at the Washington Redskins on Christmas Eve the year before.

In doing so, Peterson proved the only thing that matters is what he believed was possible. "There's a good reason none of us believed him when he said he would come back better than ever," said Paul Wiggin, a Vikings personnel consultant and a former teammate of Brown's. "The reason is no one could ever fathom it happening—to anyone ever."

Peterson said he'd return in time for the 2012 season opener. He rushed for 84 yards and two touchdowns on 17 carries in the win against the Jacksonville Jaguars. People gushed. Peterson predicted much greater things. Through 10 games he moved beyond the discussion for NFL Comeback Player of the Year and was in the mix for MVP with 1,128 yards, seven touchdowns, and a 4.97-yard average.

The best was yet to come. When he ran for 210 yards in a loss at Green Bay, the Vikings were 6–6 and needed to win out to have a chance to make the playoffs. Despite an ankle injury and a hernia that would be surgically repaired after the season, Peterson's next bit of magic was to reach into his top hat and pull quarterback Christian Ponder into the playoffs. Ponder played well in the regular-season finale against the Packers at the Metrodome. But with the playoffs on the line, it was Peterson who ran for 199 yards. With 24 seconds left in a 34–34 tie, it was Peterson who broke loose over left tackle before being dragged down 26 yards later.

Peterson needed only nine more yards to break Dickerson's single-game rushing record of 2,105. But with only three seconds left, there was only time for Blair Walsh's game-winning 29-yard field goal and an improbable 10th win.

It was the best that Ponder would ever play alongside Peterson. But in another unfortunate twist in franchise history, Ponder suffered an elbow injury, the severity of which wasn't revealed until he was declared inactive in the wild-card rematch a week later at Lambeau Field. Not even Peterson's MVP-winning season could carry backup Joe Webb, who hadn't taken a snap at quarterback during the regular season. Webb started against the Packers and completed only 11-of-30 passes in a 24–10 loss.

"You want my one word for Adrian?" asked right guard Brandon Fusco. "How about, 'wow?'"

"My word is 'violent,'" said fullback Jerome Felton.

"Is 'downhill' one word?" asked left guard Charlie Johnson. "If not, give me 'angry.' He runs like he's mad, like he's going to beat someone up."

Coach Leslie Frazier compared Peterson to Walter Payton, whom Frazier played with in Chicago. "'Focused' is how I'd describe Adrian," Frazier said. "Or, actually, 'determined' might be the better word, very determined. He's a lot like Walter."

"I'd say, 'obsessed,'" Wiggin said. "He and Jim [Brown] are so much alike. So many times, Adrian will do something and I'll say to myself, 'Jim Brown.'"

There was only one person left to weigh in with his one word. "'Vicious,'" Peterson said. "I guess you can say that."

# 6 The Purple People Eaters

One of the greatest sports nicknames of all time didn't sit well initially with Carl Eller, Alan Page, Jim Marshall, and Gary Larsen. "At first, we didn't adhere to the whole 'Purple People Eaters' identity," Eller said in 2015. "We were very strong-willed individuals. We identified individually."

But through a contest on a local radio station, a nickname was born that would become famous and bond these individuals together forever. "It was just a fan—John Q. Public," Eller said. "He or she picked the name. And it stuck forever."

The name came from the popular 1958 song written and performed by Sheb Wooley. It's a catchy tune, but some of the roughest defenders in NFL history had a tough time identifying with a "one-eyed, one-horned, flying purple people eater" cartoon character. Marshall tried his best to make "Purple Gang" the nickname that would stick. But there was no stopping the "Purple People Eaters" nickname—much like there was no stopping the Vikings' defensive line during that era.

From 1969 to 1977, the Vikings went to five NFL/NFC Championship Games and won four of them. From 1969 to 1971,

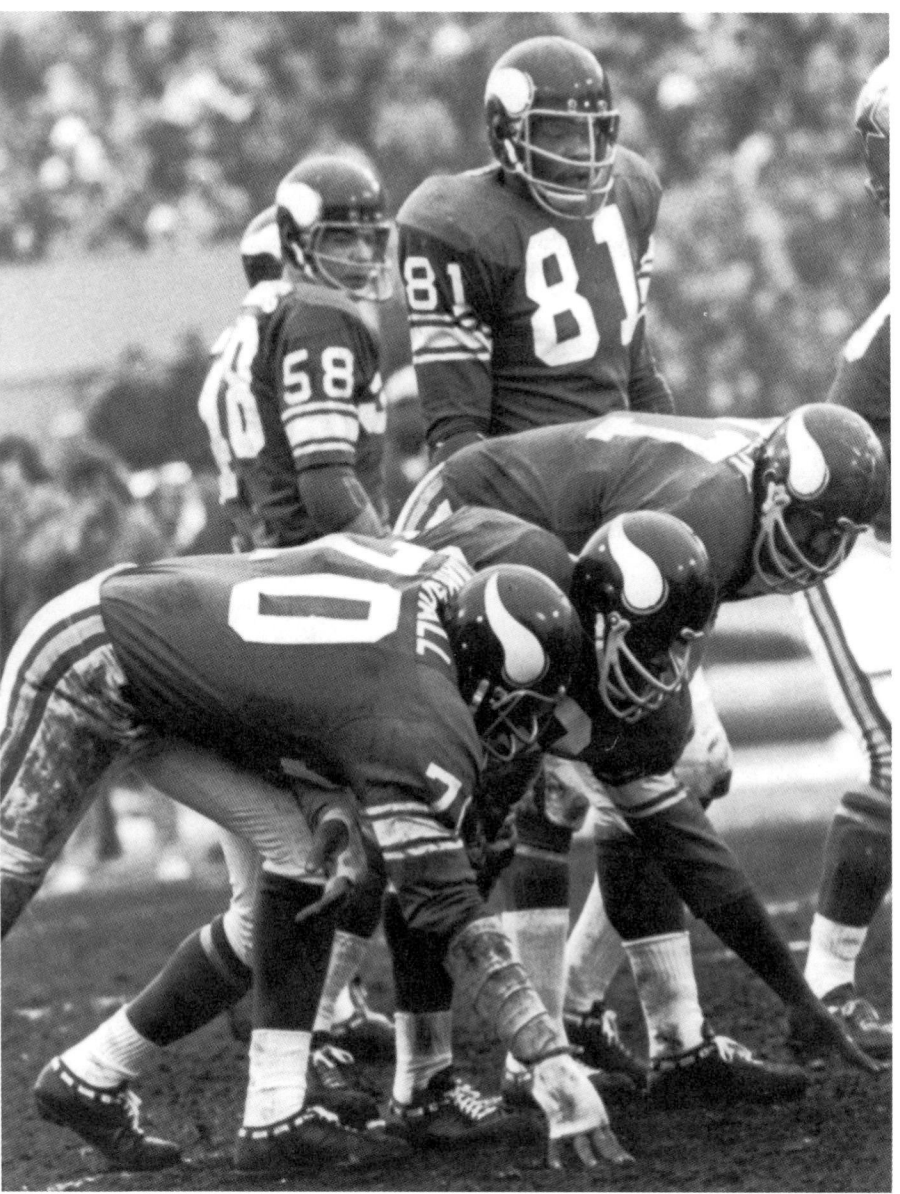

*Known as the Purple People Eaters, Minnesota Vikings defensive linemen—defensive end Jim Marshall (No. 70), defensive tackle Alan Page (88), and defensive end Carl Eller (81)—line up against the Dallas Cowboys during a 1971 playoff game.*

they surrendered 9.5, 10.2, and 9.9 points per game, respectively, and had more than twice as many shutouts (seven) as games in which they allowed more than 20 points (three). The Purple People Eaters' ability to stuff the run while living up to their motto of "Meet at the quarterback!" allowed them to control and dominate games year after year. Sacks didn't become an official stat until a later era, and most of the Purple People Eaters' careers ended before the 1978 rule changes opened up the passing game. But the Vikings still list three of their top four career sack leaders as Eller (130), Marshall (127), and Page (108).

Marshall, the right end, arrived first via the expansion draft from the Cleveland Browns in 1961. Eller, the left end, was the sixth overall pick from the University of Minnesota in 1964. Page, the right tackle, was the last of the team's three first-round picks in 1967. Page made his first start in Week 5 of his rookie season. From that point through the end of the 1977 season, Marshall, Eller, and Page played together in 169 consecutive games. The only start that was missed during that time came when Eller had a broken thumb in 1976.

When Page became a starter, Larsen, who had arrived via trade from the Los Angeles Rams in 1965, became a backup behind Page and Paul Dickson for all but one game the rest of the 1967 season. But Larsen became the starting left tackle at the start of the 1968 season and held on to the job through the midway point of the 1974 season.

Doug Sutherland stepped in for Larsen and lived up to the nickname alongside Eller, Page, and Marshall for another three-and-a-half seasons. Page was released in October of 1978, picked up by the Chicago Bears, and played through 1981. Eller was traded to the Seattle Seahawks in 1979 and played one season there. Marshall retired after the 1979 season.

"I don't know who picked that nickname, but I think ulti-mately it helped us come together and make us better as a unit and as individual players," Eller said. "It's four guys playing together. It was our identity. It's still our identity—four guys from the Vikings who dominated during a great period of time in football history."

# 7 Super Bowl VIII: Dominated Again

For the second time in five years, Bud Grant's Vikings were a dominant Super Bowl qualifier. For the second time in five years, they were dominated as a Super Bowl participant.

Some Vikings who played in all four Super Bowl losses have called Don Shula's 1973 Miami Dolphins the toughest team they faced in the Super Bowl. Those who watched the game on January 13, 1974, at Rice Stadium in Houston would have a tough time disagreeing.

Super Bowl VIII was a mismatch of brute strength from the start. The Dolphins opened with a pair of long touchdown drives sandwiched around a three-and-out in the first Super Bowl possession for quarterback Fran Tarkenton, who had returned via trade the year before.

With running back Larry Csonka and Miami's "No-Name Defense" pounding away, Miami led 14–0 after a quarter, 17–0 at the half, and 24–0 through three quarters. Quarterback Bob Griese threw only seven passes, which remains a Super Bowl record for fewest pass attempts. He completed six for 73 yards while throwing only once in the second half. *Once.* "We were prepared to throw more," said Griese, via *The New York Times.* "But we also knew what we could do. We'd run straight at them, then around them, then a trap."

Even Miami's offensive linemen seemed surprised by the ease with which they controlled the famed "Purple People Eaters" with strength, precise trap plays, and quick crossing blocks. Center Jim Langer told reporters, "It was obvious from the start that we could overpower their defense." Csonka, the first running back to win Super Bowl MVP, ran for 145 yards and two touchdowns on 33 carries. The Vikings had just 72 yards rushing.

With less than a minute left in the half, running back Oscar Reed lost a fumble on fourth and 1 from the Miami 6. Grant later defended his decision not to kick a field goal by saying the Vikings had converted similar short-yardage situations in their 27–10 NFC Championship Game win at the Dallas Cowboys. The next morning *The New York Times* wrote that, "[Grant] forgot that the Dolphins, who made history with a perfect 17–0 record last year, are hardly the Cowboys." Yes, the Vikings had gone 12–2 during the regular season, but many considered the 1973 Miami team (15–2) even better than its undefeated 1972 team.

The fumble before halftime wouldn't be the only critical error that kept the Vikings from mounting a comeback. John Gilliam's 65-yard return of the second-half kickoff was negated by a clip on Stu Voigt. Following a Vikings punt, Miami scored a touchdown for its 24–0 lead. From there the Vikings could manage only a fourth-quarter whimper when Tarkenton ran for a touchdown. Years later, as the Vikings of that era have dealt with the pain of their four Super Bowl defeats, they've relived all the mistakes many times. "We never got the bounces, never had any good luck it seemed," defensive end Carl Eller said. "It was always something—penalties, turnovers at the wrong time. We didn't play our best, but there was always something that went against us."

That may be so, but a clear difference in strength and fundamentals also was evident from the opening drive on January 13, 1974. Grant acknowledged as much after the game. "From Amos

Alonzo Stagg on, you've got to block and tackle," he said. "And they did it better than we did."

# Favre Arrives

Honestly, only one thing could have made Brett Favre's journey from Minneapolis-St. Paul International Airport to Winter Park any more surreal. "Perhaps if I had driven my son's white car," joked coach Brad Childress, whose transport of Favre to team headquarters in a black SUV was covered live via helicopter by a local television station. "Brett got a couple of texts from people saying they felt like they were watching the O.J. [Simpson] chase."

No, this wasn't a Hall of Famer going down in flames in a white Ford Bronco. This was a future Hall of Famer riding toward his former hated rival on a proverbial white horse as the fans who once loathed him cheered uncontrollably.

At 12:10 PM on August 18, 2009, hundreds of fans and dozens of reporters, satellite trucks, and cameras were staked out across the side street in front of the Winter Park facility. A helicopter whirred overhead when Childress' Escalade turned right into the parking lot. Fans raced across the street, following the vehicle as one security guard essentially threw up his hands in defeat and others looked on from the roof of the facility.

The one and only Brett Favre had arrived. Within moments the same guy, who had spent 16 seasons torturing the Vikings while winning a Super Bowl and three league MVPs for the despised Green Bay Packers, would sign a two-year, $25 million contact that would reach $28.5 million a year later.

Under Childress the Vikings had gone from 6–10 in 2006 to 8–8 in 2007 to 10–6 and NFC North champions in 2008. Having all the pieces they needed—except a quarterback—they had been pursuing Favre for the past four months. After a bitter fallout with the Packers in 2008, Favre had wanted to play for the Vikings so he could stick it to Packers general manager Ted Thompson and coach Mike McCarthy for not welcoming him back when he wanted to unretire. Thompson traded him to the New York Jets to get him out of the division and the conference.

A hot start in New York was followed by a dismal finish and no playoff berth as Favre continued to play despite a torn right biceps muscle. He had surgery after the season, retired again, and had told Childress just three weeks prior to his signing that he wasn't coming back. But he was the ultimate retirement waffler, so Childress tried one more time as the Vikings opened the preseason. Most players were caught off guard and assumed it wouldn't happen. Some looked on through the cafeteria window as the hoopla unfolded, and a living legend crawled out of the passenger's side of the Escalade. Magic would follow—at least for 17 of the next 18 games.

The breaking news and the Black Escalade Chase helped Vikings sell 8,000 single-game tickets and 2,500 season-tickets in just two hours. And, boy, did they get their money's worth. At least for one season before greatness ended in that all-too-familiar sadness.

Favre would butt heads with Childress but also have the best statistical season of his 20-year career. He'd post career highs for completion percentage (68.4) and passer rating (107.2). He'd notch 33 touchdowns and only seven interceptions—the latter a career low as a starter. The Vikings would win 12 games, claim another division title, and win their only playoff game under Childress, a 34–3 blowout of the Dallas Cowboys at the Metrodome. There would be two dramatic—and super surreal—primetime wins over the Packers. There would be a 9–0 record at home, including Favre's perfectly placed, 32-yard rocket-ball touchdown to Greg Lewis to beat the San Francisco 49ers in the final two seconds.

And all of the energy for this season could be felt the day when Favre showed up in that black Escalade and spoke to the media for the first time. Favre talked about his 10-year-old daughter Breleigh's reaction when she learned three weeks earlier that her father had told the Vikings no for presumably the final time they would ask him to come back. "She started crying," Favre said. "I can be chased by five defensive linemen, and it doesn't scare me, but when my daughter cries, it softens me up. And she said, 'Daddy, I wanted you to go back and win one more Super Bowl.'"

That was the realistic plan. And it looked like the team's destiny when it headed to New Orleans for the NFC Championship Game. Unfortunately, the word *unfortunately* gets used a lot in Vikings history. And unfortunately for the Vikings, destiny would take another dramatic wrong turn in a city that hosted two of the franchise's four Super Bowl losses.

# 2009 NFC Championship Game

Somehow, the Vikings were in control of a game that seemed so out of control. They were dominating New Orleans in yardage, first downs, and every other way—except ball security. But on this January 24, 2010 day, the Vikings, not the Saints, were marching in toward victory and what appeared to be their destiny: a fifth Super Bowl. Yes, the Vikings had fumbled six times. Yes, they had lost two of them inside the Saints' 11-yard line and another one near their own goal line. Yes, Brett Favre had thrown an interception.

But the Vikings were somehow tied 28–28 when they gained possession with 2:37 left in the NFC Championship Game. Favre had the one pick, but it was only the eighth interception he had thrown more than 500 passes over 17-plus games during that magical season. Coach Brad Childress had butted heads with his legendary quarterback on occasion, but give the man credit. He coaxed "Good Brett" to the best statistical season of his career while stifling "Bad Brett" and his maddening turnovers—up to that point, of course.

On third and 7, Favre threw a 10-yard pass to Bernard Berrian. Then he threw a 20-yard pass to Sidney Rice. So far, so good. A 14-yard run by Chester Taylor gave the Vikings a first down at the New Orleans 33-yard line. The Vikings were in field-goal range. An attempt there would be from 51 yards, which was two yards inside of Ryan Longwell's comfort zone. After two more runs gained zero yards, the Vikings faced third and 10 and called timeout with 19 seconds left.

And that's when things started to happen, things that make you wonder if this franchise is indeed cursed on the big stage. The Vikings came out of the timeout, and confusion reigned. Fullback Naufahu Tahi was in the huddle when he wasn't supposed to be. When the Vikings broke the huddle with 12 men, one of the more infamous yellow flags in franchise history was thrown. The five yards moved the Vikings out of field-goal range. But they still had a timeout left.

That didn't matter.

"Bad Brett" rolled right, ignored a wide-open running lane ahead of him, threw back across his body to the middle of the field, and was intercepted by Tracy Porter. "After the penalty we were out of field-goal range," Favre said. "I probably should have ran it. In hindsight that's probably what I should have done."

The Saints won the overtime coin toss, used a questionable pass interference penalty on linebacker Ben Leber to get in field goal range, and won on a 40-yard field goal by Garrett Hartley. Of course they did. And the Vikings lost their fifth straight NFC title game. Of course they did.

The NFL changed its postseason overtime rules the next season, allowing both teams possession of the ball unless the first team scored a touchdown. Naturally. And that wasn't the only additional anguish added to this loss well after the final whistle. Details surrounding the beating that Favre took in this game became a prime piece of evidence in the "Bountygate" scandal that rocked the Saints franchise two years later.

The Saints were caught violating the league's long-standing rule by paying players to injure opponents from 2009 to 2011. Head coach Sean Payton was suspended without pay for the 2012 season. General manager Mickey Loomis was suspended for eight games. Former defensive coordinator and bounty mastermind Gregg Williams was suspended indefinitely and spent a year out of football. The Saints also were fined $500,000 and docked second-round draft picks in 2012 and 2013.

Vikings fans have argued that Favre didn't run to the open field at the end of the NFC title game because he was hobbled by a badly sprained ankle from a hit late in the third quarter. There was no flag on the hit, but the NFL later fined defensive lineman Bobby McCray $20,000 for illegally hitting Favre low and from behind while he was being hit high by another defender.

Favre was intercepted by linebacker Jonathan Vilma on the play. According to the NFL's investigation, it was Vilma, a team captain, who offered $10,000 to any player who knocked Favre out of the game. Favre never left the game, but long before news of "Bountygate" broke, Childress complained to the league about the beating Favre took that day.

Childress outlined eight plays in which he thought roughing penalties should have been called but weren't. The league agreed with him on one play—the hit by McCray. Would an interception-negating flag on that play have changed the outcome of the game? Who knows. But we do know the Saints went on to Miami, where they beat the Indianapolis Colts in Super Bowl XLIV. And Vikings fans got another chapter added to their book of purple pain.

But even considering those dubious plays, the Vikings dominated in total yards (475–257) and first downs (31–15). It was butterfingers and a minus-4 turnover margin that were more to blame than anything else. "We turned the ball over five times. We had 12 men in the huddle at the end," defensive end Jared Allen said. "We did all kinds of things to ourselves in that game that had nothing to do with bounties."

# 10 Tarkenton Arrives on the Scene

The first regular season game in Vikings history was still more than a week away, and rookie quarterback Fran Tarkenton already felt hopelessly lost on football's highest level. "In our last exhibition game, we were playing the L.A. Rams," Tarkenton said. "And I reached out to Zeke Bratkowski because I just didn't get it."

Bratkowski was entering his eighth season as an NFL quarterback. Like Tarkenton, he had played at Georgia. Tarkenton was hoping the old Bulldog could teach him something to boost his confidence. "I had dinner with him," Tarkenton said. "I said, 'Zeke, I'm just not comfortable out there. I don't get it. I'm not instinctive.' He said, 'Well, it will happen. Be patient. It will open up and it will slow down. You just keep watching film and keep working, and it will break for you.'"

The Vikings had reported to Bemidji State University for their first training camp on July 7, 1961. It was a seven-week grind that included five exhibition games. The first four were on the road. On August 5, a crowd of 4,954 watched the Vikings get blown out 38–13 in Sioux Falls, South Dakota, by the Dallas Cowboys, an expansion team the year before. A 13–3 loss at the Baltimore Colts was followed by a 14–10 loss to the San Francisco 49ers in Portland, Oregon.

The following week featured some gamesmanship between upstart Vikings rookie head coach Norm Van Brocklin and Chicago Bears founder and coach George "Papa Bear" Halas, who had played an influential role in Minnesota getting an NFL team. Prior to their exhibition game in Cedar Rapids, Iowa, Van Brocklin didn't deliver game films to Halas on time, per NFL rules. Halas went public with the information, mocking Van Brocklin's team and telling reporters he couldn't wait to see what "that rough-and-tough football team has been doing." Halas laughed again when the Bears won 30–7.

Tarkenton and Van Brocklin never would hit it off personally or professionally. Van Brocklin's Hall of Fame career had ended the year before in Philadelphia with his second NFL title as a classic pocket passer for the Eagles. His temper and volatile personality clashed with most of his players but would become especially problematic with Tarkenton, who would carve his own Hall of Fame career outside the pocket as a new-age scrambler. "Van Brocklin wasn't my favorite person, as people know," Tarkenton said. "But he was a great, great player. And he really understood the passing game and he understood quarterbacks. He prepared me."

Fifteen days after their exhibition meeting, the Vikings and Bears would open the regular season at Metropolitan Stadium on September 17. Van Brocklin was going to start Tarkenton, even though the Vikings had traded a first-round draft pick to the New York Giants for George Shaw, the No. 1 overall pick of the Colts in 1955. Shaw had the misfortune of breaking his leg early on in 1956, allowing a young fella by the name of Johnny Unitas a chance to play. "Van Brocklin said he was going to start me, so I went over to his house every night that week and watched film," Tarkenton said. "The Bears blitzed 80 percent of the time with all kinds of screwy blitzes. Van Brocklin had drilled into me all the audibles and things to watch out for. I knew it would work if I got the chance."

But Van Brocklin's nature was unpredictable. The morning of the game, he told Tarkenton he needed to give Shaw a chance to start. Shaw didn't make it to the end of the first quarter. With the Vikings trailing 3–0, Tarkenton was sent in. "I had no nervousness," Tarkenton said. "I saw that field like I had been there for 20 years. I knew every blade of grass, every place they were lined up, what audible to call. And I think back about it, I can tell you it was the greatest upset in the history of the National Football League."

Weaving his way around slower Bears defenders, Tarkenton completed 17-of-23 passes for 250 yards, four touchdowns, no interceptions, and a fifth rushing touchdown in a 37–13 rout.

The Bears, meanwhile, threw four interceptions and lost one of their four fumbles. Halas cussed out his players and told reporters he had never seen so many things go wrong in one game during his 42 seasons of running the Bears.

Vikings would go on to lose seven straight and wrap up a 3–11 season with a 52–35 loss in Chicago. But a Hall of Fame career was hatched in the first game in franchise history.

# 11 Mick Tingelhoff

As center and co-captain on Bud Grant's four Super Bowl teams, Henry Michael "Mick" Tingelhoff's leadership was firm, forever dependable, and, for the most part, mild-mannered and quiet. "Mick was tough to rile," said longtime head athletic trainer Fred Zamberletti. "But don't get him mad. Mick could handle himself, boy."

On or off the field. And in the front office, too.

It wasn't long after Jim Finks left as general manager that his replacement, Mike Lynn, discovered just how powerful Tingelhoff's presence was throughout the organization. "Mick's contract was up, so Lynn told Mick he had to come in and talk," former Vikings running back Dave Osborn said in 2015 while sitting next to Tingelhoff during one of their weekly get-togethers at a McDonald's in Lakeville, Minnesota.

So in 1974 Tingelhoff drove to team headquarters, walked into Lynn's office, and sat down. He also continued an old habit of setting his car keys on the desk in front of him. Lynn considered his desk a source of pride. It was always decked out with memorabilia and a big bowl of cinnamon candy. "They start talking and Lynn says, 'Mick, you're really not that good anymore, so we can't really pay you because you're overpaid now,'" Osborn said. "So Mick took his arm and swept the desk. Trophies and that bowl of cinnamon candy and everything went flying."

Tingelhoff stormed out of the office. But not before punching a hole in the door. "Mick gets to his car and remembers that he set his car keys on the desk," Osborn says. "So now he has to come back in. He walks in and everybody is silent, thinking, *Boy, Mick's really going to bust things up now.*"

Tingelhoff walked into Lynn's office. He got down on his hands and knees and began quietly searching through the rubble for his keys. "I found them, got up, and walked out," Tingelhoff said with a smile. "I guess he must have paid me because they didn't get rid of me."

Grant made sure of that. "Mick and Jim [Marshall] were our two leaders," Grant said. "It's hard for me to talk about Mick without Marshall and Marshall without Mick. Mick was an introvert. Jim was an extrovert. They were different personalities but really respected and our best players. They bought the program when I came in [1967]. If I said, 'Jump,' they would be the first ones to jump, and everybody else would have to jump with them."

At 6'2", 237 pounds, Tingelhoff was an undersized but quick and tenacious blocker. He went from being an undrafted rookie linebacker out of Nebraska in 1962 to starting every regular season (240) and postseason (19) game at center over the next 17 seasons. In his final 11 seasons, the five-time, first-team All-Pro helped Grant post a 112–42–2 record while winning 10 division titles.

In 2015, 37 years after his final snap, Tingelhoff became the ninth center to reach the Pro Football Hall of Fame. "Mick Tingelhoff wasn't a Minnesota Viking," said Fran Tarkenton, Vikings Hall of Fame quarterback and Tingelhoff's presenter in Canton, Ohio. "Mick Tingelhoff *is* the Minnesota Viking."

He played and lived life with a toughness that wasn't to be messed with. "We had this crabby neighbor when we lived in Edina," said Pat Tingelhoff, Mick's son. "My brother Mike and I were running across his lawn. He grabs Mike and throws him into the bushes. We ran home crying and told Mick."

Mick wasn't happy. "Mick just nods, real quiet, and says, 'Okay,'" Pat said. "Then he walks down, knocks on the guy's door. Guy opens the door and—*Boom*—Mick dropped him."

Mike never spent another moment in the neighbor's bushes. "But Mick did call the Vikings and say, 'You better get a lawyer ready,'" said Phyllis Tingelhoff, Mick's wife.

"Mick says to me, 'What if this guy calls the cops?'" Osborn said. "Eventually, someone told him that if the guy didn't file a complaint in 24 hours, Mick would be okay." "I sweated it out for 24 hours," said Tingelhoff, laughing as Osborn told the story.

Mick started the next week. Mick always started the next week. In fact in the history of the NFL, only Brett Favre (297) and Tingelhoff's former Vikings teammate Jim Marshall (270) started more games consecutively than he (240). "Bud always said we had two centers," Osborn said. "Mick healthy and Mick hurt."

Even the late heavyweight boxer and Minnesota native Scott LeDoux admired Tingelhoff's toughness. In fact, hanging in the den of Tingelhoff's Minnesota home is a photo of LeDoux punching an opponent. It's even signed by LeDoux with the following inscription—"Mick Tingelhoff: God knows they won't throw [your] kid in the bushes again."

# 12 The Push-Off

Three tips for survival as a Minnesotan: dress warm unless Bud Grant is watching, wince whenever the 1998 NFC Championship Game is mentioned, and even if you weren't alive on December 28, 1975, always, *always* agree that Dallas Cowboys receiver Drew Pearson pushed off.

In Minnesota sports fans generally have two feelings toward game officials. They either hate them or they *really* hate them. For many veteran fans, ground zero for this ailment can be traced to Met Stadium on December 28, 1975. A field judge by the name of Armen Terzian would agree. To say fans were enraged that day is putting it mildly. One of them had the accuracy and blood-alcohol level to throw the infamous whiskey bottle that split open Terzian's head during the chaos that ensued after Pearson's push-off went uncalled and resulted in a 50-yard touchdown reception with 24 seconds left in Dallas' 17–14 playoff-opening victory.

Prior to December 28, 1975, miracle long passes that resulted in jump balls for touchdowns were called many different things. The most common was the "alley oop," a term used in San Francisco in the 1950s when 49ers quarterback Y.A. Tittle and receiver R.C. Owens became especially adept at executing the play. All that changed on December 28, 1975, when Cowboys quarterback Roger Staubach, a Roman Catholic, gave his postgame press conference in the jubilant Dallas locker room. "I closed my eyes and said a Hail Mary," Staubach said of the high-arching pass that was released from the shotgun formation at the Dallas 41-yard line to just inside the Vikings' 5-yard line. So, yeah, in case you didn't know, the term, "Hail Mary" got its launching point from the broken backs of the Vikings and their home crowd.

Cornerback Nate Wright played for Atlanta and St. Louis before finding a home in Minnesota through a trade in 1971. A reliable starter and one of the better cornerbacks in team history, he recorded 31 interceptions in 129 games over 10 seasons as a Viking. He's also remembered as the guy who was covering Pearson on the day that's remembered for the "Hail Mary" in Dallas and "The Push-off" in Minnesota.

Two snaps before the climactic play, the Cowboys were down to a fourth and 16 from their 25. Staubach connected with Pearson along the sideline for a 25-yard gain. Pearson didn't get two feet inbounds, but those doggone officials ruled it a catch, saying Wright forced Pearson out of bounds.

On the touchdown there was contact as Staubach's pass arrived. Wright ended up on the ground. Pearson somehow caught the ball by pinning it between his right arm and right hip, backing into the end zone untouched as safeties Paul Krause and Terry Brown complained vehemently to the official. Defensive tackle Alan Page argued so hard that he drew an unsportsmanlike conduct penalty and was ejected. Quarterback Fran Tarkenton was still yelling at officials when the Vikings got the ball back in the closing seconds. "From our side of the field, there is no question Nate was pushed," Grant said after the game. "No question."

Years later, Wright told the *Minneapolis Star Tribune* that Pearson admitted to him that he did push off. But Pearson was still professing innocence when the newspaper contacted him before the Vikings and Cowboys met in the 2009 playoffs. Told that 34 years later Vikings fans still insist than he pushed off, Pearson said, "That bothers me because I didn't do it. It bothers me that people harp on that as opposed to getting on Nate Wright for letting it happen. You don't see any extension of my arms. You know who gave the best explanation? Bud Grant. He said it was like two basketball players going up for a rebound."

The Vikings made the Super Bowl in 1973, 1974, and 1976. But many argue that the 1975 team was Grant's best. The defense ranked third in points allowed. Chuck Foreman was a 1,000-yard rusher, and Tarkenton won NFL Most Valuable Player.

Sadly for Tarkenton, the pain of losing a football game wouldn't matter long. After leaving the Met on December 28, Tarkenton got the news that his father, Dallas Tarkenton, had suffered a heart attack and died while watching the game on television.

# 13 Alan Page

It didn't take long for teammates to learn that the kid from Notre Dame was one heck of a football player and a steadfast football nonconformist. By the time Alan Page arrived as a first-round draft pick in 1967, the Vikings already had some strong personalities, and none were stronger than fellow defensive lineman Jim Marshall.

A seven-year NFL veteran at the time, Marshall was a boisterous, extroverted leader. He ruled over the locker room, not to mention how he broke in rookies during training camp. "It was customary for highly regarded rookies to go through a ritualistic indoctrination," Marshall told the *Minneapolis Star Tribune*. "We had 40 cases of beer and we went to a big lodge somewhere out in the country. We devised a series of drinking games to see how rookies would react the next day in practice after they were intoxicated and hungover. Would they feel sorry for themselves or overcome adversity?"

Page didn't drink, nor did he believe in what he considered the sophomoric behavior typical of most football players. When Marshall lectured him, Page left. "He thought it was silly," Marshall said. "He didn't know what it was to relinquish his principles. It was the first time I had ever heard of a rookie defying the tradition of the veterans. And for the first time, we saw the stubbornness and independence that would someday make Alan the best defensive tackle to ever play the game."

Perhaps the greatest player in franchise history, Page never missed a game in 16 seasons with the Vikings and Chicago Bears. The 1988 Pro Football Hall of Fame enshrinee earned nine Pro

Bowl berths, six first-team All-Pro selections, and was the first of only two defensive players to ever win NFL Most Valuable Player (1971). A backup in his first three games as a rookie, Page started 157 straight for the Vikings and 58 more in a row for the Bears after an ugly split with coach Bud Grant during the 1978 season.

Page's stubborn, nonconformist nature was something Grant struggled with often. Page missed parts of training camp to attend law school at the University of Minnesota from 1975 to 1978. He was an active, outspoken member of the executive council of the NFL Players Association and was instrumental in the 1974 labor dispute that canceled the College All-Star Game and led to a brief strike by veteran players during the preseason.

Grant once fined Page $50 for being late to a meeting. Page not only appealed the fine, but he also filed a grievance accusing Grant of violating rules between the league and the Players Association on minimum time off. The icy relationship finally fractured in 1978. By then, Page was training to be a marathon runner. His weight dropped from over 245 to 222. Grant wasn't pleased. On September 25 in Chicago, Grant pulled Page in the first half in favor of a young player named Duck White; Page wasn't pleased. Page started the second half but was pulled again for White; Page was furious.

In the closing minutes, the other defensive tackle, Doug Sutherland, was injured. Page was on the sideline and hadn't seen the injury when an assistant coach barked his name and told him to go in. According to a *Sports Illustrated* story in 1979, Page said, "What for?" Grant stepped in and called for another player. Eight days later, Grant released Page with a phone call. Then he shocked the Twin Cities media with a news conference to announce the move. "Alan can no longer meet the standard he set for himself," Grant said then. "He just can't make the plays anymore." When pressed for details, Grant didn't hold back. "Here is a man we had to take out in short-yardage situations, who was not strong enough to rush the passer…He was not doing his job."

The 33-year-old Page was available to any team for the NFL's $100 waiver fee, and the Bears pounced. Bears general manager Jim Finks drafted Page when he was Vikings general manager. Coach Neill Armstrong and defensive coordinator Buddy Ryan had coached Page in Minnesota. At this point Page was still trying to pass the Minnesota bar exam. He had flunked on his first attempt but would pass on his second try and join the Minneapolis firm Lindquist & Vennum.

When the Bears claimed him, Page was relieved to be out from under Grant and harbored ill feelings toward the Vikings for years. "Let's face it: I got fired by the Minnesota Vikings and I am never going to forget that," Page told the *Star Tribune* on the day he was voted into the Hall of Fame.

Page played 10 games for the Bears in 1978 and had 11.5 sacks. And if young people think Brett Favre returning to Green Bay in a Vikings uniform was surreal, older people felt the same way when Alan Page returned to Met Stadium in a Bears uniform a month after he was released. Page had five unassisted tackles and forced a fumble. But the Vikings won 17–14. Grant announced that he had awarded a game ball to Chuck Goodrum, the guard who lined up across from Page. In a typically measured and effective response, Page told reporters, "Why did they give the game ball to someone who blocked me if I was so bad they let me go in the first place?"

The following summer, Page's wife, Diane, described to *Sports Illustrated* how happy her husband was to be in Chicago and out from under Grant. "In Minnesota Bud Grant is like Mom and apple pie and the flag," she said. "It's fun to be able to sit back now and call him a turkey."

Page played through the 1981 season before retiring. Unlike so many players who struggle to give up the game, Page felt the best was yet to come. He told the *Star Tribune* that the NFL limited his intellectual growth and instead used his head "for nothing more than a hat rack and a battering ram."

In one of the most successful post-playing careers in NFL history, Page went on to become an assistant state attorney general, a University of Minnesota regent, and an associate justice of the Minnesota Supreme Court from 1993 until 2015, when he hit the mandatory retirement age of 70.

Page's final nonconformist act as an NFL player came during his Hall of Fame induction in his hometown of Canton, Ohio, in 1988. His presenter wasn't a former teammate or coach.

It was Willarene Beasley, the principal at Minneapolis North High School and the Hall's first presenter with no NFL ties. During their speeches on the steps of the Hall of Fame, Beasley and Page spent more time talking about the need to educate inner-city youth than anything Page did as a Purple People Eater.

# 14 Cris Carter

Cris Carter scored on the first touch of his first organized football game. Of course he did. It was 1973. Carter was 8 years old in Middletown, Ohio. "I was playing for Armco Credit Union over at Barnitz Stadium," said Carter, referring to the local steel company that sponsored his Pee Wee team in the stadium that is now named Cris Carter Community Field. "Coach Butch Johnson called '18 bootleg,' and I was the quarterback. I went 70 or 80 yards right down the sideline."

He crossed the goal line. Just like he would at Ohio State, when he led the Big Ten in touchdown catches in 1984, 1985, and 1986.

*Known for his sure hands and deft footwork, wide receiver Cris Carter celebrates a 16-yard touchdown reception in 1997.* (AP Images)

Just like he would in Philadelphia, where he scored on his first NFL reception and eventually caused Philadelphia Eagles coach Buddy Ryan to famously say, "All he does is catch touchdowns." Just like he would 130 times over 16 NFL seasons, 12 of them with the Vikings (1990–2001).

Carter's career ended in 2002 with the Miami Dolphins, but he still ranks fourth in NFL history in career catches (1,101) and receiving touchdowns (130). In 2013 Carter reached the Pro Football Hall of Fame, taking with him two of the greatest hands in league history and a highlight reel of precise route running, acrobatic leaps, and two signature big toes that were perfectly trained to hug the last blade of grass in bounds.

Carter discovered early in life that he wasn't like a lot of people. One day, he went fishing. Then he went the next day. And every single day after that for a month. "I have an addictive personality," Carter said. "It can be a good thing when it's channeled into something like football."

Unfortunately for Carter, there were some dark channels. He started drinking alcohol at an early age. Then he started using marijuana. At his high school graduation, he did cocaine for the first time. He didn't consider it a big deal. He figured he could handle it and didn't think he'd ever get hooked like he'd seen others in the neighborhood get hooked. When it was football season at Ohio State and players were being drug tested, Carter simply stopped smoking marijuana and drank instead.

When Carter signed with agent Norby Walters before his senior season, he lost his eligibility and was selected by the Eagles in the fourth round of the 1987 supplemental draft.

Things were going well in Philadelphia, or so Carter thought, until Labor Day of 1990, when Ryan called him into his office for a four-minute conversation that began what Carter would call the "worst day of my life." Carter had started 34 straight games. He had finished third in the NFL in touchdown catches with 11 in 1989. But Ryan had had enough. He was taking a stance against Carter's substance abuse. "My wife [Melanie] was pregnant with our first kid, my son, Duron," said Carter, who also has a daughter, Monterae. "And I had to go home and tell her I didn't have a job."

It wasn't an easy decision for Ryan. "Buddy started out by saying, 'I told my wife I was going to release you, and she began to beg and plead, 'Don't cut that kid. There's something special about him,'" Carter said. "Buddy's telling this story, and I'm starting to cry because it's cutdown day and I know I'm about to be cut."

The Eagles offered Carter a flight to any destination of his choice. He didn't know where to go. "Then they gave me a garbage bag and told me to put my belongings in that bag," Carter said. "I'm walking across Veterans Stadium, going to empty out my locker with a gray garbage bag. That was the first time in my life that anybody had ever told me that I was garbage."

On September 4, 1990—the day after the Eagles cut him—the Vikings stepped forward with a $100 waiver-wire check and a plan to get Carter some help for his substance abuse. "I don't know this for sure," said Jerry Burns, the Vikings coach at the time, "but that $100 has to rank right there at the top as the best bargain in NFL history."

After joining the Vikings, Carter became an eight-time Pro Bowler and a two-time first-team All-Pro. He had back-to-back, then-record 122-catch seasons (1994–95), eight consecutive 1,000-yard seasons (1993–2000), and five straight seasons with at least 10 touchdown catches (1995–99). From 1991 to 2000, Carter led the NFL in third-down catches (297) and third-down conversions (81 percent). His 72 career red-zone touchdowns still rank No. 2 behind only tight end Tony Gonzalez.

But the on-field success didn't come until after Carter got his life together off the field. "Oh, my goodness, I needed a lot of help,"

Carter said. "That first day in Minnesota was very, very difficult because I would say the Vikings were somewhat aware of my situation but not fully aware."

Carter credits Wheelock Whitney, one of the Vikings' owners at the time, and his assistant, Betty Triliegi, a drug and alcohol counselor who worked with the team, as two "angels" who saved his career, his marriage, his family, and his life. It was Triliegi who issued Carter a memorable challenge on September 19, 1990: stop drinking for one week. Just one week. "And that was the last day I ever drank," Carter said. "I owe everything to the Vikings. They taught me how I should live the rest of my life."

# 15 Herschel Walker Trade

One player, one final piece to the puzzle, is all that stood between the Vikings and a fifth Super Bowl appearance in the fall of 1989—or so Vikings general manager Mike Lynn thought. On October 12 of that year, he pulled the trigger on what remains the most infamous trade in team history, if not sports history. "I did what I thought was the right thing at the time," Lynn said on the 20th anniversary of the Herschel Walker trade. "I have no regrets."

Neither did Lynn's trade partner, Jimmy Johnson, who predicted the magnitude of the deal's lopsidedness on Day One. As the brash rookie coach of the Dallas Cowboys that day, Johnson bragged to a disbelieving Dallas media that he had just committed "The Great Train Robbery." History might suggest he was being understated.

In what remains the largest and most complex trade in NFL history, the transaction ultimately involved 18 players and draft picks. The Vikings gave up five players—three of them defensive starters—and eight draft picks, including three first rounders, three second rounders, and a third rounder.

Johnson used those picks to build the NFL's team of the 1990s. He selected players, he traded picks to move up, and he traded down for even more picks. Eventually, Johnson had landed the likes of NFL career rushing leader Emmitt Smith, defensive tackle and No. 1 overall pick Russell Maryland, safety Darren Woodson, cornerback Kevin Smith, wide receiver Alvin Harper, and line-backer Dixon Edwards. The Cowboys went from 1–15 in 1989, the first year under owner Jerry Jones, to winning Super Bowls after the 1992, 1993, and 1995 seasons. "When you look at what we gave them, I think Mike Lynn built the Cowboys' dynasty of the '90s," former Vikings safety Joey Browner said. "I can't help but think those were Super Bowls that possibly could have been won here in Minnesota."

Meanwhile, the Vikings went 21–23 with Walker, the big running back they coveted, before releasing him in May of 1992. Their only playoff appearance with Walker was a 41–13 loss at San Francisco in the divisional round in 1989. Walker rushed for 29 yards that day. "You can't blame Herschel," said former Vikings receiver Anthony Carter. "The ball was in Mike Lynn's hands, and it was one of the horrible trades in sports history. All the blame for that goes on one individual, and that's Mike Lynn. Sorry to say that, but it's the honest to God truth."

Even 20 years after the trade, Lynn said he "still hasn't figured out" how the Walker trade went so awry. "All that we lacked on that team was a big back, and Herschel was the best big back in the league," Lynn said. "He gained 1,500 yards the previous year. He was in marvelous shape when he got here. It should have worked out."

It did—for one game. In Walker's debut, a 26–14 victory against the Green Bay Packers at the Metrodome, Walker ran for 148 yards on 18 carries, the first 100-yard game by a Vikings running back in 30 games. On his first carry, he literally ran out of his shoe while gaining 47 yards. "Everybody sure thought it was a great trade that day," Lynn said. "But something happened. I don't know what it was, but whatever he had, he didn't have it any longer. It was like a great horse not having it—just gone overnight or in a week."

Walker would suit up 43 more times in purple. He'd average just 49.9 yards rushing per game. Work ethic and attitude weren't the problem, according to teammates and coach Jerry Burns. But his running style simply didn't mesh with the system run by Burns and offensive coordinator Bob Schnelker.

Walker was a Heisman Trophy winner at Georgia, a star in the USFL, and a Pro Bowl player who had a combined 2,019 yards rushing and receiving with the Cowboys in 1988. All of his success came as a classic I-formation tailback who lined up eight yards deep with a fullback in front of him. "That was a problem when he got here," Hall of Fame guard Randall McDaniel said. "We ran traps and counters all the time. We were a split-back formation, which is a totally different set-up. We asked Herschel to move closer to the line, split the backfield, and do things he just wasn't used to doing."

Walker never rushed for 1,000 yards in a season with the Vikings. After being released he ran for 1,070 yards with the Philadelphia Eagles in 1992. He returned to Dallas for the 1996–97 seasons and retired as a Cowboy. Walker's ineffectiveness was only half of the immediate blow the Vikings sustained in the trade. On a returning playoff team that was only two years removed from the NFC Championship Game, it also cost Vikings starting linebackers Jesse Solomon and David Howard, starting cornerback Issiac Holt, leading rusher Darrin Nelson, and defensive end Alex Stewart.

The Vikings were 3–2 at the time. Some players didn't find out until reporters began calling for reaction. "And some of us were sitting in the meeting rooms when they started calling out players who were in the trade," Carter said. "It was devastating. We lost a lot of good football players that morning."

Meanwhile, in Dallas, Johnson was cooking a scheme that would increase his long-term bounty immensely. Five of the picks he received in the trade—two first rounders, two second rounders, and one third rounder—were conditional. In the agreement—one that New York Giants general manager George Young joked "may be longer than the Magna Carta"—the Cowboys could use the five players in the deal for the season and then either keep them or the conditional picks. "I thought they would keep a number of those players," Lynn said 20 years later. "So I didn't think the number of draft choices would be as great as it was."

Lynn had been rushed into the deal. Johnson already had a generous offer from Cleveland Browns general manager Ernie Accorsi and used it to put a tight deadline on Lynn. "When we made the trade, Darrin Nelson didn't show up," Johnson said. "He didn't want to play on a bad team or whatever. I didn't care. I wasn't going to keep him anyway. I wanted those [conditional] picks. He didn't like the trade, so I said, 'Fine, hit the road.' We traded him to San Diego."

Johnson then told his assistants that the other four players from Minnesota were not to start. "They were the best players we had," Johnson said. "But I knew if we started them, the coaches would like them and try to talk me into keeping them. And then the fans would say, 'Why is this guy releasing our best players?'"

Johnson wasn't done manipulating Lynn. After the season he called Lynn and told him he liked the players but was going to cut them all and keep the picks. "If I cut the players at that point, Mike got nothing," Johnson said. "He had no choice but to make another trade to salvage something and let me keep the players and the conditional picks."

Lynn hung up before eventually agreeing to tweak the trade. In February of 1990, Johnson gave Lynn a third and a 10th-round pick in 1990 and a third-round pick in 1991 so he could keep Solomon, Howard, Holt, and the conditional picks outlined in the original trade. "Based on the value of all the picks we got and the value of Minnesota's picks, it was off the chart," Jones said 20 years later. "If you added up the value for those three years [1990–92], we had more draft-value points in those three years than we had in our next 10 drafts combined."

History has judged the Walker trade as the move that built a Cowboys dynasty. Johnson said that's an oversimplification. "In my five years in Dallas, I made 51 trades," Johnson said. "That's more than the rest of the league made combined. And you can't really trace the Herschel Walker trade because of all the other trades that came with all the picks and players after it. It became like the branches of a tree."

# 16 Jim Marshall

Officially, the Vikings retired Jim Marshall's jersey at the Metrodome during a 35–27 win against the San Diego Chargers on November 28, 1999. Unofficially, an equipment manager named Jimmy "Stubby" Eason decided on his own 10 years earlier that no other living creature would ever step on an NFL field wearing a Vikings jersey with the No. 70 on it.

To this day, the Vikings have had only two equipment managers. Once Marshall retired after 20 seasons, 282 consecutive games, and 270 straight starts, Eason decided not to issue the jersey in 1980. Stubby died of lung cancer in 1981, but his understudy, Dennis Ryan, had gotten the message and held firm until the team finally followed suit.

Yes, Jim Marshall—defensive end, ironman, team co-captain, and tone-setter—meant that much. "Jim should be in the Hall of Fame," center and fellow longtime co-captain Mick Tingelhoff said shortly after he finally gained entry to Canton, Ohio, in 2015. "More than anyone else, he should be in there."

Marshall was a 21-year-old out of Ohio State when he played one year in the CFL in 1959. When he retired from the NFL after the 1979 season, he was a 42-year-old grandfather who never missed a game, including none of the 19 he played in the postseason. When the NFL had a 12-game schedule in 1960, Marshall didn't start but played every game for the Cleveland Browns. He was traded to the expansion Vikings in 1961 and started every game when the NFL had a 14-game schedule (1961–77) and two more years when the league went to a 16-game schedule. Brett Favre, the only person in NFL history with more consecutive starts (297) than Marshall, played all 20 of his seasons during the 16-game era. "I was always blessed," Marshall told the *Minneapolis Star Tribune* years after his retirement. "When it got close to game time, regardless of whether I was in the hospital or how badly banged up I was, something always seemed to happen to allow me to play."

Off the field the free-spirited Marshall has pushed the limits of his health and mortality to the point where former teammates have joked about the "nine lives of Jim Marshall." Soon after he retired, Marshall was injured when he crashed his glider plane. Another time, he was trapped on a Wyoming mountaintop during a snowmobile trip and survived while another man in the traveling party froze to death. "The very nature of my life makes these close calls happen," Marshall said. "I did a lot of things that people didn't do at the time, so I was labeled a kook, a nut. But my zest and quest for life is still there and so is that spark. We ruin so many people each year by not allowing them to create the genius inherent to our species. We see lives through limited minds instead of opening up and going full tilt."

Like a lot of players and people of that era in the 1970s, Marshall also turned to drugs as a socially acceptable way to push the limit. The NFL didn't test for them, and teams looked the other way as long as a player showed up and did his job. And no one did that better than Marshall, so, as you might imagine, the Marshall home was a place to be. Eventually, Marshall got himself clean after a downward spiral included a 1990 arrest in Duluth, Minnesota, for possessing 56 grams of cocaine. "When cocaine hit in the late '70s, no one knew much about it," defensive end Carl Eller told the *Star Tribune*. "Those days got fairly wild. Cocaine was certainly made available and accessible and it became a way of fitting in."

Vikings fans old and too young to have seen Marshall play still idolize him as a great player, a true leader, and perhaps the ultimate symbol of the team's history of rugged toughness.

Of course, an equipment manager named Stubby knew way back in 1980 that the legend of Jim Marshall would live forever. "He destroyed all the No. 70s after Jim retired," former Vikings coach Bud Grant told the *Star Tribune*. "And he never ordered another one."

# 17 Visit Kezar Stadium and the Wrong-Way Run

If you're ever in San Francisco and want to stand on the most infamous 66 yards of game-related real estate in Vikings history, head for the southeastern corner of Golden Gate Park. Located in the middle of a neighborhood is Kezar Stadium, former home of the San Francisco 49ers and the spot where former Vikings great Jim Marshall ran the wrong way with a fumble back on October 25, 1964.

The stadium looks considerably different since a $9 million renovation changed it from a 59,942-seat former NFL venue to its current 10,000-seat look for local high school teams. Originally opened on May 2, 1925, Kezar Stadium became the original home of the 49ers when they began play in the All-America Football Conference in 1946 and hosted the first four games of the Oakland Raiders' AFL existence in 1960.

The 49ers' last game at Kezar Stadium was a 17–10 loss to the Dallas Cowboys in the NFC title game on January 3, 1971. The "alley-oop" play was born here in the 1950s when 49ers quarterback Y.A. Tittle realized he could throw the ball up for grabs and receiver R.C. Owens would come down with it in the end zone. For those who prefer movie history, several scenes in the popular 1971 film *Dirty Harry* were filmed at Kezar Stadium. Midfield is (spoiler alert) where Clint Eastwood, playing Dirty Harry, shot Scorpio, the film's bad guy.

Although things have been changed, somewhere in those blades of grass over half a century ago, Marshall made one of the more blooper-worthy mistakes the game has ever seen. In 1994 NFL Films produced the *NFL's 100 Greatest Follies* video. Yes, Marshall's mishap ranked No. 1—a cruel ranking for a well-respected man who played 20 seasons, retired with the NFL record of 282 consecutive games played, and was the leader of the famed "Purple People Eaters" that led the Vikings to four Super Bowls in the 1970s.

The Vikings still won the game 27–22. Early in the fourth quarter, Marshall forced a fumble that fellow defensive end Carl Eller returned 45 yards for a touchdown to give the Vikings a 27–17 lead. But it was the next fumble moments later that would live in infamy.

Backup 49ers quarterback George Mira scrambled and completed a pass to Billy Kilmer, a young running back at the time. Kilmer was stripped of the ball in a collision with Vikings defensive back Karl Kassulke and linebacker Rip Hawkins at San Francisco's 31-yard line.

The ball shot forward three yards. Marshall jumped over a fallen player, scooped up the ball, and never broke stride. Linebacker Roy Winston is seen heading the other way to lead the blocking. Stunned teammates on the sideline ran alongside Marshall yelling for him to turn around.

Up in the radio both, 49ers play-by-play announcer Bob Fouts was calling the game. His 13-year-old son, Dan, the future Hall of Fame quarterback for the San Diego Chargers, was keeping stats. "Kilmer fumbles the football, and it's picked up by Jim Marshall, who is running the wrong way!" Bob Fouts yells during his call. "Marshall is running the wrong way! And he's running it into the end zone the wrong way! He thinks he's scored a touchdown! He's scored a safety!"

49ers guard Bruce Bosley was the first player to reach Marshall. He patted him on the back and said, "Thanks for the favor." The Vikings' only good fortune was Marshall flipping the ball out of play rather than dropping it where the 49ers could have recovered for a touchdown.

"I couldn't hear our guys yelling that I was going the wrong way," Marshall said. "I had to jump over a guy to get the ball. And just before that, I was going the other way on the pass rush. I just got mixed up. I can't remember even picking up the ball. The thing was that confusing. I saw my teammates running down the sideline. I thought they were cheering for me. I think it dawned on me as I was crossing the goal line. Maybe I flipped the ball over my head to get it out of bounds. I don't really know."

# 18 Carl Eller

In the fall of 1956, Ben Warren was the head football coach at Atkins High School in Winston-Salem, North Carolina. He was on his way to practice when Bobby Mooreman, a sophomore defensive tackle, approached with a scouting report on a quiet freshman he just met. "There's a boy named Carl Eller, and he's huge," Warren remembers Mooreman saying. "He's shy, won't say two words. Carl just didn't have the confidence to go out for the team."

Warren found out that Eller liked to hang out on the playground after school every day. The next day, Warren took a recruiting trip to the playground. "I said, 'You interested in playing football?'" Warren said. "And Carl said, 'I'll think about it.'"

Forty-eight years later, in 2004, Eller was enshrined into the Pro Football Hall of Fame. An All-American at the University of Minnesota and a five-time All-Pro with the Vikings, the man known as "Moose" had let his dominance at left defensive end do most of his talking.

Eller played 15 seasons for the Vikings (1964–78) as one of the most feared members of the famed Purple People Eaters. A first-round draft pick of the Vikings and the AFL's Buffalo Bills, the 6'6", 247-pounder was strong enough to stop the run and quick enough to still hold the Vikings' team record for sacks (130.5).

Eller was born in a tobacco town in the segregated South. His father died when Carl was a young teenager, leaving Carl and his mother, Ernestine, to live with Carl's grandparents.

Ernestine said Carl was known around town as one of the hardest workers, always picking up odd jobs between his family chores. Carl also had a love of the theater, joining the high school drama club and landing the lead role in the senior play. "I shared Carl with the drama teacher," Warren joked. "I don't know what kind of actor he was. But as a football player, you just didn't see kids like Carl back then. He was 6'5", 6'6", 225, and so quick. Other teams either double-teamed him, triple-teamed him, or ran away from him. And when they ran away from him, he'd catch up to them anyway."

Eller won a state title as a senior and went undefeated during his final two seasons. Soon, he would learn about a man named Murray Warmath and how he was bucking the national establishment as a major college coach willing to recruit African American players. Like most recruiters who came through Winston-Salem that fall, Bob Bassons, a Warmath assistant, was looking at a running back named Jay B. Sharp. "Bob said to me, 'I like Jay B.,'" Warren said. "And then he pointed at Carl and said, 'And I want him, too.'"

Eller's size and strength even caught the NFL by surprise on many a Sunday in 1964. "I remember playing him that first time and thinking, *I don't know how much longer I want to hang around*," said Green Bay Packers Hall of Fame tackle Forrest Gregg, who was in his eighth season in 1964. "There was a play in which I moved to left guard, and my job was to pull and kick out the left end. I didn't get past the center. I took my first step and hit a wall. I looked up and it was No. 81, Carl Eller."

Bob Brown, the Hall of Fame offensive tackle who played for the Philadelphia Eagles, Los Angeles Rams, and Oakland Raiders, joined Eller in the Hall of Fame's class of 2004. He was asked to rank the defensive ends he played against. "Well," he said, "I'd rank the top five defensive ends I played against as Carl Eller, Claude Humphrey, L.C. Greenwood, Deacon Jones, and everybody else."

Eller was a Hall of Fame finalist 12 times before he finally was selected. In his 13th stint as a finalist, the Vikings campaigned heavily on Eller's behalf. Their strategy included asking some of the tackles who played against Eller to write a letter on Eller's behalf and send it to members of the selection committee. "You're darn right I wrote a letter for Carl," said Hall of Famer Dan Dierdorf, who sent a handwritten letter. "If you took some clay and tried to sculpt the perfect defensive end, I don't know if you'd do any better than what God did with Carl Eller. He was perfect."

# 19 Super Bowl IX

The Vikings were too good, too intimidating, too well-balanced to be dominated on the game's biggest stage for the third time in six seasons, right?

Wrong.

In 1974 the Vikings went 10–6 to win the NFC Central for the sixth time in seven years. They rushed for 363 yards in two playoff wins over the St. Louis Cardinals (30–14) and the Los Angeles Rams (14–10). Then they headed for New Orleans for Super Bowl IX against the Pittsburgh Steelers, who were playing in their first ever title game in 41 years.

Sure, there was some bad karma. The Vikings were man-handled in the Super Bowl the year before and were returning to Tulane Stadium, site of their Super Bowl IV upset loss, because construction on the nearby Superdome was behind schedule.

And things went south from the opening coin toss. Not only did the Vikings lose that, but they also inadvertently elected to play against the wind on a 46-degree day with gusts up to 25 mph. "I couldn't figure out which way the wind was blowing," coach Bud Grant told reporters after the game. "It was swirling around so. As soon as the game started, I knew I took the wrong end."

The Vikings didn't make it past their own 40-yard line in the first quarter. Things got worse in the second quarter. The Steelers led 2–0 at the half because quarterback Fran Tarkenton fumbled while mishandling a pitch near his goal line. He fell on the loose ball in the end zone with 7:11 left in the quarter.

In 60 minutes of football, the only points the Vikings' No. 3-ranked offense scored were those two points for the other team. Tarkenton threw three interceptions while the Vikings mustered only 17 yards rushing and 119 overall. Running back Chuck Foreman was held to 18 yards on 12 carries and also fumbled the ball away on first and goal from the Pittsburgh 5-yard line with the Steelers leading 9–0 in the fourth quarter. "They took away just about everything we do well," said Tarkenton, who completed only 11-of-26 passes for 102 yards.

Defensively, the vaunted Purple People Eaters kept the Vikings in the game but were overpowered in a second straight Super Bowl. In Super Bowl VIII, Miami Dolphins running back Larry Csonka won MVP honors while setting records for carries (33) and yards rushing (145). In Super Bowl IX Pittsburgh's Franco Harris won MVP while breaking both records (34 for 158).

Those who witnessed that game in person say the frustration of being the first team to lose three Super Bowls was palpable. As the game ended, defensive tackle Alan Page, standing on the sideline, slammed his helmet to the artificial turf before jogging off the field. "It doesn't bother me all that much to lose," he told reporters. "What does bother me is that we had some players who didn't want the win when it was there."

The Vikings turned the ball over five times, including Bill Brown's fumble of the second-half kickoff. That led to a nine-yard touchdown run by Harris. The Vikings finally scored when Matt Blair blocked a punt that was recovered by Terry Brown in the end zone. Fred Cox missed the point-after attempt to make it 9–6.

The Steelers answered quickly, driving 66 yards in 11 plays to take a 16–6 lead on a four-yard pass from Terry Bradshaw to Larry Brown with 3:31 left. The drive wasn't without controversy or a rise in Grant's blood pressure. A 30-yard third-down completion from Bradshaw to Brown appeared to have ended with a fumble and Vikings possession. One official ruled it a fumble but was overruled by linesman Ed Marion. "There was no question [Brown] was not down," Grant said after the game. "The official who called it was across the field and behind him, and the official who ruled it our ball was in front of the play. When they didn't give it to us, it became a very big play, bigger than any we could make. Neither team got here playing this kind of football. It was just a succession of errors by all three teams today."

# The 2010 Season Implodes

On August 17, 2010, Brett Favre stepped to a microphone at Winter Park to announce he would return for a 20th NFL season. The team pumped its collective fist, fans rejoiced, and even the media nodded in unison. After all, what could possibly go wrong?

You mean besides *everything?*

"We had everybody back," then-coach Brad Childress said five years later. "But that's why you tell those guys every year that each year stands on its own merits. You're either getting better or you're getting worse. You don't stay the same in the NFL."

Amen.

A week after Favre returned, the fantasy of 22 returning starters picking up right where they left off in the NFC Championship Game seven months earlier began to unravel. Sidney Rice, who had caught 83 passes for 1,312 yards and eight touchdowns during the magical 2009 season, was having hip surgery at the Steadman Clinic in Vail, Colorado. Rice had put off surgery for an injury sustained in the NFC title game loss in New Orleans and would play only six games, catching 17 passes for 280 yards and two touchdowns.

But the bad news would only snowball throughout the disastrous 2010 season. Looking back, it all seemed downhill after the Vikings lost the season-opening coin toss and allowed the Saints to move 77 yards in five plays for a 7–0 lead en route to winning the rematch 14–9 in the NFL's season kickoff game.

A week later, the Vikings scored only 10 points in their home opener. Favre, who had thrown only seven interceptions the year before, threw three and lost a fumble in a 14–10 loss to the Miami Dolphins.

The beating Favre had taken in the NFC title game was a prominent piece in the Saints' infamous "Bountygate" scandal. Favre had to have ankle surgery following the game and was telling teammates before training camp began that the ankle still didn't feel completely healed. It would bother Favre throughout the season. But at the time, the Vikings, quite frankly, thought it was just Favre being Favre. A year earlier, he had said essentially the same thing about the torn biceps tendon in his throwing arm only to unretire after one year with the New York Jets and produce one of his finest seasons.

The Vikings were convinced that a second run with Favre would pay off. When mid-August arrived and Favre still hadn't left Hattiesburg, Mississippi, or announced another retirement, coach Brad Childress excused kicker Ryan Longwell, left guard Steve Hutchinson, and defensive end Jared Allen from practice so they could climb aboard ownership's private plane and go expedite Favre's decision.

Meanwhile, Rob Brzezinski, Vikings executive vice president of football operations and salary cap expert, was working on sweetening the financial pot for No. 4. Ultimately, Favre's base salary was increased by $3.5 million to $16.5 million while another $3.5 million of incentives was tacked on. At the end of a long day with three of his best friends on the team, Favre famously gave in and, according to Hutchinson, simply said, "Let's do it."

Unfortunately for the Vikings the 0–2 wrong-way start would never correct itself. Receiver Percy Harvin's migraine headaches returned, causing him to miss two games. During the Week 4 bye, Childress underestimated Randy Moss' volatility when he pushed the front office to bring Moss from New England back to Minnesota for a third-round draft pick. Moss lasted less than a month, catching 13 passes for 174 yards and two touchdowns during a 1–3 stretch.

On November 1, a day after Moss criticized Childress and teammates following a 28–18 loss at the Patriots, Childress released Moss. His anger got the best of him in a unilateral move that surprised ownership and defied team protocol established specifically for those kinds of situations. That decision played a significant role in Childress being fired the morning after the team fell to 3–7 with a humiliating 31–3 home loss to the Green Bay Packers. Only 368 days earlier, Childress was given a contract extension through the 2013 season while his team's record stood at 8–1.

Leslie Frazier was named interim head coach and finished the year 3–3. But the nightmare didn't end with Childress' firing. The Metrodome roof collapsed on December 12, forcing that day's home game against the New York Giants to be played the following night in Detroit's Ford Field. Favre, who had injured his throwing shoulder the week before against the Buffalo Bills, wasn't able to play, ending his NFL-record streak of consecutive regular-season starts at 297.

The Vikings also had a game in Philadelphia delayed until Tuesday night because of the threat of heavy snow. In Week 15 with the Metrodome still out of service, they played their first outdoor home game in 29 years, losing 40–14 to the Chicago Bears at TCF Bank Stadium, home of the Gophers.

Favre had been ruled out the Friday before that game. But he talked his way into playing. In what was the final snap of his career, Favre was literally knocked out when his helmet was bounced off the frozen turf on a sack by Corey Wootton. "It was the first time in my career I was ever completely knocked out," Favre told *Sports Illustrated* years later. "It was like 10 to 15 seconds. The field was as hard as a stone. I hit myself on the side of the head, and the next thing you know I'm snoring. Eric Sugarman, our trainer—we call him Sug—comes out, and he's like, 'Hey, buddy,' and I said, 'I was just snoring.' He goes, 'All right, c'mon, come with me.' I got up and saw some Bears guys clapping—[Brian] Urlacher and a couple of those guys—and I'm like, 'What are the Bears doing here?' I went straight to the shower, grabbed some hot chocolate and a hot dog, and from that point I never missed it. I knew it was time."

Favre would finish his 20th and final season standing on the sideline in a loss at Detroit. The Vikings finished 6–10 with Favre as bad as he was good the year before. He threw 11 touchdown passes and 19 interceptions while posting a 69.9 passer rating.

He also spent the year dealing with the embarrassment of the NFL investigating him for allegedly sexting and leaving inappropriate voice messages for Jets employee Jenn Sterger during the 2008 season. The NFL said it couldn't prove that Favre sent the photos but did fine him $50,000 under its personal conduct policy for not cooperating with the investigation.

"You look back on it, he was distracted in that second year," Childress said six years later. "We sent the guys down there, and his heart wasn't there. I think he had one mission [beating the Packers] in mind that year he came to us in 2009. I think he was in a completely different spot in his life in Year Two. That's a good lesson for when you talk to guys about each year standing on its own. It's not just a matter of somebody crowning you king in the beginning."

# 21 Stormin' Norman

Players from the Vikings' early days tend to remember the coins and the noises they made while jingling inside the pockets of their fidgety, volatile young coach, Norm Van Brocklin. "He always had his hands in his pockets and he always had a ton of coins," running back Dave Osborn said. "He was a nervous guy, too. So he was always rattling those coins around."

"The Dutchman" also had an infamous temper that could really make those coins sing and dance. "During a game the ref made a bad call, or something didn't go right," Osborn said. "Van Brocklin threw his hands up, but they were still in his pockets. Well, he threw his hands up so hard that he ripped both pockets off. Quarters and nickels and dimes and pennies went flying all over the official."

Vikings Hall of Fame center Mick Tingelhoff roared with laughter listening to Osborn tell the story five decades later. "Stormin' Norman, that's what we called him," Tingelhoff said. "Every other word was a cuss word, always yelling and calling us girls and all that stuff."

On December 26, 1960, Van Brocklin's 12-year playing career ended with the Hall of Fame quarterback and his Philadelphia Eagles handing Vince Lombardi's Green Bay Packers their only NFL title game loss. Twenty-three days later—with no coaching background and limited offseason college personnel work for the Eagles—Van Brocklin was named Vikings head coach. He was 34.

Weeks earlier, a similarly inexperienced Bert Rose was named Vikings general manager. Rose was the promotions director for the Los Angeles Rams and, more importantly, a close friend of new NFL commissioner Pete Rozelle, the former Rams public relations director, who helped orchestrate the hire. The Vikings reportedly interviewed three others for the head coaching job: Northwestern's Ara Parseghian, newly-hired team scout Joe Thomas, and Bud Grant, the young coach of the CFL's Winnipeg Blue Bombers.

Even in a simpler era, the teaming of Van Brocklin and Rose raised eyebrows. During his introductory press conference, Van Brocklin was asked about this shocking lack of experience and whether he was worried about going straight from the playing field to the head coaching ranks. The reigning NFL Player of the Year barked, "I don't worry about anything."

Soon, the unease would belong to the players, particularly quarterback Fran Tarkenton, who would clash with Van Brocklin more than any other player. Tarkenton's scrambling instincts and refusal to muffle them never sat well with Van Brocklin, a classic pocket passer who had claimed passing titles, thrown for a league-record 554 yards in a game, and won two NFL titles with two different teams.

But as a coach, Van Brocklin lasted 84 games through the 1966 season, finishing 29–51–4 without a playoff appearance. He resurfaced in Atlanta in 1968, coaching the Falcons for seven seasons. He did beat the Vikings twice but finished 37–49–3 before exiting with a 2–6 record in 1974.

Van Brocklin's best season was 1964, when the Vikings finished 8–5–1. Unfortunately, Van Brocklin's collapse beneath the pressure of elevated expectations for 1965 ultimately undid any bright future he might have had in Minnesota. The Vikings lost the opener 35–16 at the Baltimore Colts and the home opener against the Detroit Lions 31–29 the following week. They were 2–3 when they won three straight heading into the rematch with Baltimore at home.

But a day after losing to Baltimore 41–21, Van Brocklin called reporters into his office and said he was resigning immediately. "I want to get out of football," he told reporters. "I have no intention of reconsidering. I've taken the team as far as I can. I can't get the team over the hump. It's been going this way for five years. We come to the big game and we blow it."

Within 24 hours he had reconsidered and was back. But it was clear he had lost what was left of the players' respect. He was a tough-talking, hard-drinking, fists-flying man's man, but he'd never shake the moment he quit after a disappointing loss. The

Vikings finished 7–7 in 1965 and stumbled to 4–9–1 in 1966. On February 11, 1967, Van Brocklin resigned again. Only this time no one tried to talk him out of it.

# 22 Trading Tarkenton

After six seasons together, there was nothing left of the fractured relationship between coach Norm Van Brocklin and quarterback Fran Tarkenton. To this day Tarkenton, the Hall of Fame scrambler, credits Van Brocklin, the Hall of Fame pocket passer, with helping him understand the quarterback position and the pro passing game. But as Tarkenton said in 2015, "Everybody knows Van Brocklin wasn't my favorite person."

Tarkenton was the team's third-round draft pick (29th overall) in its 1961 expansion season. Van Brocklin was the young, volatile coach who went straight from winning the 1960 NFL title as a player in Philadelphia to running that expansion team. Yes, they butted heads.

"But he butted heads with everybody in our locker room," Tarkenton said. "God bless his soul, but he was a dysfunctional human being, totally dysfunctional. Bill Wade, a guy who played with him in Los Angeles, a very religious guy and a good friend of mine coming out of high school, was drafted as a quarterback when Van Brocklin was in L.A. He says, 'You're going to hate this guy's guts. He's dysfunctional.' Mick Tingelhoff was our first guy to make All-Pro. We had our offense together in the meeting room. When Mick made that team, Van Brocklin says in front of the whole group, 'Tingelhoff, you made the All-Pro team. All-Pro, my

*Though the Vikings traded quarterback Fran Tarkenton to the New York Giants in 1967, the scrambling quarterback would return to the team five years later and play seven more seasons.*

ass. You're All-Pro barnyard' because Mick was a country boy who grew up on a farm. He just treated people like crap."

Tarkenton said there was a point during the 1966 season when he thought the two would be able to coexist beyond that season. "He brought me into his office with about four games left and said, 'You know, we got to get ourselves together here, you and I, because we have some players here and we can really win. We just got to work better together,'" Tarkenton said. "I said, 'Boy, that's great. I'm all for that.' I went home and told my wife this is the greatest thing ever."

And?

"He never spoke to me the rest of the season," Tarkenton said. "He stopped coaching. [Vikings assistant coach] Lew Carpenter and I put in the offense. Van Brocklin never spoke to me again, never said a word."

After a win over the Green Bay Packers, Tarkenton threw five interceptions in a loss to the Detroit Lions and was benched in favor of Ron Vander Kelen in the following week's loss to the Los Angeles Rams. Two weeks later second-year quarterback Bob Berry started against the expansion Atlanta Falcons and threw five interceptions before Van Brocklin went back to Tarkenton.

By the spring of 1967, Tarkenton had enough. "I had just turned 27. I took a trip back to Minneapolis, sat down with Van Brocklin, and said, 'I'm not going to play for you.' I need to be traded. He said he wasn't going to trade me. I didn't yell. I didn't scream. I just said, 'I have no respect for you. I wish you well, but I'm not going to play here.' I walked out, got on a plane, and went home."

Tarkenton's phone rang the next day. It was Vikings general manager Jim Finks. "He says, 'Fran, Dutch [Van Brocklin] tells me you had a great meeting,'" Tarkenton said. "I said, 'He told you what?' He says, 'He told me you had a great meeting and got everything worked out. I'm so happy.' I said, 'Finksie, I told him I wasn't going to play there anymore. For all the reasons you know.' Finks says, 'Oh, my God. Let me get back to you.'"

News of Tarkenton's demand for a trade went public. On February 11 Van Brocklin resigned unexpectedly. Tarkenton says he was fired. Either way, Tarkenton knew he couldn't return to Minnesota. "They wanted me to stay," Tarkenton said. "I said, 'Ain't going to do it, Finksie. I'm not going to have Van Brocklin's blood on my hands. I can't come back after this.' I didn't leave Minnesota because I wanted to leave Minnesota."

On March 7 Tarkenton was traded to the New York Giants for two first-round picks and two second-rounders. Finks acquired running back Clinton Jones and receiver Bobby Grim in 1967, Hall of Famer Ron Yary with the No. 1 overall pick in 1968, and guard Ed White with a second-round pick in 1969.

Five years later Finks brought Tarkenton back to Minnesota through a trade for Grim, quarterback Norm Snead, fullback Vince Clements, and picks in the first round in 1972 and the second round in 1973. Tarkenton and Bud Grant teamed up and went to three Super Bowls before Tarkenton retired after seven more seasons.

# 23 Fred Cox, the Father of the Nerf

Fred Cox retired after the 1977 season and yet 39 years later he's still the Vikings' career scoring leader by more than double the amount of the next highest scorer. An eighth-round draft pick of the Browns, Cox originally was slated to compete as a blocking fullback for the great Jim Brown as a rookie in 1962. But a back injury early in training camp changed that. Coach Paul Brown moved Cox to kicker.

Raised in the small mining town of Monongahela, Pennsylvania, Cox kicked and punted in high school and at the University of Pittsburgh. He was good, but even he knew he didn't have a shot to unseat Lou "the Toe" Groza, Cleveland's Hall of Fame kicker and left tackle. "Anybody with any real common sense would have known the odds were stacked against me," Cox told the Vikings website in 2011. "But Groza is the reason I eventually made it as a kicker. I spent all of training camp up until the last exhibition game with him and I learned more from Lou Groza in that period of time than I learned in all my years of kicking before and after that."

The Browns traded Cox to the Vikings before the final preseason game in 1962. Cox impressed coach Norm Van Brocklin, but this was 1962, and the notion of a kicking specialist wasn't popular. "Norm Van Brocklin made no bones about it," Cox said. "He told me that he wanted to keep me, but we could only have 36 players, and we were too young a team to be able to keep a guy who just kicked."

So, Cox was released.

In their 1961 expansion season, the Vikings drafted a kicker, Mike Mercer, in the 15th round. He lasted the entire season despite making only nine of 21 field goal attempts. A year later Mercer missed all five of his attempts while Jim Christopherson of Wadena, Minnesota, made 11 of 20 in his only season with the team. Christopherson, who played at Concordia in Moorhead, Minnesota, would return to his alma mater as head coach in 1969. He coached through the 2000 season, compiling a 218–101–7 record with two NAIA national titles and was inducted into the College Football Hall of Fame in 2007.

Cox returned to training camp in 1963. This time he made it and would stick around for 15 seasons as one of the league's last straight-on kickers. He led the league in scoring (121) and field goal accuracy (70.3) in 1969 and in scoring (125) again in 1970. His 62 percent career mark on field goals was considered reliable for his era. Cox, who played in all four of the Vikings' Super Bowls, posted 1,365 points and 282 field goals, and both are team records. The point total is 695 better than Hall of Fame receiver Cris Carter's 670. It's also 29th in league history, while the field goal total is 30th.

Cox's interests were broader than football. His back injury in 1962 caused him to go back to school and get his degree as a chiropractor in 1972. He had a practice for 20 years. But his most

## Walsh Goes Back to First Grade

As you can imagine, Twitter wasn't a comforting place for Blair Walsh when he missed the 27-yard field goal with 22 seconds left in the 10–9 wild-card playoff loss to the Seattle Seahawks in January of 2016. Fans were brutal toward him.

But not all of them. Certainly not the first-graders at Northpoint Elementary School in Blaine, Minnesota. While the venom spewed via Twitter, mature understanding and compassion flowed from the crayons of the children in Judie Offerdahl's classroom. Sensing a teachable moment on empathy, Offerdahl asked her students to write letters that could be sent to Walsh, the 26-year-old kicker who had stood up and accepted responsibility for the loss in the locker room after the game.

The children put crayons to paper and wrote things such as, "Everyone makes mistakes sometimes," "I missed a basket before," and "One time I made a mistake when I was doing a cartwheel. I felt embarrassed. Try, try again." And one little girl simply wrote: "For Blair Walsh. Keep on trying. Puppies are cute."

When Walsh found out what the first graders had done, he stayed in town a few days longer so he could set up a classroom visit with the kids just four days after the painful loss. "I wanted to show these kids that I cared and I didn't want to wait until spring," he said that day. "It was very touching to me...I will cherish the cards forever."

Walsh also told the kids that the failure won't define his career. "This isn't the end," he said.

fortunate move was answering the door when a gentleman by the name of John Mattox came knocking for advice on an idea of a movable goal post for kids. One thing led to another and, bingo, Cox came up with the idea for the Nerf football, which began selling in 1972 and never stopped, becoming the No. 1-selling football of all time. "It's safe to say that I don't know how much money I've made over the years from it, but I can tell you that it's been considerable," Cox said.

He still receives quarterly checks from Hasbro, which owns the product. "They sell them all over the world," Cox said. "Three years ago [in 2008], I know they sold over eight million of them."

# 24 Korey Stringer's Death

The Vikings had just assembled on the practice field in Mankato, Minnesota, when they paused for a moment of prayerful silence the morning of July 31, 2011. It had been 10 years since one of their own, right tackle Korey Stringer, had died from heatstroke. On July 30, 2001, the 27-year-old, 335-pounder practiced on that very field for the last time.

On a hot, humid day with a 110-degree heat index, Stringer, a six-year veteran coming off his first Pro Bowl season, pushed and pushed until his body temperature hit 108.8 degrees and couldn't be cooled. He was taken by ambulance to Immanuel St. Joseph's hospital in Mankato, where he died at 1:50 AM the next day.

On July 31, 2011, the only active player on the team who had known Stringer and played with him was 13-year veteran tight end Jim Kleinsasser, the team's second-round pick in 1999. "I've sat down and talked to the guys about Korey because my hope is he will never be forgotten in Vikings history," Kleinsasser said. "I tell them what he was like as a player but more importantly what he was like as a person. He was a great person, great in the community, caring, funny. We still have Korey's locker preserved [behind glass] back at Winter Park. Maybe me talking to them will make it mean a little more when they walk past it every day."

In addition to the preserved locker, the team also re-named its annual media good guy award after Stringer, retired his jersey number (77), and placed him in its ring of honor.

Born May 8, 1974, in Warren, Ohio, Stringer went to Ohio State, where he was consensus All-American in 1994. The Vikings selected him in the first round of the 1995 draft and were determined to build a strong line around him. They reached the NFC title game in 2000, the year Stringer reached his only Pro Bowl. Determined to be more of a team leader, he reported to training camp in 2001 at 335 pounds, his lightest as an NFL player.

On the first day of training camp, Stringer became ill from the heat and vomited several times before leaving practice early. Later that night he appeared to be fine as he walked through the players' dormitory. The second day of camp was the first day in full pads. Coaches and teammates ribbed Stringer about a photo in the *Minneapolis Star Tribune* of him doubled over while struggling with the heat the day before.

Stringer was determined not to leave practice early again. He practiced for more than two and a half hours and, according to media reports at the time, refused several suggestions that he take some breaks. He even joined his fellow linemen in a post-practice running session before motioning to head athletic trainer Chuck Barta that something was seriously wrong. Stringer was taken to an air-conditioned trailer at 11:30 AM. He died less than 16 hours later. He left behind a wife, Kelci, and a three-year-old son, Kodie.

Kelci filed lawsuits against the Vikings and the NFL. The suit against the Vikings was dismissed, while the one against the league was settled in 2009. The only disclosed part of the settlement was the NFL's agreement to promote a heat-illness prevention program that would change how teams now handle players in the sweltering heat.

Stringer's teammates, many of whom didn't find out until being called into a team meeting at 6:00 AM, were devastated. The Vikings never recovered that year, finishing 5–11 with Denny Green getting fired and replaced by offensive line coach Mike

## Tragedy Cut Kassulke's Career Short

The Vikings were assembled in Mankato, Minnesota, for the start of the 1973 season when coach Bud Grant called everyone together to announce that safety Karl Kassulke had been in a motorcycle accident on his way to training camp a few hours earlier and might not survive. Grant broke down in tears.

Kassulke survived the accident, but he was paralyzed from the waist down. He would go on to inspire thousands as part of Wings Outreach, a Christian ministry to the disabled, before his death on October 26, 2008 at age 67.

Born March 20, 1941, in Milwaukee, Kassulke became one of the NFL's hardest-hitting safeties and one of the more popular Vikings players during a 10-year career from 1963 to 1972. A standout at Drake, he was drafted by the Detroit Lions in the 11th round in 1963 and joined the Vikings before the start of the regular season.

Unfortunately, some might remember Kassulke's name from the popular NFL Films segment. In Super Bowl IV, Kansas City Chiefs coach Hank Stram agreed to be the first NFL coach to wear a microphone during a game. Stram used the opportunity to joyfully mock the heavily favored NFL-champion Vikings during the AFL-champion Chiefs' 23–7 upset in the last Super Bowl before the merger. At one point during the game, the Vikings' defense was confused when Stram cackled, "Kassulke was running around there like it was a Chinese fire drill."

Kassulke played 131 games, intercepting 19 passes. He made the Pro Bowl in 1971 but would play only eight more games in 1972 before his accident.

Tice with one game left in the season. Receiver Randy Moss, one of Stringer's closest friends, wept while speaking during the news conference the day Stringer died. "I don't even know where to start," said Moss, a black cap pulled down over his face. "It's like he was here today, gone tomorrow. I think the reason that it is hard for me is just because the only thing I've been thinking about for the last 24 hours was, if he does die, what is going to happen to his son? I don't know how many people are thinking like me, but I don't even know how and when I am going to get over this because it's hard. We know Korey Stringer, No. 77, is going to be missed running through the tunnel on gameday, having his number called."

## 25 Sing Prince's Purple Prose

At the risk of claiming to understand how Prince's mind worked, the Minneapolis native wasn't thinking of his hometown NFL team when he wrote the 1984 Oscar-winning hit song "Purple Rain." Although you have to admit the opening lyrics would be fitting if they were sung from the Vikings to their loyal, but frustrated followers:

*I never meant to cause you any sorrow*
*I never meant to cause you any pain*
*I only wanted to one time to see you laughing*
*I only wanted to see you*
*Laughing in the purple rain*

The song was written for the popular movie by the same name. Each verse is about the people in the life of Prince's movie character.

But that doesn't mean Prince hadn't penned a song about his favorite NFL team before his death in 2016. It happened in January of 2010, after the Brett Favre-led Vikings beat the Dallas Cowboys 34–3 in a divisional playoff game at the Metrodome. Prince called it "Purple and Gold," and it goes like this:

*The veil of the sky draws open*
*The roar of the chariots touch down*
*We are the ones who have now come again*
*And walk upon water like solid ground*
*As we approach the throne, we won't bow down*
*This time we won't be denied*
*Raise every voice and let it be known*
*In the name of the purple and gold*
*We come in the name of the purple and gold*
*All of the odds are in our favor*
*No prediction 2 bold*
*We are the truth if the truth can be told*
*Long reign the purple and gold*
*The eyes say ready 4 battle*
*No need 4 sword in hand*
*We are all amped up like a rock n roll band*
*Ready 2 celebrate every score*
*Ready 2 fight the elegant war*
*Ready 2 hear the crowd roar*

Unfortunately for Prince and his fellow Vikings fans, the Vikings lost to the New Orleans Saints in the NFC title game a week later and are still looking for their next playoff win six years later.

# 26 Max Winter

Max Winter didn't miss the boat—figuratively—as a Minneapolis businessman seeking an NFL franchise in the late 1950s—or literally—as a 10-year-old child emigrating with his mother to the United States from Austria-Hungary in 1914. Halfway across the Atlantic, World War I broke out in Europe. No other passenger ships made it out in time. "I'm glad we didn't miss the boat," Winter would tell people years later, according to the *Minneapolis Star Tribune*. "If we had missed that boat, my entire life would have been changed. I'd have never gotten to the United States."

Winter's work ethic came from a father who settled in Minneapolis ahead of him and worked as a street corner apple salesman to save enough money for the steerage class fare to bring his family to America. Young Max would grow no taller than 5'5" but would become a giant as a local entrepreneur and a founding father of professional basketball and football in the Twin Cities.

Winter made his fortune opening The 620 Club, a popular nightclub at 620 Hennepin Avenue in 1933. He became a sports promoter, boxing manager, and big thinker in terms of putting the Twin Cities on the nation's sports map. It started in 1947, when he became part-owner, president, and general manager of the Minneapolis Lakers, who won the National Basketball League title in 1948 before shifting to the rival league and winning five of the next six titles in the Basketball Association of America and then the National Basketball Association.

Winter's interest in bringing the NFL to Minneapolis began in 1955 when he saw a game in Chicago. When things didn't work out initially with the NFL, Winter joined the efforts in forming the rival American Football League. On August 14, 1959, it was announced that six AFL teams, including Minneapolis, would start play in the fall of 1960. Winter's team even participated in the inaugural AFL draft held in Minneapolis later that year. Meanwhile, George Halas, Chicago Bears owner and one of the original co-founders of the NFL, stepped in behind the scenes and convinced Winter and his partners to abandon the AFL in favor of a shot at approval for an NFL franchise.

The expansion fee and start-up costs for an NFL team were $1 million. Winter and businessmen Bill Boyer and H.P. Skoglund were the original three partners. To cover the cost, they added *St. Paul Pioneer Press* publisher Bernie Ridder and former Duluth Eskimos owner Ole Haugsrud. In January of 1960, NFL owners met to consider adding Dallas and Minneapolis as the 13th and 14th franchises. But first they had to name a new commissioner to replace Bert Bell, who had died in October. On January 26 Pete Rozelle, who started out as Los Angeles Rams PR man and later worked as their general manager, was selected after 23 ballots were cast.

Two days later Dallas was approved as the 13th NFL team and would begin play that fall. Convinced that his group had been shot down, Winter squirmed during a break in the action. But later that night, Minnesota was awarded an NFL franchise that would begin play in 1961. The team was incorporated simply as "Minnesota Professional Football."

On August 5, 1960, Bert Rose, a promotions director with the Rams and a friend of Rozelle's, was named Vikings general manager. Rose lasted until 1964 and is overshadowed immensely by his Hall of Fame successor Jim Finks. But it was Rose who named Minnesota's team. He recommended the nickname to the team's board of directors because, "it represented both an aggressive person with the will to win and the Nordic tradition in the northern Midwest." And on September 17, 1960, the name "Vikings" was born.

To this day, Vikings headquarters is known as "Winter Park." But like so many endings in franchise history, Max Winter's final days were ugly. Finks left in 1974 when his attempts to gain minority ownership were rebuffed. In July of the following year, Winter promoted Mike Lynn to general manager after 10 years with the team. Nine years later, Winter turned over more control to Lynn and ended up regretting it until he died at 92 on July 26, 1996.

Winter, who owned nearly 50 percent of the shares in the team, decided in the mid-80s to sell to Irwin Jacobs and Carl Pohlad. The other owners at the time, John Skoglund and Jack Steele, were aligned with Lynn. They challenged Winter in court, arguing that the other owners had right of first refusal on buying the shares. Winter eventually won in court, but Lynn assembled a group of 10 to pay Jacobs and Pohlad double for their shares and eventually take control of the team. In September of 1987, the new board of directors voted 6–3 to dump Winter as team president and replace him with Wheelock Whitney.

Winter's reaction to the news could describe a number of endings in team history. "I'm deeply hurt," he said.

# 27 Favre vs. Packers

Brett Favre sitting in a chapel hours before kickoff and worrying himself sick isn't an image that comes to mind when one thinks about the fun-loving gunslinger's 20-year Hall of Fame career. Then again, No. 4 had never played the Green Bay Packers before and never charged into the Metrodome wearing a purple jersey while looking across the field at the team for which he played 16 seasons, won three MVPs, and a Super Bowl.

This was his moment. This was his time to prove in person to Packers general manager Ted Thompson and coach Mike McCarthy that they had made the wrong decision when they wouldn't accept

## Not Exactly Favre vs. Rodgers

The Associated Press introduced its NFL Defensive Player of the Year award in 1971 as a way of recognizing that side of the ball since a defender had never won league Most Valuable Player. Then came Alan Page, the best defender on one of the best defenses in NFL history. The Vikings defensive tackle not only won the first NFL Defensive Player of the Year award, but he also won league MVP in 1971. The only other defensive player to win the latter was New York Giants linebacker Lawrence Taylor 15 years later.

In 1971 the Vikings offense ranked 18th in scoring (17.5 points per game) but went 11–3 because of a Page-led defense that ranked No. 1 in points allowed (9.9). They allowed more than 20 points just one time, held nine opponents to 10 or fewer points, and posted three shutouts in their first nine games.

The last of those shutouts came on November 14, 1971, and produced what had to be the worst quarterback matchup in the history of the Vikings-Packers rivalry. Minnesota's Gary Cuozzo took on Green Bay's Scott Hunter, who was eventually replaced by Zeke Bratkowski.

Only 11 passes were completed that day. Cuozzo completed 5-of-11 for 42 yards. Hunter completed 5-of-8 for 61 yards with two interceptions. Bratkowski completed 1-of-3 with another interception.

Packers rookie running back John Brockington ran for 149 of Green Bay's 245 yards rushing. The Vikings were outgained in total yards (301–87) and first downs (15–5). But the defense forced four turnovers, and the Vikings won 3–0 in a classic black-and-blue NFC Central Division struggle. The Vikings won the division with Cuozzo going 6–2 as a starter that year. But they lost to the Dallas Cowboys 20–12 in their playoff opener at home. That solidified the team's decision to bring quarterback Fran Tarkenton back from New York via trade before the 1972 season.

his decision to unretire and return to the Packers in the summer of 2008. A year after playing for the New York Jets because the Packers had blocked his attempts to join the Vikings, this was the day Favre would outshine his former understudy, Aaron Rodgers, in prime time on *Monday Night Football*.

So, yeah, Brett Favre admits he was as nervous as he had ever been in his career. "I didn't think I would be," he said after the game. "As the week progressed, I felt fine. But I got to the hotel [on Sunday], and it kind of dawned on me. I had church today at

*Quarterback Brett Favre leaves Lambeau Field victoriously on November 1, 2009, having completed a season's sweep over his former team.*

3:00 and was sitting there throwing all kinds of prayers out. I said, 'Man, I'm losing it.'"

The surreal setting included pink cleats in honor of breast cancer awareness, but it was impossible to take an eye off the purple No. 4 jersey and what it was doing to the green and gold. Five days before his 40th birthday, Favre completed 24-of-31 passes for 271 yards, three touchdowns, no turnovers, no sacks, and a 135.3 passer rating as a crowd of 63,846 lost its collective minds and voices. "The Good Lord answered my prayers," said Favre, who lifted the Vikings to a 4–0 start while becoming the first quarterback to beat all 32 NFL teams.

Favre had plenty of help from a Vikings defense that sacked Rodgers eight times. Defensive end Jared Allen had a career-high 4.5 sacks, including one for a safety that gave the Vikings a 30–14 lead midway through the fourth quarter. Running back Adrian Peterson was held to 55 yards by the Packers' new 3-4 scheme. He also had the ball ripped from him and returned 42 yards for a game-tying touchdown by linebacker Clay Matthews late in the second quarter.

Favre didn't flinch. He countered with an eight-play, 80-yard touchdown drive that included a Charles Woodson end zone interception that was nullified by a questionable pass interference penalty. One play later Peterson scored from a yard out for a 21–14 lead.

In the third quarter, Favre threaded a deep ball to Bernard Berrian for a 31-yard touchdown and a 28–14 lead. Rodgers finished with 384 yards passing but also had the safety and two turnovers that led to 14 points.

Favre tried to downplay the revenge factor, but there was no coincidence that he chose kicker and fellow former Packer Ryan Longwell to share a sideline body bump with after his first touchdown pass. "He handled his emotions well; his demeanor was great," Vikings coach Brad Childress said. "It's a great thing for a defensive lineman to get out of his mind and sling snot but not so good for a quarterback. I thought he handled that part well."

Less than a month later, on November 1, another surreal setting unfolded with Favre being booed in Lambeau Field as he jogged onto the field in his Vikings uniform. The game itself was much the same with Favre playing flawlessly as the Vikings won 38–26. Despite the jeers Favre threw four touchdown passes without an interception or a sack. Rodgers threw three touchdown passes and didn't turn the ball over but was sacked six more times. "I hate to lose to whoever is at quarterback for them," Rodgers snapped after the game. "I hate losing to the Vikings."

Afterward, Favre didn't seem to revel in playing the villain at Lambeau. "Packer fans cheer for the Packers first; I know that," Favre said. "But I hope that everyone in the stadium watching tonight said, 'I sure hate those jokers on the other side, but he does play the way he's always played.'"

# The Scrambler

Long after their crazy, zig-zagging chases across NFL fields had ended, Fran Tarkenton and Pro Football Hall of Fame defensive lineman Deacon Jones were sitting around one day talking about the mobility of the modern quarterback. "Old Deacon told me, 'They think they got mobile quarterbacks today? They don't know what a mobile quarterback is!'" said Tarkenton, whose 18-year career included 13 with the Vikings (1961–66, 1972–78).

Until Tarkenton came along, the NFL hadn't seen a passer run so much and so well to extend so many big plays. When Tarkenton retired, he held every major career passing record. But his enduring nickname was "the Scrambler." The 6'0", 190-pounder was remarkably durable while running 675 times for 32 touchdowns, a 5.4-yard average, and 3,674 yards, which still ranks fourth all-time among quarterbacks. "We'd play old Deacon in that Coliseum out in L.A., and he'd be worn out by the end of the first quarter, chasing after me all over the place," Tarkenton said. "He and Merlin Olsen, they'd be telling Carl Eller, 'Tell that quarterback of yours to slow down.'"

Tarkenton said instincts allowed him the confidence to run while circumstance forced him to do so during the early part of his career. "I played on an expansion team the first [six] years," he said. "And then I went to the Giants for five years, and they just didn't have anything going on. They were 1–12–1 the year before I got there. Then they traded two No. 1 picks and two No. 2 picks to get me. I really didn't have a chance."

Tarkenton held passing records for years after his retirement. But as the NFL evolved into a pass-first league, his numbers began to slide. "I've had people say, 'I didn't realize you set all those passing records,'" Tarkenton said. "They knew me as what? A scrambler. I was a scrambler, but I was a passer first. I bought time. You can't win as a quarterback without being a great passer. And I was a great passer."

Every time his legs took off, Tarkenton says his eyes were searching for targets downfield. That wasn't enough justification for Tarkenton's first coach. Norm Van Brocklin was a Hall of Fame quarterback who had won NFL titles with traditional pocket passing. He went from winning the 1960 NFL title as a player with the Philadelphia Eagles to coaching the rookie Tarkenton in 1961.

Their relationship deteriorated over the years. One of the reasons was Van Brocklin's distaste for Tarkenton's style of play. "I had the ability also to run and to buy time and to make first downs," Tarkenton said. "When you have that ability, you use it. Roger Staubach had that ability. How'd it work out for him? Joe Montana had that ability. How'd it work out for him? Steve Young had that ability. How'd it work out for him? Aaron Rodgers has that ability today. It's a great asset. But I was kind of the first one to do anything like that. It was like you're not supposed to play quarterback like that. It was like it was against the rules to break out of the pocket and run. I was like some freak of nature at the time."

# 29 Jim Finks

Jim Finks reached the Pro Football Hall of Fame after five decades of turning around the CFL's Calgary Stampeders and the NFL's Vikings, Chicago Bears, and New Orleans Saints. What he did in Minnesota in 1967 was one giant step toward Canton, Ohio. That year alone, Finks hired Bud Grant, selected Alan Page with a draft pick from Los Angeles, signed Joe Kapp, and actually turned Fran Tarkenton's trade demand into a positive by fetching the picks that produced Clinton Jones, Bobby Grim, and Ron Yary.

Other than that he also used his own first-round pick on Gene Washington and his seventh-rounder on Bobby Bryant, a cornerback who played 13 seasons, participated in all four Super Bowls, and finished with 51 career interceptions. And, oh yeah, Tarkenton returned in a Finks trade in 1972 and led the Vikings to three more Super Bowls.

*Whew.*

If that weren't enough, consider that Finks conducted the 1967 draft from a room at Fairview Southdale Hospital, where he was being prepped for gallbladder surgery. Scouting director Jerry

Reichow and Grant were the only others involved in the draft, which included three first-round picks. Jones was No. 2 overall, Washington No. 8, and Page was No. 15, the pick Finks got for trading running back Tommy Mason, whose knee injuries had robbed him of the player he once was. "The last thing Jim was concerned about was his own ailment," former Vikings owner Bernie Ridder told the *Minneapolis Star Tribune* in 1995, when Finks was enshrined in Canton posthumously. "I'll never forget Jim drafting Alan Page, Gene Washington, Clinton Jones, and Bobby Bryant from his hospital bed that day. That really put the Vikings on the treadmill and elevated our team."

Finks was born on August 31, 1927, in St. Louis. In 1945 he became the T-formation quarterback at Tulsa. In 1949 the Pittsburgh Steelers selected him in the 12th round and stuck him at defensive back. In 1952 he was back at quarterback when he tied Otto Graham's record of 20 passing touchdowns on the way to his lone Pro Bowl.

Finks retired after seven seasons and became an assistant coach at Notre Dame in 1956. He went to Calgary in 1957 briefly as a player/coach before becoming general manager that fall.

While in Canada, Finks befriended Grant, an adversary who got the Winnipeg head coaching job at age 29 in 1957. Grant turned down the Vikings' first offer to coach the expansion team in 1961, but he'd change his mind after winning four Grey Cup titles and getting the call from Finks to come south.

After one losing season in 1967, Finks and Grant built the foundation of a team that would win 11 division titles and go to four Super Bowls in 14 years. Finks arrived in Minnesota in 1964, replacing Bert Rose. The Vikings had won 10 games in three seasons. Finks' first draft pick was Carl Eller. Finks' last first-round draft pick in Minnesota was Chuck Foreman in 1973. Finks was named NFL Executive of the Year when the Vikings went 12–2 on the way to their second Super Bowl. But, unfortunately for the Vikings, the Finks era ended right there.

Finks resigned in 1974 when owners Max Winter, J.P. Skoglund, and Bill Boyer blocked his attempts to gain minority ownership of the team. Finks had been leading efforts for a new stadium in downtown Minneapolis, which would significantly increase the value of the team. He felt he deserved a piece of the action, but the owners were reluctant in part because of a bad experience when the former coach Norm Van Brocklin had been given minority ownership.

Making matters worse, Finks joined the rival Chicago Bears as general manager. A year later he drafted Walter Payton. Two years after that, the Bears made the playoffs for the first time in 14 years. Finks left Chicago in 1982, but he drafted 19 of the 22 starters on the 1985 Bears team that went 15–1 and won the Super Bowl.

After a couple of years as president and CEO of the Chicago Cubs, Finks took over the New Orleans Saints in 1986. They hadn't had a winning record in their 19 seasons. A year later they went 12–3, earning Finks another NFL Executive of the Year award. Meanwhile, Finks continued to smoke a lot of cigarettes. Grant, a non-smoker, always tried—to no avail—to get his friend to quit. In 1993 Finks' career ended when he was diagnosed with lung cancer.

He died on May 8, 1994. He was 66. Fourteen months later it was his son, Jim Jr., who gave the acceptance speech on the steps of the Pro Football Hall of Fame. The son pulled out an old, neatly folded piece of paper on that day in Canton, Ohio. It was the same piece of paper that his dad always carried with him in his wallet. The crowd of Vikings, Bears, and Saints fans listened as Jim Jr. read from the piece of paper. "If we are ever unlucky enough to have it made, then we'll be spectators and not participants in life," he read. "It's the journey, not the arrival, that counts. Does the road wind uphill all the way? Yes, to the very end."

# 30 Super Bowl XI

On January 9, 1977, the Vikings were manhandled for the fourth time in their fourth Super Bowl. They left the Rose Bowl with a staggering four-game cumulative disadvantage in points (95–34), yards rushing (862–227), and turnovers (minus-12). Bud Grant-coached teams that had gone 45–10–1 in those four seasons had somehow managed to go AWOL in 36 percent of the first 11 Super Bowls. Thirty-nine years later, as the NFL celebrated a half century of Super Bowls, the Vikings still were searching for their fifth appearance.

Super Bowl XI was the most lopsided of the four low points. The Oakland Raiders amassed records for first-half yards (288) and total yards (429) on their way to a 32–14 victory in front of 103,438 fans. "I don't know how you can play in four of these things and lose them all," Vikings offensive tackle Ron Yary told reporters in the locker room. "Not only lose them all, but play bad football. I don't know how or why it happened, but for the first time in all the years that I've been playing football, I'm embarrassed."

The Vikings had won the NFC Central for the eighth time in nine years. They beat the Washington Redskins 35–20 and the Los Angeles Rams 24–10 to set up sure Super Bowl redemption—or so they thought. "I can't bear the idea of losing this game again, and nobody on the team can," said Ed White in *Minnesota Vikings: The Complete Illustrated History* by longtime Twin Cities columnist Patrick Reusse. "Nobody thinks about that as a serious possibility. It's been a burden all these years. So much that all you want to do is stand there and tell the world, 'We've won it. We're a great football team and we've won it.'"

The Vikings didn't win it—again.

In the first quarter, Fred McNeill blocked and recovered a punt on the Oakland 3-yard line. Two plays later fullback Brent McClanahan fumbled the ball away. In four Super Bowls, the Vikings turned the ball over 15 times while their defense forced

## Don't Feel Sorry for Bud

Yes, he went 0–4 in Super Bowls as head coach of the Vikings. But, no, it didn't change his life, or have any impact on it, as he has noted repeatedly through the years. "Winning is great, but if we had won those four Super Bowls instead of losing four, there is nothing in my life that would have been any different," Grant told the *Minneapolis Star Tribune* as he prepared to enter the Pro Football Hall of Fame in 1994. "I don't think it would have meant any more to me monetarily. When I walked out of here [in 1985], I was the highest-paid coach in the country."

Born in Superior, Wisconsin, on May 20, 1927, Grant grew up with little money during the Depression. His father, Harry Peter Grant Sr., had a steady job as a firefighter, but Bud worked odd jobs as a child to help the family get by. That experience affected the decisions he would make later on in life, such as initially spurning the Philadelphia Eagles as the 14th overall draft pick to play in the NBA for the Lakers in Minneapolis, where Grant could make additional money pitching town-ball baseball in the summers.

Grant also had good fortune when it came to timing. On July 6, 1945, he enlisted in the Navy and went to the Great Lakes training base near Chicago. A month later World War II ended. Grant was spared combat and started to develop his interest in coaching while playing under Paul Brown on the powerhouse Great Lakes team.

Although he coached 18 seasons, Grant often was praised for keeping football in perspective. His teams routinely were the last to report for training camp because, ever the outdoorsman, Grant enjoyed hunting and fishing as much as football and coaching. "You've got to keep in mind this is entertainment," Grant said in 1994. "Ask the die-hard fan who is vitally interested in Super Bowl Sunday who played in the game three years ago, and he won't remember. When it's over, it's gone; there are no residuals…Nothing is older than yesterday's sports page."

only three takeaways. The Raiders turned McClanahan's fumble into an early second-quarter field goal that grew into a 16-0 half-time lead.

Running back Chuck Foreman had rushed for 1,155 yards and 13 touchdowns during the 1976 season. But once again he was ineffective in the Super Bowl. Facing a rare three-man defensive front that helped Oakland go 13–1 during the regular season, Foreman had only 44 yards on 17 carries. In four Super Bowls, the Vikings averaged 57 yards rushing per game. Their opponents averaged 216. Oakland's Clarence Davis had 137 yards rushing in Super Bowl XI.

Tarkenton fell to 0–3 in Super Bowls. By this time he was 37 years old and led all the NFL's major career passing categories. His eight-yard touchdown pass to Sammy White made it a 19–7 game late in the third quarter but was followed by two interceptions.

Defensively, the Purple People Eaters were the league's No. 2 scoring defense (12.6 points allowed per game). No team had scored more than 23 points against the Vikings all season. But the Raiders rolled up 32 while rushing for 266 yards and two touchdowns on 52 carries.

After the game Vikings players sat stunned. In some ways that feeling remains four decades later. "It really hurts," Foreman told reporters after the game. "I don't know how I'm going to handle it."

# 31 A.P. and the Chaotic 2014 Season

Mike Zimmer climbed the outside steps to his Winter Park office, opened the door, took a deep breath, and said something that made it seem silly that he was asked to talk about the difficulty of staying focused during one of the more tumultuous opening months for a first-year head coach in NFL history. "It was five years ago today," Zimmer said on October 8, 2014. "Five years ago today is when my wife [Vikki] died. So for me today obviously is a hard day. But when I think about all the things I'm thinking about with her, I know I still have to go out there and focus on doing what I have to do, football-wise."

Five years earlier, Zimmer was the one who found Vikki when he got home from his job as Cincinnati Bengals defensive coordinator. She was 50 and hadn't been sick. Three days later, Bengals players gave Zimmer a game ball after he helped them beat the rival Baltimore Ravens.

Zimmer's head coaching debut at any level had gone perfectly on September 7, 2014. The 58-year-old orchestrated a 34–6 win in St. Louis with every piece of his team in place, except for special teams coordinator Mike Priefer, who was serving his two-game suspension for making an anti-gay remark. Nose tackle Linval Joseph, who had been shot in the calf as an innocent bystander during an incident at a downtown Minneapolis nightclub after the first preseason game, had returned to give full strength to Zimmer's roster. "The weird thing about it is the OTAs, training camp, and everything else was so smooth," Zimmer said. "Everything was kind of like how I envisioned it would be. And then the St. Louis game was pretty much the same way. And then I don't know, whatever the word is, but it kind of hit the fan."

Zimmer lost his starting quarterback, right guard, and tight end in one game. He released receiver Jerome Simpson when news of more legal trouble surfaced days before Simpson was set to return from a three-game suspension. He started three different quarterbacks in 12 days. He got blown out 42–10 in Lambeau Field on national television and picked up the phone one early morning to discover that defensive tackle Tom Johnson had been arrested on suspicion of disorderly conduct. Johnson was later cleared.

But none of that compared to the news that running back Adrian Peterson, the team's best player and the foundation upon which everything was built, was indicted on felony child abuse charges by a Texas grand jury and removed from the team on September 12, five days after the opener. Peterson was deactivated for Week 2 and spent the rest of the season in exile. He bounced between the commissioner's exempt list and a suspension after pleading no contest to a reduced misdemeanor charge. He was reinstated in the spring of 2015 and led the NFL in rushing at age 30. "That was pretty much a blind side," Zimmer said of the grand jury indictment. "I thought it was a done issue."

Zimmer joked that he already had enough material to write a book about his head coaching career, which was 35 days into its first regular season. Two games into his head coaching career, Zimmer had 10 satellite TV trucks parked outside his team's headquarters and a horde of reporters wanting to know more about Peterson's situation and caring nothing about the team's 30–7 blowout loss to New England in the home opener. At one point during the Monday news conference, Zimmer pleaded, "How 'bout those Patriots?"

"Yeah," Zimmer said, "it's pretty odd when you're asking people to ask you about getting your butt kicked."

The team's internal support of Peterson wavered initially because of the unprecedented nature of the charges and a strong backlash from sponsors that objected to corporal punishment and Peterson whipping his four-year-old with a wooden switch. But eventually, the team's support solidified because of Zimmer and general manager Rick Spielman were steadfast in their belief in Peterson as a person and his value as the league's best running back. "I want to stick with the players," Zimmer said. "And I've told the players this. If they'll fight for me and they're good guys and they make a mistake, I want to stick with them. I want to fight for them. And I want to show that I have their back."

Zimmer finished 7–9 in his first season but was given credit for turning around a woebegone defense while developing a promising rookie quarterback in Teddy Bridgewater. The tough times didn't deter Zimmer, who gained an extra dose of toughness by being in Atlanta in 2007 when head coach Bobby Petrino quit during his first season. "I'm trying to instill the toughness that I want these guys to have," Zimmer said. "I don't want them to see me saying, 'Woe is me' over the stuff that has happened. I've seen a coach quit on his team. So regardless of how bad it gets, I'll never use anything as an excuse. I can't let our football team see that the guy who supposedly is leading them is going to flinch the first time I get a punch thrown at me."

# 32 Viking Durability

There was a point in NFL history when the top three players in consecutive games started were Jim Marshall (270), Mick Tingelhoff (240), and Alan Page (215). Even decades after their careers were over, they remained in the top six with Marshall and Tingelhoff in the top three behind Brett Favre (297), who ended his career in purple. "Some guys are just tougher than other guys," former Vikings coach Bud Grant said. "Some guys can just play, and some guys get a hangnail and they can't play. All these guys played at a high level every down, every week."

Marshall and Tingelhoff already were Vikings when Grant arrived from the CFL in 1967. Together, the three of them instilled a level of toughness that—combined with great talent and good luck—established an unmatched level of roster-wide durability for one team in NFL history. "The main ingredient of most great players is durability," Grant said. "You don't achieve greatness without being able to play a lot of games. Durability is the greatest ability you can have."

Page, a first-round draft pick in 1967, said all the key ingredients came together for the Vikings in the 1960s. "The first thing you have to be is lucky," Page said. "No. 2 is you have to be good to survive that long. And No. 3 you have to play well as a team. You have to come to know each other and take advantage of each other's strengths."

Strong leadership on those teams also played a significant role. In establishing his program, Grant tabbed Tingelhoff and Marshall as his captains. They controlled the rest of the team in different ways. "There are two types of leaders," Page said, "the introvert and the extrovert. But true leaders lead by example. Mick was the introvert but certainly was a doer. Jim was more of an extrovert, but he also was a doer."

There was a certain level of toughness on those teams that didn't require a lot of verbiage to maintain. "Having people that talk all the time, when all is said and done, more is said than done," Page said. "That doesn't get you very far. It's about people who put themselves on the line. And you could see it. You could feel it. You didn't have to hear Mick or Jim say anything. You knew where they were physically, mentally, and emotionally. You would be well served to get yourself in the same place."

Through the years the Vikings have continued the tradition of durability on a number of occasions. Guard Randall McDaniel is 13th on the list of consecutive starts (202). In terms of games played, Marshall had 282 and Tingelhoff 240. Meanwhile, Fran Tarkenton played in 246 games, Ed White 241, Cris Carter 234, Chris Doleman 232, Paul Krause 226, Carl Eller 225, McDaniel 222, John Randle 219, Page 218, Matt Birk 210, Grady Alderman 204, and Scott Studwell 201. "There's no question [durability] rubs off," said Studwell, who still remembers facing Tingelhoff in practice as a rookie in 1977, Mick's 16th season. "When a leader goes to work every day and shows up and performs every Sunday, just the fact you know they're going to be there, it rubs off on everybody. If those guys are going to be there every day, you better make sure you're there every day, too."

Tingelhoff didn't even miss a preseason game until his final season in 1978. He was in the hospital with a leg infection, and it ended a streak of 328 preseason, regular season, and postseason starts. "There was a time against Green Bay when Mick tore his calf muscle the Saturday before the game," longtime head athletic trainer Fred Zamberletti said. "There was no way he should have played. But Mick would fight you down to the last straw when it came to coming off the field. So I taped him from his butt clear down to his toes. We went to Green Bay, and, of course, he played."

# Bud Grant, a Man of Few Words

The Vikings' winning percentage would change dramatically over time when Bud Grant arrived from Canada, following Norm Van Brocklin's unexpected resignation on February 11, 1967. The verbiage and vitriol spewing from the man in charge would change immediately.

"Stormin' Norman," Vikings Hall of Fame center Mick Tingelhoff said in 2015. "That's what we called Van Brocklin. He was always cussing, always calling us girls and stuff, just yelling at you all the time."

"And he liked you, Mick," said former Vikings running back Dave Osborn, who was sitting next to Tingelhoff.

Having never been a head coach, Van Brocklin jumped from the mountaintop to the expansion Vikings less than a month after winning the 1960 NFL title as quarterback of the Philadelphia Eagles. Six seasons later he left town with a 29–51–4 record (.369) and no playoff appearances.

## Bud Grant's Garage Sale

Bud Grant was a couple weeks from turning 88 when he joined Twitter in May of 2015 to announce another one of his garage sales. Wait...*what?*

Yes, the Vikings Hall of Fame coach is on Twitter (@HPBudGrant). And, yes, he's like the rest of us. The clutter accumulates inside his home in Bloomington, Minnesota, so he has garage sales to make a few bucks while getting rid of things, signing autographs, and spending time with waves of adoring fans. Grant typically posts hand-written garage sale signs throughout the area and hangs a banner in the yard that simply reads "Grant." And, naturally, each day's sale doesn't begin until Grant blows his old coaches whistle.

Twitter was Bud's way of drumming up some more customers. About a year later, he had over 7,000 followers. A man of few words, Bud has proven to be a man of few tweets as well.

Grant has a tough time comprehending his fame. At his 11th garage sale in 2015, he told the *Minneapolis Star Tribune* that he had just sold the shell box that he used for duck hunting for 50 years. Some excited fan got a story for the rest of his life, while Bud seemed baffled that he made money on something most people would have thrown away. "When you have birthdays, Christmases, you get a lot of presents," Grant said. "You accumulate stuff."

*The laconic head coach, Bud Grant, won 168 games, including 10 playoff victories with the Vikings.*

Grant arrived as a veteran CFL coach with a plan, four Grey Cup titles with the Winnipeg Blue Bombers, steely blue eyes, and that classic stoic demeanor. "Bud was clean, quiet," Tingelhoff said. "A lot different than Stormin' Norman."

Once again, Tingelhoff became one of the head coach's favorite players. He and defensive end Jim Marshall were Grant's co-captains through the rest of their careers. Tingelhoff and Grant became close off the field as well. "If you don't like Mick Tingelhoff," Grant said, "it's not Mick. It's you."

They shared a love for the outdoors. That made them regular hunting and fishing partners over the years. Like his coaching style, Grant the outdoorsman practiced an amazingly efficient ability to communicate his vision for the hunt. "Mick and a teammate went hunting with Bud in Nebraska," said Jerry Edelman, a friend of Mick's from his days at the University of Nebraska. "They agreed ahead of time that they wouldn't say a word on the drive down until Bud spoke first."

No matter what, neither player would so much as clear his throat until the coach said something. They made it from the Twin Cities to the Iowa border. Then they made it almost through Iowa without a single word being spoken by three men in the cab of an old pickup truck. "Finally, they had to stop for gas," said Dave Osborn, a longtime friend of Tingelhoff's.

Bud pulled up to the pump. As he opened the door, the silence was broken with six words. "Bud's first words were, 'It was full when I left,'" Osborn said. "That was Bud. That's all he needed to say to make them understand the situation perfectly. They were paying."

# 34 Joe Kapp

Joe Kapp could have gone out of bounds. And he should have gone out of bounds. But he wouldn't have been Joe Kapp if he had turned down a fight.

Kapp, the Vikings' 31-year-old quarterback, tried a few unsuccessful moves before deciding to just plow into Jim Houston, the Cleveland Browns' 240-pound All-Pro linebacker. Kapp was flipped into the air, but his knee caught Houston in the jaw. Once the bodies settled, it was the linebacker who didn't get up. Houston left the 1969 NFL Championship Game with a concussion, Kapp stayed in and led the Vikings to a 27–7 win at Met Stadium and a spot in Super Bowl IV. "I guess I hit him with my purse," Kapp would write in an article for *Sports Illustrated*, the same publication that also ran a cover story of Kapp with the headline, "The Toughest Chicano."

Fran Tarkenton is the most celebrated quarterback in franchise history. But even the Hall of Famer has to take a seat behind Kapp when it comes to beloved characters in franchise history. Kapp was a tequila-loving, tough-talking, fists-a-flying swashbuckler with multiple nicknames, including "Hennepin Avenue Joe," a Minnesota version of the "Broadway Joe" Namath craze from the same era.

After Tarkenton was traded before the 1967 season, a new coach (Bud Grant) and a new quarterback (Kapp) arrived from the Canadian Football League. In Year 1 they went 3–8–3. In Year Two they took the Vikings to their first playoff appearance in franchise history. In Year Three they dominated everything except, of course Super Bowl IV, where they lost 23–7 to the Kansas City Chiefs.

Kapp's style was rough around the edges and anything but pretty. But in 1969 he complemented the Purple People Eaters perfectly. The Vikings scored a league-high 379 points while allowing a league-low 133. The season began with a loss to Tarkenton and the New York Giants. But then a 12-game winning streak would start in dramatic fashion against the Baltimore Colts on September 28, 1969. The Vikings won 52–14 with Kapp throwing for a

## Kapp vs. Wiggin in "The Play"

Cal's miracle five-lateral kick return for a touchdown through the Stanford marching band isn't a Vikings memory, but it has significant Vikings ties. When Cal pulled that 25–20 upset on November 20, 1982, at California Memorial Stadium, the head coaches were Joe Kapp and Paul Wiggin. Kapp, the Vikings' quarterback in Super Bowl IV, was in his first season at Cal. Stanford had Wiggin, who was a Vikings assistant coach (1985–91) before joining the personnel department in various roles, including his current consulting position.

Wiggin's Cardinal were 5–5 but favored by six points over the 6–4 Golden Bears because of a powerful offense led by a guy named John Elway. Elway was a lock to be the No. 1 overall pick in the 1983 draft and needed the win to secure his first and only bowl berth. Elway had directed touchdown drives of 77 and 73 yards but trailed 19–17 when he got the ball at his 20-yard line with 1:27 left. In what would become a classic Elway drive, he completed a long pass on fourth and 17 to set up the go-ahead field goal.

Strangely, Wiggin called a timeout with eight seconds left to get his field goal unit on the field. Had he let the clock run down another four seconds, he wouldn't have had to kick off because time would have expired. And a Stanford tuba player wouldn't have been run over in perhaps the most famous play in college football history. Cal used several laterals on that ensuing kickoff return to score the winning touchdown, even though the Stanford band had come onto the field midway through the return, thinking that the game was over.

That bizarre and climactic win would be the highlight of Kapp's coaching career at his alma mater. He coached five seasons, finishing 20–34–1 and posting just one winning record. But he was 3–2 against Stanford.

record-tying seven touchdown passes. Kapp and seven other players still hold that record. "I ran the offense," Kapp told the *Minneapolis Star Tribune*. "I looked at more film than anybody despite having the reputation of spending all of my off time at Duff's Bar."

Kapp became the first Vikings quarterback to win a playoff game when Minnesota beat the Los Angeles Rams 23–20 on December 27, 1969. A late drive by Kapp gave the Vikings a 21–20 lead. A sack for a safety by Carl Eller and an interception by Alan Page sealed the victory. Against Cleveland, the Vikings ran 45 times for 222 yards. Kapp ran for 57 yards and a touchdown while also throwing a touchdown pass.

Unfortunately for the Vikings and Kapp, the dominators were dominated in the Super Bowl a week later. But 1969 will never be forgotten in Vikings lore—nor will the battle cry, "40 for 60!" At the time NFL rosters were limited to 40 players. Early on that season, Kapp said success required 40 players giving full effort for 60 minutes. He kept repeating it until "40 for 60" became the catchphrase for the Super Bowl run.

Kapp further endeared himself to teammates and fans during the team's awards banquet that season. When Kapp was handed the team's Most Valuable Player award, he handed it back. "There is no most valuable Viking," he said at the time. "There are 40 most valuable Vikings…We have '40 for 60.' I just can't accept this."

Unfortunately for the Vikings, Super Bowl IV would be Kapp's final game with the team. With his contract expired, Kapp and his hard-ball agent, John Elliott Cook, demanded a five-year, $1.25 million deal with $250,000 up front. The Vikings wouldn't pay what was an outrageous sum at the time. And the "Rozelle Rule" basically eliminated free agency with the unbearable compensation that a team had to pay to sign another team's unsigned player.

Finally, during the season, Kapp was traded to the Boston Patriots. The Vikings received a first-round draft pick in 1972 and safety John Charles. Kapp went 1–9 with the lowly Patriots in

1970. When Boston tried to make him sign a standard players' contract in 1971, Kapp walked out of training camp and took his case to court, filing a $2 million suit against the NFL and commissioner Pete Rozelle. Kapp did win his argument that the "Rozelle Rule" was unfair. But he got nothing in damages and never played again.

# 35 Visit Howard Wood Field

Metropolitan Stadium, the Vikings' first home field in Bloomington, Minnesota, died long ago and was replaced by the Mall of America. But one can still visit the very first field upon which Hall of Fame quarterback Fran Tarkenton and the entire Vikings organization made their NFL debuts. About 197 miles west of Minneapolis sits Howard Wood Field in Sioux Falls, South Dakota, where, on August 5, 1961, the Vikings played their first preseason game, losing to the Dallas Cowboys 38–13 in front of only 4,954 fans on a sweltering, 92-degree Saturday evening.

How South Dakota ended up with its one and only NFL game at a venue that still exists as a 10,000-seat football and track facility is one of the peculiar tales in team history. It starts with a man named Bob Burns, a high school coaching legend in Sioux Falls. He was coaching Augustana College, which played its games at Howard Wood Field, when he stopped at a Minneapolis bar called the 620 Club during a recruiting trip.

The bar was owned by Max Winter, who was part of the ownership group that founded the Vikings. While eating, Burns overheard Winter talking about needing a new venue to play the first preseason game. At the time NFL teams routinely played exhibition contests at neutral sites. Burns, an outgoing character, spoke up when Fargo-Moorhead, was mentioned as a possibility. When Burns suggested they play the game at Howard Wood Field, "they all laughed at me," Burns told the *Argus Leader*, the newspaper in Sioux Falls.

Burns asked how much the Vikings would need to be persuaded to come to Sioux Falls. He was told $40,000. Winter didn't think Burns would come up with the money. Burns made some calls back to Sioux Falls and within hours he had the money. Burns became the game's promoter and organizer. Bleachers were added to increase capacity to 16,500, but that proved to be wishful thinking. Ads in the *Argus Leader* said the game would be a "whale of a battle" and a "must-win" for both teams. But the NFL wasn't nearly as popular at the time, the heat was scorching, and many people balked at the price of the tickets—$5.50 for the grandstand and $3.50 for the bleachers.

Burns needed to sell 10,000 tickets to break even. He didn't even make it halfway.

If that weren't bad enough, Vikings coach Norm Van Brocklin made things more miserable with complaints about, well, everything. He didn't like the field and he nixed Burns' idea of dividing the only locker room between the teams. Van Brocklin told Burns to tell Tom Landry, coach of the Cowboys, that they would have to dress for the game at the Cataract Hotel before busing to the stadium.

Yeah, Tom wasn't too happy.

There were other requests that Burns couldn't afford to grant. "The Vikings also wanted 200 soft-lead pencils and 40 typewriters in the press box," he told the *Argus Leader*. "I told them, 'We haven't got 40 typewriters in the state of South Dakota!' The whole thing was a comedy. We couldn't spend any more money, but they kept on asking for things."

But there was a game. With 11:13 left in the first quarter, the Cowboys, who had gone 0–11–1 in their expansion season the year before, scored the game's first points on a 15-yard run by L.G. Dupre. No one in the stands would have known the significance of the 21-year-old Tarkenton, a rookie from Georgia, entering the game with the Vikings trailing 31–6 in the fourth quarter. He quickly threw a 36-yard touchdown pass to Don Ellersick. A month later he came off the bench to replace George Shaw and lead the Vikings to a 37–13 upset of the Chicago Bears in the team's first regular season game.

Howard Wood Field was renovated in 2003. Field Turf has replaced the grass upon which the Vikings played. But you can still go to Sioux Falls, sit in the bleachers, and look at the field where a Hall of Fame career and the Vikings franchise itself got its start.

# 36 Purple Pass Rushers

Pro Football Hall of Famer John Randle was asked years ago to define the key ingredient that can be found in every great pass rusher. He answered almost as quickly as he used to shoot through gaps on his way to terrorizing quarterbacks. "It's like this," he said. "A great pass rusher looks at 1,000 doors. He's been told there is a sack behind just one of those doors. It might be the first door. It might be the last door. The great pass rusher opens every single door just as hard as he did the first door."

In that case the Vikings have a rich tradition of opening doors and dropping quarterbacks with the likes of Carl Eller, Jim Marshall, John Randle, Alan Page, Chris Doleman, Jared Allen,

Keith Millard, and many more. "Great pass rushers are relentless, like the big game hunter born to stalk his prey," Marshall said. Added Doleman: "They all have the inner 'want-to' on every single play of their careers."

When the NFL started keeping sacks as an official stat in 1982, it's probably fitting that a Viking led the league. The Purple People Eaters era was over, and the team's next wave of great pass rushers was a few years off. But in 1982 Doug Martin led the NFL with 11.5 sacks in the lone All-Pro season for the ninth overall draft pick in 1980.

Although their careers ended before sacks were official stats, Eller and Marshall are commonly recognized as the team's top two sack leaders with 130 and 127, respectively. Randle, who joined the team in 1990, ranks third with 114 of his 137.5 sacks coming as a Viking, while Page is fourth with 108.

In 1989 Doleman led the league with 21 sacks but didn't even win NFL Defensive Player of the Year. That honor went to Millard, who had 18 sacks lined up next to Doleman, who ranks fourth in NFL history with 150.5 sacks, and 96.5 of those came as a Viking. In 1997 Randle would lead the league with 15.5 from the tackle position. And in 2011 Allen would break Doleman's team record with 22 sacks, falling half a sack short of the single-season NFL record held by Michael Strahan. Allen would go on to post 85.5 of his sacks in six seasons as a Viking.

For decades, some of the best line battles in the NFL probably occurred on the Vikings practice fields. During the Purple People Eaters era, the Vikings also had offensive lines that included Ron Yary, Mick Tingelhoff, and Ed White. Then in the late 1980s and early 1990s, when Doleman and Millard were punishing quarterbacks, the Vikings had Randall McDaniel at left guard and Gary Zimmerman at left tackle. "Those guys didn't take plays or time off, and I didn't take plays or time off," Doleman said. "We made each other better. That's one of the things about being a great player—you have to work every single day."

Allen also was asked what goes into making a great pass rusher. He said each person's style can be totally different but achieve the same results. Being tall and slender, Allen knew he couldn't rely on raw power to get to the quarterback. He also wasn't a straight speed rusher, so he always incorporated mixed martial arts into his training regimen to help him with his hand techniques. "John Randle had a great hump move, but I'm not a guy who is going to hit you with my left arm and send you rolling down the field," Allen said. "So I'm big into hands. I know if I can stop your hands, I can stop your feet. And as a pass rusher, once you get a guy to stop his feet and punch his hands, you can break him down and get to the quarterback."

It's also hard to compare pass rushers from different eras, said Marshall, who played for the Vikings from 1961 to 1979. "Pass rushers today have so many more restrictions and have to walk that fine line between aggression and all the rules and fines that are designed to protect the quarterback," Marshall said. "Back in the Purple People Eaters days, the fines we would have faced playing the way we did, our entire salaries would have been spent in fines by midseason."

# 37 Take a Love Boat Cruise on Lake Minnetonka

Fans can't necessarily recreate the most infamous cruise in Vikings history. At least not legally. But they can sail the high seas of Lake Minnetonka aboard the same yachts that were at the center of the Love Boat scandal that rocked their favorite team in 2005.

Al & Alma's Supper Club and Charter Cruises, located just west of the Twin Cities in the tiny waterfront community of Mound, offers what it calls "the perfect fusion of spectacular scenery and attentive award-winning service" aboard its fleet of six yachts. With individual yacht capacities from 60 to 149 guests and a combined 400 for all six yachts, Al & Alma's can accommodate individuals to large private groups for a variety of cruises throughout the day and night. For more information check out their website at al-almas.com.

A lasting link—good, bad, or mostly sordid—between Al & Alma's and the Vikings began at about 9:30 on the night of October 6, 2005. That's when, according to police reports, 17 Vikings players and several female companions boarded the 64-foot cruising yachts named the Avanti and the Avant Garde. The cruise was scheduled for three and a half hours, but the alarmed yacht captains called it a night and headed for shore after 90 minutes when they learned of drunken players engaging in sexual acts out in the open with strippers who had been flown in for the team's annual rookie party. Veteran cornerback Fred Smoot organized the party and booked the yachts for the team's bye week.

Unfortunately for the Vikings and embattled head coach Mike Tice, it was yet another black eye for a team that already was viewed as having run amok. As fate would have it, the embarrassing news would break a week later on the very day that first-year owner Zygi Wilf was concluding a two-day organizational summit on how to get the Vikings to operate as a "first-class organization."

Since 2002, when wide receiver Randy Moss' tendency to misbehave included bumping a traffic officer with his car and later pleading guilty to two misdemeanors, the Vikings often looked out of control. A Super Bowl ticket-scalping quandary entangled some of the coaches, including Tice, who was fined $100,000. And the crown jewel, at least until the Love Boat set sail, was running back Onterrio Smith being detained at the Minneapolis-St. Paul International Airport with a device called "The Original Whizzinator," which is designed to beat drug tests and includes vials of dried urine and a fake penis. Months later, Smith was suspended for the entire 2005 season after violating the league's substance policy for a third time. Smith never played again for the Vikings, and Tice was fired in the locker room moments after the season-ending win against the Chicago Bears.

As for the Love Boat Scandal, four players—Smoot, left tackle Bryant McKinnie, running back Moe Williams, and quarterback Daunte Culpepper—were charged. The charges against Culpepper were dropped, and Smoot and McKinnie pleaded guilty to misdemeanor disorderly conduct. Williams was convicted of disorderly conduct. Smoot and McKinnie were fined one game check apiece. Williams was out of the league when the case was resolved in 2006.

Vikings fans might disagree, but there was some levity that came with this ugly chapter in Vikings history. Two weeks later Carolina Panthers receiver Steve Smith was punishing Smoot with 11 catches for 201 yards when he scored a touchdown, sat down on the ground, and pretended to row a boat.

Vikings center Matt Birk also had one of the more memorable lines. Birk, who wasn't on the cruise, had spent years patiently giving his reaction to reporters every time other players made news for the wrong reasons. When asked for his reaction to teammates flying in strippers from Atlanta for the party, Birk put on a serious face. "I just think," he deadpanned to reporters in the locker room, "it's a slap in the face to all Minnesota strippers."

# 38 Cris Carter's Family

Cris Carter was standing on the stoop outside Apartment B at the People's Place Apartments on Lafayette Avenue in Middletown, Ohio, in May of 2013. The town was celebrating "Cris Carter Day" to honor the new Pro Football Hall of Famer. Carter, who had stopped by the poor section of town to visit his childhood home, was looking up at the second-story window and reminiscing with his brother, John, about the time they broke their mother Joyce's edict about being home before dark. "Mom locked the door, and [John] sent me up on the roof of that porch to go through the window," Cris said. "Mom hears me and she's waiting there at the window with a belt in her hands. I didn't know whether to go in the window or jump off the roof."

Joyce Carter raised seven rambunctious kids by herself in that small two-bedroom apartment. But she was the boss. Her oldest child, Butch, a former NBA player and head coach, threw a temper tantrum at school and was sent to the principal's office to be swatted on the backside. He left, went home, and told Joyce what had happened. She not only brought him back to school, but she also held him down so the principal could swat him.

Joyce had to leave high school when she was 17 because she became pregnant with Butch. But she was a stickler for academics. When she was close to 40, she returned to school, got her master's degree, and became a teacher. "Mom was known for taking you off the team if you had a C-minus," John Carter said. "She'd say, 'A C-minus is nothing more than a D. They just didn't want to give you a D because they knew I'd take you off the team.' She pulled my brother George off the team for a C-minus right before [basketball] tournaments his freshman year. And the C-minus was in French, which George shouldn't have been taking no French anyway. But Mom said, 'You decided to take it. Off the team you go.'"

Joyce started out in Troy, Ohio, about 50 miles away. When Butch was eight, Joyce and her husband, Clarence, divorced. Joyce ended up moving to Middletown, which had a rich scholastic sports tradition. She took a job in daycare at the Robert "Sonny" Hill Community Center about a quarter mile from her apartment. The small basketball court at the center became the Carter kids' home away from home.

Long before Middletown celebrated "Cris Carter Day," it was known as the home of Butch Carter. Butch was named the state's top high school basketball player in 1976. He signed with Indiana University, was drafted in the second round by the Los Angeles Lakers in 1980, played seven seasons for four teams, and later became a head coach. "Butch was our only father figure," said Cris, who is nine years younger. "Every dime he made growing up, he gave to my mom, so we'd have food on the table. Butch didn't think I noticed, but when we'd eat, there were seven of us, and Butch wouldn't eat until he knew there was enough for the rest of us kids."

A lot of times, the only thing to eat was oatmeal. "To this day," says Butch, "I still can't look at a bowl of oatmeal."

Butch also was a mentor to Cris athletically. Cris' explosive personality and a fiercely competitive side boiled over during his first Pee Wee football game when he threatened to beat up teammates who weren't giving as much effort as he was. It was Butch who sat him down and had a talk about the importance of being a good teammate.

Butch has called his father a "quitter," but when it comes to Joyce, all of the Carter kids remember their humble beginnings and the family motto instilled in them by Joyce: "Carters Don't Quit!" "People ask, 'How did you do it all by yourself?'" Joyce said. "I tell them I didn't. I had God. There's no way I would have survived these kids without God in my life."

# 39 John Randle

John Randle never forgot that he came from nothing or how he became everything no one thought he'd ever become. It fueled the work ethic that generated the relentless motor that didn't stop working when the games ended on Sundays. "There was this time John was shopping at Cub Foods," said John Teerlinck, the Vikings defensive line coach from 1992 to '94. "John is walking down the aisle, and there's this woman coming toward him with a grocery cart." Randle was a rookie free agent out of Division II Texas A&I University in 1990. A bundle of quick-twitch muscle in a compact body, this young, aspiring defensive tackle took it to heart when his mentor, the unconventional Teerlinck, told him to use even the most mundane everyday situations to practice his pass-rushing moves. Of course, the poor woman pushing the cart in Cub Foods didn't know this. "John moves toward her and starts putting a stutter-shake spin move on her cart," Teerlinck said. "She froze. She didn't know what to think, so she starts screaming and yelling for the manager."

NFL quarterbacks knew the feeling. Randle posted 137.5 sacks, a record for a defensive tackle, while playing 11 seasons for the Vikings and three more with the Seattle Seahawks. He was first-team All-Pro six times, a Pro Bowler seven times, and a member of the NFL's 1990s All-Decade team, a decade in which he never missed a game. In 2010 Randle became the 14th person to go from rookie free agent to Pro Football Hall of Famer. Two of his classmates were the incomparable Jerry Rice and Emmitt Smith.

## Randle Took Trash Talking to New Heights

People have always asked Robert Davis what John Randle was like in high school back in the mid-1980s. "I tell them he never said a word," said Davis, Randle's football coach at Hearne (Texas) High School. "They can't believe it. They saw the face paint and all the trash talking he did on television with the Vikings. But John didn't get noisy until he got to the pros."

Did he ever.

An NFL Films dream come true, Randle didn't participate in just any old garden variety trash talking. "The guy did his homework on you," former Chicago Bears guard Tom Thayer said. "As an offensive lineman, you got used to defensive linemen talking all the time. But with John he'd read the press guide and find some detail about you that he'd use during the game. I always found it to be pretty funny, but not everybody did."

He did the same thing in practice every day, said fellow Pro Football Hall of Famer Randall McDaniel, who had to block Randle as the Vikings' left guard. "Johnny doesn't have an off switch," McDaniel said. "He'd be yapping, and the guys in the huddle would be saying, 'Randall, you got to shut that guy up.'"

Some players tried to turn the tables on Randle. "I loved it when that happened because usually that got the quarterback involved," Randle said. "Someone would try to talk trash to you. Then the quarterback would say, 'Be quiet,' so he could call the signals or whatever. Then the next thing you know, everybody's telling each other to shut up and they'd call a timeout. I'd just walk away and watch the mess I caused."

Randle sometimes got too carried away. At the Metrodome in the 2000 playoffs, he celebrated a sack of New Orleans Saints quarterback Aaron Brooks by crawling on the field and lifting his leg as if he were a dog peeing. The sack was free. The celebration cost him $7,500.

*Undersized, but tenacious, defensive tackle John Randle sports his trademark eye black during a 1997 game against the San Francisco 49ers.*

John Anthony Randle was born December 12, 1967, the youngest of three boys to Martha Randle, a large Christian woman who didn't spare the rod. John's father, Edward Wilson, a mechanic, lived nearby with his other family and never was a part of John's life. "Ninety percent of who I am is because of my mom," Randle said. "We had nothing. But she never gave up."

Mumford, Texas, was a 176-person speck alongside Farm to Market Road 50 near the Brazos River. There was no stoplight, one store, a cemetery, and cotton as far as the eye could see. About 200 yards off the highway was a small, white three-bedroom house sitting on cinder blocks. It was built decades earlier for the summer help who worked in the cotton fields. There was no indoor plumbing, an outhouse out back, an aluminum roof, thin wooden walls with no insulation, and a kitchen so small that Randle could extend his arms and nearly touch the walls on both sides. In the living room was a wood stove and one bed that John shared with his older brothers, Dennis and Ervin, who played eight NFL seasons as a linebacker for the Tampa Bay Buccaneers and Kansas City Chiefs. "The wash room was what we called the 'No. 10 [gallon],' a bath tub that we hung on a nail on the back of the house," Dennis said. "When it was bath time, you got the tub off the nail, brought it into the kitchen, and mom would warm the water on the stove."

Martha earned $23 a week as a maid. She also worked the cotton fields in the summer, making $3.75 an hour. John often worked alongside her when he wasn't playing football at Hearne High School. Martha also knew how to force her sons back onto the right path. One day, tired from having to always hitchhike 12 miles home from practice, Randle came home early and told his mother he quit the football team so he could hang out with friends. Martha sent him back immediately. "My mom was 6'1", about 210 pounds, tough, and fast," Ervin said. "You didn't go against her. You didn't have a say. She said it, and it was done."

Randle rejoined the football team. When it came time for college, Randle's options were limited. "The big schools weren't looking for short, 227-pound defensive linemen," said Randle, who transferred to Texas A&I from Trinity Valley Community College. When it came time for the NFL, 28 NFL teams drafted 332 players not named John Randle. The Vikings were lucky to have a scout named Don Deisch, who happened to be scouting Portland State when he noticed Randle on the other side of the ball.

Randle hit Minnesota at full speed and never slowed down. "Johnny made me a Hall of Famer because if I ever took a play off in practice, he would have embarrassed me," guard Randall McDaniel said. "Johnny's motor never stopped, ever."

Randle returned to the Twin Cities to live after his playing career. He maintained his high motor but channeled it into his 10-handicap golf game and helping his wife, Candace, and their twins born on May 31, 2004. His daughter, Ryann, was born healthy, but his son, Jonathan, nearly died weeks later because of complications from a birth defect. Jonathan's kidneys weren't working. But on Father's Day 2004, three hours before Jonathan was scheduled to undergo a desperate procedure that had a 10 percent success rate, the kidneys began working, and Jonathan would be fine. After all, Randles always were at their strongest when cast as underdogs. "I was supposed to last three weeks in training camp and be cut," Randle said. "I never forgot what that felt like."

# 40 Ahmad Rashad and the Miracle at the Met

The first piece of the famous 1980 "Miracle at the Met" Hail Mary connection was acquired on a Monday morning on September 13, 1976. The Vikings had just returned from New Orleans with a 40–9 victory to kick off what would be an 11–2–1 season. But a 31-point victory against the Saints didn't hide Bud Grant's need for a quality receiver.

Ahmad Rashad was quality and then some.

At the time Vikings fans weren't too happy. The Vikings owed the expansion Seattle Seahawks a player in return. Seattle liked Bob Lurtsema. Yes, Minnesota's very own "Benchwarmer Bob." By then, Lurtsema was three years into being the beloved backup/ advertising pitchman. His funny name, self-deprecating humor, and backup status behind the stars of the Purple People Eaters defensive line made him perfect as an NFL player posing as the common man in ads for TCF Bank. "Moose [Carl Eller] broke his thumb the day before, and they still traded me," Lurtsema laughed years later. "Of course, they knew what they were doing. Moose still played the following week, naturally, and they got Ahmad Rashad."

Rashad was born Bobby Moore on November 19, 1949. He converted to Islam and changed his name in 1972, the same year the St. Louis Cardinals selected him fourth overall in the draft. Two years in St. Louis were followed by two years with the Buffalo Bills, the brief stint in Seattle, and seven seasons as a Viking.

As a Viking, Rashad caught 400 of his 495 career passes for 5,489 of his 6,831 yards and 34 of his 44 touchdowns. None was more memorable than the one he made on December 14, 1980 at

Met Stadium. The Cleveland Browns, known as the "Kardiac Kids" because of their thrilling finishes that year, were 10–4 and dominating the 8–6 Vikings on a cold afternoon on the Bloomington prairie. When running back Cleo Miller scored with about seven minutes left, the Browns led 23–9. But that's when Cleveland began playing not to lose.

The Vikings raced back. They scored a touchdown, got an interception from Bobby Bryant, and scored another touchdown. After the Browns punted, the Vikings had the ball at their 20 with 14 seconds left, no timeouts, and a 23–22 deficit. Quarterback Tommy Kramer, who joined the team after Rashad as the No. 1 draft pick in 1977, was calm and well-protected. He threw a 10-yard pass to tight end Joe Senser, who executed a perfect hook-and-lateral to running back Ted Brown, who added 24 more yards before going out of bounds at the Cleveland 46.

Five seconds remained. Kramer had thrown for 410 yards and three touchdowns. But the best was yet to come—at least from a Minnesota perspective. The play was called "Squadron Right, Squadron Fly." Lined up to the right were Sammy White, Terry LeCount, and Rashad, who at that point had eight catches for 96 yards and a touchdown.

The perfect pocket allowed Kramer time and room to step up and throw deep. The ball came down at the 2-yard line, near the front right end zone pylon. LeCount went for the ball in a scrum of players but didn't have a chance. Three Browns defenders were there to make the play. Safety Thom Darden leaped and tipped the ball. But that's when the sea of bodies seemed to split, allowing Rashad to calmly reach out, snare the ball with his left hand, and softly backpedal a yard into the end zone before being mobbed by teammates.

The victory gave Grant his 11th and final division title. The Browns would clinch their title the following week in Cincinnati. But Rashad remains a villain on the shores of Lake Erie.

"It was quite a game, no doubt about that," Rashad was quoted as saying in Jim Bruton's book *Vikings 50: All-Time Greatest Players in Franchise History*. "And fans in both Minnesota and Cleveland still, after more than 30 years, remember how the game ended. I can recall several times on airplanes people coming up to me and saying, 'I'm from Cleveland and I hate you.'"

# 41 Darrin Nelson's Drop

The Vikings didn't need a miracle catch with 56 seconds left in the NFC Championship Game at Washington on January 17, 1987. Trailing 17–10 in a sloppily-played game, they only needed running back Darrin Nelson to catch a Wade Wilson pass to his fingertips at the goal line on fourth and 4 from the Redskins' 6-yard line. A catch and the Vikings either score with a chance at the tying PAT or they have first and goal inside the 1-yard line. A drop and, well, it's another heart-stomping finish to a Vikings season. "Life goes on," receiver Anthony Carter said after the drop. "Only we're not going to San Diego [for the Super Bowl]."

Unlike other seasons when the Vikings were a dominant team that fell short, Jerry Burns' 1987 team had no business making it this far during an up-and-down season marred by a players' strike and three games played by replacement players. The Vikings were 2–0 before losing all three replacement games. General manager Mike Lynn, an ardent critic of the league's decision to stage replacement games, made little effort while fielding perhaps the league's worst replacement roster.

When the strike ended, the Vikings won five of six. Then they lost three of four to slip into the playoffs at 8–7. But then they went to New Orleans and routed the Saints 44–10 in a wild-card game. Then they went to San Francisco and upset the No. 1-seeded 49ers 36–24 in the divisional round. Suddenly, a trip to Washington to face the No. 3-seeded Redskins seemed like another step toward San Diego.

But the Vikings started dropping passes against the Redskins, including seven in the second half. Wilson was sacked eight times. The running game disappeared with 76 yards. And yet the Vikings forged a 7–7 halftime tie on a 23-yard pass to Leo Lewis. They were tied 10–10 before Washington quarterback Doug Williams threw a seven-yard touchdown pass to Gary Clark with 5:06 left. The Vikings moved the ball until they stopped themselves. Again. "This was the story of our season," left tackle Gary Zimmerman told reporters after the loss. "We'd get down to the goal line and not score."

Life went on for Carter but not before he voiced his frustration over Nelson being the intended target at the end. Carter caught two passes on the final drive, seven for 85 in the game, and had caught 10 for 227 in the 49ers upset the week before. Meanwhile, no one felt worse than Nelson. "It's called '83 Option,'" Nelson said of the final play. "It's for me or Anthony. I saw the ball coming and thought I had it…I guess I dropped it."

The Redskins went on to beat the Denver Broncos 42–10 in Super Bowl XXII. The following summer the Vikings reported to Mankato as a 6–1 favorite to win the Super Bowl. Only the Cleveland Browns at 4–1 had lower odds. "Don't tell me we're six yards away from the Super Bowl," Burns told reporters on reporting day. "We're 16 games away."

# 42 Randall McDaniel

They came, year after year, as unsuspecting targets with $10 bills practically earmarked for the pocket of Vikings left guard Randall McDaniel. "Bunch of suckers is what they were," said left tackle Gary Zimmerman. Defensive backs usually were prime targets. They had the speed, the cockiness, and the desire to win a bet with an offensive player. McDaniel would challenge them to a 40-yard race and then shame them into giving him a 10-yard head start. They assumed they could run down a 276-pound guard. They never did. "Randall was probably the greatest athlete to play guard in the history of the NFL," said former Vikings offensive coordinator Brian Billick. "There wasn't anything you couldn't do with Randall because he could do it all."

McDaniel played left guard for 12 seasons (1988–1999) in Minnesota and two more with the Tampa Bay Buccaneers. The Pro Football Hall of Famer earned nine consecutive All-Pro selections and started 12 consecutive Pro Bowls. Hall of Fame quarterback Warren Moon, who played for the Vikings from 1994 to 1996, joked that McDaniel should have been catching screen passes instead of blocking for running backs who caught them. "One time, against New Orleans at the Metrodome, Randall turned the corner, and there was no one for him to block," Moon said. "In that situation he's taught to turn it upfield, and the back will catch up to him. Well, Amp Lee couldn't catch him. It was strange seeing a man that big run that fast."

Before he was a Hall of Fame guard, McDaniel was an all-state tight end, an even better all-state basketball center, and a record-setting all-state track and field athlete in Arizona.

His track career didn't begin until after his freshman year when Bob Grey, the track coach at Agua Fria High School in Avondale, Arizona, just happened to be walking by when he saw McDaniel and some other basketball players hanging around the high jump pit. Suddenly, McDaniel did a front flip over a bar set at six feet. "And he did it flat-footed in street clothes while holding his books," Grey said.

McDaniel and Grey talked, and McDaniel told Grey that he was faster than any sprinter he had on the track team. Grey asked him to come back the next day and prove it. But there was a problem. McDaniel needed track spikes and he wore size 15 shoes. The biggest pair Grey had was size 13. "So I cut out the back of the 13s and taped them on his feet," Grey said. "Then he went out and beat every sprinter I had."

McDaniel gave up baseball for track. Eventually, he threw the shot 55 feet and the discus more than 160 feet. He also was an all-state sprinter. "I was 220 pounds," McDaniel said. "I'm sure other runners were thinking, *No way this guy can run*. I'd just smile at them. The race would end, and I'd look across at the guys and say, 'Surprised y'all, didn't I?'"

McDaniel ran a school-record 10.64 seconds in the 100-meter dash and made the state finals one year. Vance Johnson, who would play 11 seasons as a wide receiver for the Denver Broncos, also made the finals from another school. "Randall probably would have won that state meet," Grey said. "But he was still wearing those shoes we taped on him. He was even with Vance or leading a bit when one of those shoes blew out. He was running down the track with his shoe and the tape flapping all over the place."

After joining the Vikings as the 19th overall draft pick out of Arizona State in 1988, McDaniel mixed a strong work ethic with a combination of size and athleticism the NFL has rarely seen at guard. "Randall was a beast," said former Buffalo Bills defensive end Bruce Smith, the NFL's all-time sack leader and fellow member of the Hall of Fame's class of 2009. "I cannot remember facing another guard that possessed the ability, the tenaciousness, the strength. He was just incredible. Once he locked on to you, you weren't going anywhere."

# 43 Paul Krause

Paul Krause was asked about the viability of his NFL career interception record when his 19-year wait finally ended and he was entering the Pro Football Hall of Fame in 1998. "I'm very proud of the record," the former Vikings free safety said in Canton, Ohio, that day. "I hope it's not broken, even though records are made to be broken."

Then again, maybe some of them aren't.

Charles Woodson was a rookie in 1998. He played cornerback and safety in the NFL for 18 seasons before retiring after the 2015 season at age 39. He left the league with 65 interceptions—still 16 shy of Krause's 81. And, remember, Krause played a 14-game schedule for all but two of his seasons. With Woodson's pursuit of the record over, the position of active leader was turned over to 32-year-old DeAngelo Hall, who sat in 63rd place with 43 interceptions. No player under 30 was even in the top 252.

The Big Bang moment that created the NFL's pass-crazed present came in 1978 when key rule changes opened things up. Yet with more passes being thrown than ever before, the guy with the most interceptions played from 1964 to 1979.

Krause grew up in Burton, Michigan, where he was a four-sport star who reportedly fielded 140 college scholarship offers. He went to Iowa and on to the Washington Redskins as their second-round pick (18th overall) in 1964. Krause immediately proved that no one had a better understanding of how to be in the right place at the right time. He led the league with a career-high 12 interceptions and earned the first of three All-Pro first-team selections as a rookie.

## The Reason—or Lack Thereof—the Redskins Traded Krause

As quarterback of the Cleveland Browns from 1946 to 1955, Otto Graham was great. As head coach of the Washington Redskins from 1966 to 1968, Otto Graham fell short of good. The latter helps explain why Paul Krause was dealt to Minnesota in what Redskins historian Mike Richman called "arguably the worst trade in Redskins history."

The 6'3", 200-pound Krause played four seasons in Washington. He led the league in interceptions as an All-Pro rookie in 1964. He went to two Pro Bowls and had 28 interceptions through only four seasons. But after the 1967 season, Graham traded Krause to the Vikings for linebacker Marlin McKeever and a seventh-round draft choice. Krause played 12 more seasons for the Vikings, still holds the NFL's career interception record of 81, and was enshrined in the Pro Football Hall of Fame in 1998.

So what happened?

Blame Graham, according to Richman. In an article on Redskins. com, Richman wrote: "Redskins' defensive backfield coach Ed Hughes didn't think much of Krause's playing ability and persuaded Graham to make the trade, according to Sam Huff, a Redskins middle linebacker and defensive captain during Krause's stay in Washington. Plus, team president Edward Bennett Williams, who admired Krause's ability, was out of town when Graham pushed the eject button. When Williams returned, there was nothing he could do."

Krause was bitter about the trade and toward Graham, who went 17–22–3 during his Redskins stint. "I didn't care for Otto Graham," Krause is quoted as saying in Richman's article. "Graham listened to one of his defensive coaches who didn't know what he was doing. Then Graham traded me, so I don't think he knew what he was doing either. He wasn't a great football coach."

Krause intercepted passes in seven straight games that year. He joined the Vikings in 1968 and had interceptions in six straight games that season. Krause played in eight Pro Bowls and helped the Vikings to four Super Bowls. He's in the Vikings' Ring of Honor and on the Redskins' 70th anniversary team.

The knock against Krause—and most likely the reason he waited so long to enter the Hall of Fame—is he wasn't involved in tackling that much. He played a deep safety role. Former Vikings assistant and head coach Jerry Burns, who coached Krause at Iowa, was asked about that once. "As Bud Grant said, 'Paul personified the term free safety,'" Burns told the *Minneapolis Star Tribune*. "He would read a quarterback's eyes…play a hunch…use his intelligence to make plays. Some people will say, 'He was really just a center fielder.' So was Willie Mays."

# 44 Gary Zimmerman

Gary Zimmerman played more seasons and earned more All-Pro honors with the Vikings than the Denver Broncos, but the left tackle didn't carry anything purple with him into the Pro Football Hall of Fame in 2008. "When I went to Denver, it's like the dog that gets put to the pound, and your new owner treats you good," Zimmerman said. "The way Mr. [Pat] Bowlen treated everybody in the organization was unbelievable. Coming from where I came from in Minnesota, they didn't treat people quite as well, so you know, I thought it was that way across the league. And then to go to Denver and to have your eyes open like that, it was just unbelievable, the respect and dignity. It just made you want to win for the guy."

When the Vikings lined up in Mankato, Minnesota, in 1992, the left side of their offensive line was Randall McDaniel at guard and Zimmerman at tackle. Across from them on the right side of the defensive line was tackle John Randle and end Chris Doleman. That's four Hall of Famers all in their prime going head-to-head for the same team. But it wouldn't stay that way beyond 1992.

Zimmerman, who joined the Vikings in 1986 after two seasons in the USFL, was traded to Denver after an ugly contract dispute with Vikings second-year CEO and president Roger Headrick. It wouldn't be the only rocky relationship in the tumultuous reign of Headrick, a businessman with no football background, who assumed control of the Vikings on January 1, 1991. "When Roger came in, I thought everything was focused around the dollar," Zimmerman told the *Rocky Mountain News* in 1993. "They just treated people like dogs."

In December of 1991, the team was restructured as 10 people, including Headrick, became co-owners. Coach Jerry Burns retired, and Headrick replaced him with Dennis Green, who was only the second black head coach in NFL history at the time. When Green went 11–5 and won the NFC Central in his first year, some thought Headrick deserved consideration for NFL Executive of the Year. From 1992 to 1996, the Vikings would make the playoffs four times in five seasons. But they would go 0–4 in the playoffs as talent drained from the roster under Headrick and general manager Mike Lynn. After the 1992 season, for instance, one of the league's best offensive lines lost center Kirk Lowdermilk and left guard Brian Habib to free agency and Zimmerman, who had two years left on his contract but was traded during the preseason after a heated exchange with Headrick caused him to threaten retirement.

Zimmerman played seven seasons for the Vikings, where he started 169 consecutive games and made three of his five first-team All-Pro squads. Overall, he was a seven-time Pro Bowler and a member of the NFL's All-Decade teams for the 1980s and 1990s. He retired after the Broncos beat the Green Bay Packers 31–24 in Super Bowl XXXII on January 25, 1998.

In return for Zimmerman, the Vikings got picks in the first and sixth rounds in 1994 and the second round in 1995. They selected cornerback Dewayne Washington (first round), tight end Andrew Jordan (sixth), and safety Orlando Thomas (second) in 1995.

As for Headrick his stint in Minnesota didn't include the fairy tale ending; instead local locksmiths figured prominently. After a failed attempt to buy the team outright, he was forced to resign when new owner Red McCombs assumed control in the summer of 1998. McCombs' new president, Gary Woods, had the locks changed late on a Friday night when one of the front-office sec-retaries witnessed Headrick removing chairs from his office after hours. Woods wanted Headrick to pack up during office hours. "That stuff was my property," Headrick told the *Minneapolis Star Tribune*. "I brought that with me eight years ago and I never charged the company for it. I told [Woods] that, and all he said was, 'Well, I didn't know that.' I told him I was not going to wait until Monday to get that stuff. He has nothing to stand on. Zero."

Woods said changing the locks was standard procedure, as far as he was concerned. "Roger called from Winter Park [on a Saturday morning] and was extremely upset, screaming at me," Woods told the *Star Tribune*. "He wanted to get in, and I told him he could come back during normal business hours on Monday. He said he was going to get his own locksmith and drill out the cylinders. And I said, 'I can't tell you what to do, but I don't think that would be very wise to do.' And he said, 'I'm going to do it anyway.' It never occurred to us to call the police or anything like that, but he did get his own locksmith and got in and hauled stuff away. We have no idea what he took. We're obviously going to take inventory.

We really don't know what he took. But he had a 24-foot U-Haul, which seems like a lot."

# 45 Eat at Tinucci's—Where Randy Moss Wouldn't Take His Dog

Whoever said, "There's no such thing as bad publicity" has two strong believers in Gus and Mark Tinucci, brothers and co-owners of Tinucci's Restaurant & Catering, a third-generation operation in the Twin Cities suburb of Newport. The restaurant is a place to go if you're in the Twin Cities and have a hankering for something Randy Moss said he wouldn't feed his dog. *Now there's a commercial, eh?*

A week before he was waived during his failed second stint in Minnesota, the moody wide receiver verbally attacked Gus Tinucci, who was in the locker room catering the weekly Friday post-practice meal. "What the [expletive]? Who ordered this crap?" Moss yelled at Tinucci, according to Yahoo! Sports, which first reported the incident, citing unnamed players. "I wouldn't feed this to my dog!"

Within a week Gus did more than 50 radio interviews around the country as business soared. He became a sympathetic figure among Moss' teammates, including Brett Favre, as well as fans of the Vikings and human decency. On the first Saturday night after the news broke, Tinucci's had about a three-hour wait for tables. T-shirts were made that read, "Tinucci's caters to the best. No Moss." Hundreds sold for $10 a pop. And, of course, doggie bags were re-named "Randy bags." Moss never apologized to Tinucci, but maybe it's Tinucci who should have said thank you to Moss.

The most amazing part of Moss' second stint in Minnesota is how quickly it burned to the ground for both Moss and coach Brad

Childress. On October 4 Moss was a New England Patriot. But the public grousing about his contract situation reached its breaking point after he complained about not catching a pass in a 41–14 win against the Miami Dolphins. Two days later, Patriots coach Bill Belichick shipped Moss to Minnesota for a third-round draft pick.

## All You Can Eat

On December 6, 2015, the Vikings played half asleep in a 38–7 home loss to the Seattle Seahawks. And if that weren't enough to keep coach Mike Zimmer up all night, the Vikings also had a game four days later in Arizona against a Cardinals team that was 11–2 and sported the league's top-ranked offense.

Zimmer also knew that all four of his safeties, star linebacker Anthony Barr, and run-stuffing nose tackle Linval Joseph wouldn't be healthy enough to practice the next day. Two safeties would have to be added to the 53-man roster, including Anthony Harris, a rookie free agent who would be promoted from the practice squad and start against the Cardinals.

Notorious for watching game tape into the wee morning hours and sleeping in his office, Zimmer was asked the day after the Seahawks loss if he had spent the night in his office. "I did go home last night for a little bit and I went to McDonald's on the way home because I was hungry and I ordered two cheeseburgers and only got one," Zimmer said. "That's the kind of week it's been."

Reporters asked him why he didn't use his status and ask the servers, "Don't you know who I am?"

"They probably did," he joked. "That's why I got one."

Reporters used Twitter to post the incident and Zimmer's humorous reaction. Local TV stations produced stories on it. Within hours McDonald's had responded, tweeting that it would send 100 burgers to Zimmer and the Vikings. "That's not how we show love," the tweet said. "We're sending Coach Zimmer and the @Vikings 100 free burgers. Now it's THAT kind of week."

McDonald's might want to note that while the short-handed Vikings didn't beat Arizona, the hard-fought 23–20 loss was an inspiration that helped the Vikings close the regular season with three wins and a division title.

Childress hailed the move as what the Vikings needed to jumpstart a 1–2 team that was coming off the NFC title game. Reporters, skeptical of a marriage between the enigmatic Moss and the inflexible coach, peppered Childress with questions that essentially cried out, *"Are you sure you know what you're getting into?"* At one point Childress even laughed and said, "We're already talking about a mutiny?"

Well, yeah.

On November 2, less than a month later, Childress released Moss, who caught 13 passes for 174 yards and two touchdowns as the Vikings went 1–3. Twenty days later Childress was fired after a 31–3 home loss to the Green Bay Packers.

Moss behaved himself around Childress initially. But things changed quickly and bottomed out following a 28–18 loss at New England. Upset over the loss and catching only one pass for eight yards, Moss entered the locker room and reportedly yelled to owner Zygi Wilf that Childress should be fired. Later, Moss told reporters he would do an interview, but only if he asked and answered his own questions. Moss was upset that reporters had gotten him fined $25,000 for not cooperating with the league's media policy.

While "interviewing" himself, Moss professed his love for the Patriots and Belichick while criticizing Childress. Childress was fed up with everything from the occasional lack of effort to the Tinucci's incident to the insubordination after the Patriots loss. Childress released Moss the next morning without discussing it with ownership. It was a clear violation of the personnel protocol that was in place at the time. Childress announced the move by saying it was in the best short and long-term interest of the team, even though ownership was instrumental in the Moss trade.

# 46 Unsung Heroes

1,049.

That's how many consecutive Vikings games Fred Zamberletti attended before an illness prevented him from traveling with the team to Washington for a game in 2011. That includes preseason games, regular-season games, playoffs, Super Bowls, you name it. Freddie was the team's head athletic trainer from its inception in 1961 until 1998. He was medical services coordinator until 2003 and has been a consultant and team historian ever since.

When he was with the team full time, missing work wasn't an option—ever. This, after all, was a team of ironmen led by the likes of Mick Tingelhoff and Jim Marshall who never took a day off. "I missed three out of four kids being born," Zamberletti told the *Minneapolis Star Tribune*. "We didn't have anybody else in those days. If you were sick, didn't feel good, funerals or anything else, you still went to work and you didn't miss."

When the team was formed in 1961, Zamberletti was joined behind the scenes by an equipment manager named Jimmy Eason. Everybody called him "Stubby," and the *Star Tribune* once described him as a "squat, runty little guy who limped onto the field to retrieve the tee after Vikings kickoffs. He limped because he got one of his legs blown off on the invasion beach of Salerno, Italy."

Stubby was tough but beloved. He also smoked too much and died of lung cancer in 1981. Dennis Ryan, his 21-year-old understudy, was promoted and still holds the job. So in 55 seasons, the Vikings have had just *two* equipment managers.

In 1983 Ryan was preparing for the team's preseason game at London's Wembley Stadium. He found the "language barrier" to be a tad challenging. "I was asking them how we get our coaches up to the press box," Ryan said. "They looked at me like I was crazy. I told them it was very important that our coaches are up there so they can see over the field. They were all confused and they started talking about bringing in a crane and all this stuff. That's when I found out they call their buses 'coaches' over there. I told them that's okay, we didn't need to put our buses in the press box."

In 1999 Zamberletti received one of his greatest compliments when Marshall's No. 70 was being retired. Over 20 seasons from 1960 to 1979, Marshall played all 282 games consecutively, starting 270 in a row, a record surpassed by only Brett Favre. "Nowhere does that record mention the name Fred Zamberletti," Marshall said in 1999. "But Fred Zamberletti deserves that record as much as I do."

# 47 Ron Yary

Imagine the NFL draft being held quietly just 16 days after the Super Bowl. No scouting combine. No pro day workouts. No dot.com mock draft du jour to overhype the process from January through late April. Such a time existed on January 30, 1968, when the Vikings had the No. 1 overall pick. Before the Vikings made their choice, not a single person asked Southern California offensive tackle Ron Yary to tiptoe through a three-cone drill, do a broad jump, or bench press 225 pounds 30-some times. "Heck, I didn't even start lifting weights until 1980," Yary said decades later. "When I was a boy, they told us not to lift weights. You'd get too muscle-bound."

There was no Wonderlic test. And not a single team asked Yary if he thought of himself as a cat or a dog. "That's the one that gets me," Yary said. "All of this psychological testing and all this introspective of the players they do today. It hasn't done the NFL much good, has it? They still pick hoodlums."

The notion of televising the draft in 1968 would have been laughable. For Yary, there was no trip to New York City, no bear-hugging the commissioner and holding up a Vikings No. 1 jersey. In 1968 only three people in Minnesota sat in a room picking players over the phone when it was their turn to do so. No one called it a "War Room." It was just a small room big enough to fit coach Bud Grant, general manager Jim Finks, and personnel director Jerry Reichow. "You do have to be a little lucky in this business," Grant said. "But I thought I could tell who a good football player was. We didn't have to deal with a lot of opinions. Every committee is best when it's small. A committee of one is best of all."

When the Vikings were on the clock, the nation didn't hold its breath. Grant called Yary's apartment and asked whether Yary wanted to play for him. Yary said yes, and, well, that was pretty much it. "We didn't have all the refinements they have now," Grant said.

And yet, even with all of the advancements, the draft remains a mystifying crapshoot. In 2007, with reams of information available, the No. 1 pick overall was JaMarcus Russell, one of the all-time draft busts. Thirty-nine years earlier, the No. 1 overall pick was Yary, who became one of the greatest right tackles in NFL history. "I forget the skill-position players that were available in 1968. [Hall of Famer Larry Csonka was picked eighth by the Miami Dolphins.] But I do know Ron was a safe pick for us," Grant said. "He had a competitiveness that stood out. They have a word they use today that we didn't use back then. It's called a pancake. Ron wanted to pancake every guy he ever played against every play."

Yary played 15 NFL seasons, including 14 as a key member of a Vikings team that went to four Super Bowls. He played in seven Pro Bowls and was first-team All-Pro six times. The scouting process grew over the years as the financial commitment to players exploded. In 2010, the last year before the league's rookie salary cap, quarterback Sam Bradford was given $50 million in guaranteed money as the No. 1 pick. Yary's first year's salary was $18,000 with a $100,000 signing bonus. "I once added up everything I made playing football, Super Bowl money, postseason honors, playoff money," Yary said. "It was about $1.2 million. At the time I did that, [then-Vikings left tackle Bryant] McKinnie made that much every 4.2 games."

# 48 Dennis Green

*Distraction? You want a distraction?* Well, it doesn't get much more distracting than what Vikings coach Dennis Green did on October 24, 1997. With the Vikings at 5–2 and enjoying a rare patch of calm waters, Green released his self-published book, *No Room for Crybabies*. It hit the bookstores with a self-described bombshell final chapter in which Green wrote 10 pages describing his plan to sue the team's board of directors unless it sold him 30 percent controlling interest in the team, which had 10 owners at the time.

Green had arrived in the Twin Cities on January 10, 1992. Wearing his new Vikings cap and a Super Bowl ring from his assistant coaching days in San Francisco, he stepped to the podium for his news conference and announced, "There is a new sheriff in town." Five years later the marshal had called his bosses into the street for a showdown.

The bosses weren't happy, and there was speculation that Green would be fired sooner than later. "My personal opinion is that he's shot himself in the foot," Vikings co-owner Philip Maas told the *Minneapolis Star Tribune*. "I know if one of my employees did that he'd be gone tomorrow. Or gone this afternoon."

Green was upset with ownership because he believed two of the owners, Jaye Dyer and Wheelock Whitney, had reached out to Notre Dame head coach Lou Holtz, their friend and former University of Minnesota head coach, to replace Green. The accusations were denied, but Green wasn't buying it and considered it an insult and, ironically, a distraction that hurt the team.

The Vikings were indeed for sale. And Green did indeed save his job probably because the Vikings won their next three games, finished 9–7, and beat the New York Giants on the road in a wild-card game. The chaos continued, though, after the season. Upset with Green and his co-owners, CEO Roger Headrick fought with Green to the point where he said their differences were "irreconcilable." Green had one year left on his contract and was demanding a long-term deal because of the uncertain ownership situation. Eventually, Headrick, who was angling to buy the team outright, assured Green that he would be the coach in 1998 no matter what, so Green agreed to finish out his contract.

Then things went from strange to goofy. Author Tom Clancy stepped in with a $200 million offer that the board of directors accepted. Headrick scrambled and put forth a $205 million offer, claiming he had right of first refusal as a part-owner. That didn't stop Clancy from whirling into town for a news conference and an arrogant stiff-arm to the team's CEO. He said Headrick's views and opinions on the Vikings were as irrelevant as Saddam Hussein's. "The best legal advice that I'm getting is [Headrick] is dead in the ground with a wooden stake in his heart," Clancy said.

Within months Clancy's bid would suffer the same fate. The author didn't have the money. Finally, on July 3 the board announced the $250 million sale to San Antonio businessman Red McCombs. A month later the NFL approved the sale, ending one of the more bizarre 10 months in franchise history.

Green and McCombs hit it off, and Green got a three-year contract extension. With harmony at the top and a franchise-altering rookie by the name of Randy Moss taking the league and the Twin Cities by storm, the Vikings went a franchise-record 15–1. "I don't have the inclination to worry about what other people are doing a year later," Green said late in the year when asked about his differences with the previous owners. "I'm just trying to do what I can to be a great member of this team and this organization, and that's where my satisfaction is."

The Vikings, of course, were racing toward their fifth Super Bowl until they tripped over the Atlanta Falcons in the NFC title game at the Metrodome. Green reached another NFC title game two years later but never led the Vikings to the Super Bowl.

# 49 Dave Osborn

As a rookie running back Dave Osborn liked to create as much space between himself and volatile coach Norm Van Brocklin as he did between himself and an oncoming tackler. "A lot of us always made a point on gameday to stay as far away from Van Brocklin as we could," Osborn said. "I was playing special teams my rookie year, and Tommy Mason gets hurt."

Mason, the No. 1 overall draft pick in the team's 1961 expansion season, was a three-time Pro Bowl running back at the time. But on this date, November 7, 1965, "Touchdown Tommy" would injure his right knee. He would miss the final two games of that season, play only seven more games for the Vikings the following year, and never be the same player he once was. "I was probably the third or fourth running back my rookie year," Mason said. "But for some reason, when Tommy got hurt, Van Brocklin looks around and yells, 'Osborn!' I remember thinking, 'Uh-oh, what's he yelling at me for?'"

Van Brocklin instead was giving Osborn his big break. "I came running up there, and Van Brocklin put his arm around me, great big arm, big hand," Osborn said. "He looked me in the eye. I'm thinking, *Wow, he's going to give me some great encouragement.* Then he says, 'Get in there and see what you can fuck up.' Then he pushed me onto the field. I went stumbling out there. And 12 years later, I was still out there."

Osborn and Bill Brown became good enough running mates that general manager Jim Finks was able to trade Mason, tight end Hal Bedsole, and a second-round draft pick to the Los Angeles Rams for tight end Marlin McKeever and the 15th overall draft pick in 1967. With that draft pick, Finks picked a guy named Alan Page.

Osborn played for the Vikings through the 1975 season, rushing for 4,320 yards as one of the grittiest overachievers in franchise history. The summer he was released, he was on a hunting trip when he found out that the rival Packers were interested in him. When Green Bay quarterback Bart Starr called him personally, Mason went to join the Packers for one more season.

Osborn grew up on a farm in Cando, North Dakota. Early on, he attended a one-room schoolhouse with eight grades and no transportation. "Things were different," he said. "I remember riding a horse to school." Osborn had no aspirations of playing college football, let alone professionally. But he was always faster than the kids around him.

Osborn developed as a versatile athlete on his way to becoming 6'0", 206 pounds. But in ninth grade, he failed his football physical because of a heart murmur and spent the season as the student manager. A broken collarbone shortened his junior season, and a giant snowstorm canceled a chunk of games his senior season. With few college options, he went to the University of North Dakota, where he was good enough for the Vikings to select him in the 13th round of the 1965 draft. "My first contract was for $9,000," Osborn said. "It's not like today. We had other jobs in the offseason."

He sold advertising for the *St. Paul Pioneer Press*. He sold cars and eventually owned a car dealership. He sold office machines. He did whatever it took to make a living while helping the Vikings to two of their four Super Bowls. "I think the most I made was $60,000," Osborn said. "But I think a lot of us would have played for free back then."

Osborn also became one of the most popular players on the roster, not to mention one of its more active pranksters. In 1976 when he returned to Metropolitan Stadium as a member of the Packers, Osborn arrived early, slipped into the Vikings' locker room, and tied his former teammates' jerseys and socks in knots. The Vikings knew exactly who had invaded their locker room.

# 50 Adrian Peterson Rushes for 296

In his first NFL game, Adrian Peterson caught a screen pass and went 60 yards for a touchdown against the Atlanta Falcons at the Metrodome. In his fifth game, he ran for 224 yards at Soldier Field in Chicago.

In his eighth game, he had 43 yards rushing at halftime. Yeah, November 4, 2007, was shaping up as a pretty nondescript home game against the San Diego Chargers. But that would change in a hurry. Peterson exploded in the second half, rushing for 253 yards on 18 carries. And he could have had many more. Backup Chester Taylor, a 1,200-yard rusher the year before, had five of the team's final seven carries for 47 yards in a 35–17 rout. "I was just sitting over there on the sideline," Chargers running back LaDainian Tomlinson said. "I was thinking, *I've never seen anything like it.*"

No one had. Peterson's 296 yards on 30 carries (a 9.9 yard-per-carry average) broke the NFL single-game record of 295 set by Jamal Lewis of the Baltimore Ravens against the Cleveland Browns four years earlier. Tomlinson, the league's reigning MVP at the time, had 40 yards on 16 carries (2.5). "I don't want to watch *SportsCenter* tonight, I know that," Chargers strong safety Clinton Hart said. "You just don't think it can happen because it's never happened. Ever."

Meanwhile, in the other locker room, teammates were left shaking their heads once again over this 6'1", 220-pound rookie. "You don't know what the kid is going to do next," safety Darren Sharper said. "Every time he touches the ball, you don't know. It could be the play of all time."

Chargers defensive coordinator Ted Cottrell, who had held the same position with the Vikings two years earlier, called the afternoon a "perfect storm," in which defensive injuries at all three levels collided with a red-hot, once-in-a-generation running back. The first injury blow was to outside linebacker Shaun Phillips, who was inactive with a groin injury. The second blow came early in the game when cornerback Quentin Jammer, a reliable tackler in run support, left with a hamstring injury. And the final and most devastating blow came right before Peterson barrelled around right end for his 64-yard touchdown romp with 12 minutes, 55 seconds left in the third quarter. Right defensive end Luis Castillo, the best run stopper in the Chargers' 3-4 scheme, wasn't in the game to set the edge. He was out with a serious ankle injury. "What happened in the second half," said Cottrell, "is Castillo got hurt. That really hurt."

Before Castillo went down, Peterson had 49 yards and a 1-yard touchdown on 14 carries. With Castillo out, Peterson had 247 yards and touchdowns of 64 and 46 yards on 16 carries.

Add it all up, and the Vikings' 378 rushing yards were the most by a Vikings team and the most against a Chargers team. The Vikings' previous record had stood for 43 years, while the Chargers' mark had been around for 32 years. "That," linebacker Shawne Merriman said, "is embarrassing."

To this day, then-coach Brad Childress won't hesitate when asked about his most vivid memory from that game. "Antonio Cromartie taking our missed field goal back 109 yards for a touchdown right before halftime," said Childress, referring to Cromartie's record-setting play as time expired in the first half. "That put us down 14–7."

Ask Childress what he remembers most after that, and, well, Peterson surfaces. "There was a stretch run play that they could not defend, so we stayed with it," Childress said. "When Adrian is running circles around the defense, you stick with it."

Peterson had eight carries for 107 yards in the third quarter. At the 10:07 mark of the fourth quarter, he surpassed 200 yards, albeit on a 12-yard carry that ended with him fumbling the ball away. At that point, Peterson became the first rookie in NFL history to rush for 200 yards twice. "I wasn't thinking about the record at all," Peterson said. "Oh, no, I was just out there playing ball."

Peterson's 26th carry was the 46-yard touchdown. His next carry went seven yards. A one-yard loss on the next play was negated by a holding call on Ryan Cook. Peterson was pulled and replaced by Taylor, who had four straight carries for 34, five, zero, and two yards for a touchdown with 4:22 left. Peterson, meanwhile, sat just 37 yards from the record.

The Vikings got the ball back with 1:58 left. Peterson went up the middle for 35 yards. Taylor got the next carry for six yards. In the meantime Vikings public relations director Bob Hagan had called down to the sideline to have one of his staff members inform Childress that Peterson was only two yards from the record.

With 1:04 left, Peterson went up the middle for three yards. The Vikings took a knee with 17 seconds left, and the record fell. "Adrian has a bright future," the Hall of Fame-bound Tomlinson said. "He's off to one heck of a start."

# 51 Mike Tice

*"Beep! Beep! Beep!"*

Reporters covering the Vikings at Winter Park on January 3, 2005, looked up when they heard that familiar deep voice with the New York accent imitating the sound that a service vehicle makes when it's backing up. "What am I?" coach Mike Tice said as he walked backward past a doorway. "I'm backing into the playoffs!"

Then came the even more familiar Tice laugh. Sort of a half chuckle, half giggle projectile from the towering frame of a 6'8" former NFL tight end. A year earlier Tice's Vikings led the NFC North for every snap of the season until the final fateful one in Phoenix. Arizona Cardinals wide receiver Nate Poole caught a 28-yard touchdown pass from Josh McCown as time expired on fourth and 24 to knock the 9–7 Vikings out of the playoffs and hand the Green Bay Packers the division title.

In 2005 Tice's Vikings were in the playoffs for the first and only time despite a 21–18 regular season-ending loss in Washington the day before Tice began beeping for reporters. Another 3–7 finish didn't matter. Neither did an 8–8 record or the further humiliation of receiver Randy Moss walking off the field against the Redskins with two seconds left and the Vikings lining up for an onside kick.

In a surreal setting, players, coaches, and reporters covering the game stood inside FedEx Field and watched the New Orleans Saints and Carolina Panthers decide Minnesota's playoff fate. After about 30 minutes, the Saints won 21–18 to give the Vikings the NFC's final playoff berth. "We're not going to go and do cartwheels and do something stupid like open up a bottle of champagne," Tice said at the time. "But we still got in."

The roller coaster of emotions was typical of Tice's head coaching career. Unpredictable joy often butted up against unforeseen pitfalls and vice versa, on and off the field, as Tice posted a 33–34 record (1–1 in the playoffs) from the last game of the 2001 season to his firing in the locker room moments after the 2005 season finale.

The only person to work for the Vikings as a player, an assistant coach, and a head coach, Tice was a brash, tough-talking New Yorker who was beloved by passive-aggressive Upper Midwesterners who typically don't like brash, tough-talking New Yorkers. But his teams were wildly inconsistent.

In 2003 the Vikings were the talk of the league when they were 6–0. Ten games later, in stunning fashion, they joined the 1978 Redskins as the only teams in NFL history to start 6–0 and miss the playoffs. By season's end team officials were still preparing for a home playoff game when the Vikings led the Cardinals 17–6 with six minutes left. But Arizona would convert three fourth downs, including a two-yard touchdown pass; recover an onside kick;

and overcome back-to-back sacks by Kevin Williams and Lance Johnstone to set up the final sucker punch play with no timeouts and McCown scrambling about with no time on the clock. Poole got only one foot down in the end zone before being forced out by Denard Walker and Brian Russell. It was a touchdown, per the force-out rule in place at the time. The NFL would change that rule five years later. "There was never a time when I felt that we were going to lose that game," Tice said. "Not until the last play."

That year the NFL had four teams that shared the league's worst record of 4–12. Tice's Vikings went 9–7 while losing to each one of those 4–12 teams, including the Cardinals.

A lot of Tice's coaching career didn't make sense. He was 0–4 at Soldier Field against Chicago Bears teams that missed the playoffs three out of four years. But he was 3–2 at Lambeau Field against Packers teams that made the playoffs three out of four years.

One of those wins at Lambeau Field was a wild-card playoff stunner that featured Moss pretending to moon the crowd. The Vikings had lost to the Packers twice that year by the same 34–31 score. But they won the third meeting 31–17 in a dominant performance that came less than a week after Tice playfully beeped for reporters while backing into the playoffs.

# 52 Chris Doleman

Every enormously-paid left tackle should thank Chris Doleman for what he did, where he did it, and who he did it to on January 9, 1988. It was on that date in San Francisco that 49ers coach Bill Walsh presumably assumed playoff victory for the NFC's top seed

*Defensive end Chris Doleman, who recorded 150.5 sacks, 44 forced fumbles, and 24 fumble recoveries during his Hall of Fame career, rushes upfield against the Los Angeles Rams.*

during the 1987 strike season. The 49ers were 13–2 and led by quarterback Joe Montana and wide receiver Jerry Rice, who had set the NFL record for touchdown receptions (22) while playing in only the 12 non-replacement games.

This was a Hall of Fame trio working the West Coast Offense at peak efficiency and explosiveness until it ran into the Vikings and their rhythm-busting right defensive end.

Doleman punished left tackle Bubba Paris, sacking Montana twice and knocking him down several more times as the No. 5-seed Vikings pulled off a 36–24 upset in the divisional round.

Walsh had seen enough. Tired of seeing his Super Bowl plans ruined by edge rushers such as Lawrence Taylor and Doleman, Walsh led the charge on behalf of the bank accounts of future blind-side protectors. Steve Wallace replaced Paris the following season and was given a five-year, $10.7 million deal, which was unheard of for an offensive tackle at the time.

A year later the 49ers beat the Vikings in the regular season 24–21 and 34–9 in the divisional playoff round rematch en route to their third Super Bowl title. Eight years later Doleman would join the 49ers. Two years after that, at age 37, Doleman had 15 sacks—the second-highest total of his career—for San Francisco.

Doleman's career sure didn't start that way. In fact, he was a nondescript outside linebacker with half a sack in his first 19 NFL starts. As the fourth overall draft pick in 1985, the word "bust" was starting to make its way to the tips of tongues. But then something happened that would nudge Doleman into a fateful turn toward Canton, Ohio, and the Pro Football Hall of Fame. "We were making a run for the playoffs in 1986, and, sure enough, Mark Mullaney went down," said Doleman, referring to the Vikings' 12-year veteran and first-round pick in 1975. "So the coaches asked me, 'Can you rush the passer?'"

Yes, he certainly could. Doleman started the final three games at right end in 1986. He had a sack in each one of them. A year later he was first-team All-Pro with 11 sacks in 12 games during the strike season.

Doleman played 232 games, missing only two because of injury, and made eight Pro Bowls with three teams: Vikings (1985–93, 1999), Atlanta Falcons (1994–95), and 49ers (1996–98). A three-time first-team All-Pro and a member of the NFL's 1990s All-Decade team, he also finished with 150.5 sacks (fourth all time) as well as 44 forced fumbles, 24 fumble recoveries, eight interceptions, and three touchdowns. "Chris didn't care who he was playing against," said former Vikings teammate and Hall of Famer John Randle. "He knew he was going to show the guy for 60 minutes, 'I'm Chris Doleman and I'm going to *kill* you.' You looked in his eyes and you instantly got confidence."

Randle wasn't the only tackle who reaped the benefits of playing next to Doleman. In 1989 with Doleman notching 21 sacks, a franchise mark that stood until Jared Allen had 22 in 2011, Keith Millard had 18 sacks and won NFL Defensive Player of the Year. Dana Stubblefield won the same award as Doleman's 49ers teammate in 1997.

Doleman played on 12 winning teams and was part of four defenses that ranked No. 1. Even at the end, when he returned to the Vikings for one final season, he started 12 games and had eight sacks at age 38. And just think—it all started with a sudden need at right end near the end of Doleman's second season. "After the first game, the coaches said, 'You looked pretty good at this position. Would you want to do it here on out?'" Doleman said. "I was just starting to get a feel for the linebacker position because I had never played in the 3-4 the Vikings were playing. But I have to admit, when I did move down to [end], it felt like home. It really did."

# Tingelhoff's $500 Signing Bonus

In 2015 the NFL's highest paid center was Mike Pouncey of the Miami Dolphins at $8.95 million a year. His signing bonus was $5 million. In 1962 Mick Tingelhoff signed a deal with the Vikings for $9,000 a year. His signing bonus was 500 bucks. And he never would have even known about the bonus if it weren't for his head coach's sharp tongue and famous temper.

It was coach Norm Van Brocklin who sent a scout to Lincoln, Nebraska, with $500 and instructions to give it to Tingelhoff as incentive to sign a rookie free-agent contract. The scout pocketed the money, gambling that Tingelhoff would be desperate enough to sign without it.

The scout was right.

Mick and Phyllis Tingelhoff had met at the University of Nebraska. When Phyllis arrived from Indiana in a purple convertible, Mick's eye was caught. Soon, they were married in college, and Mick needed a job. They knew nothing about the NFL draft, and it would be decades before the draft would become a national obsession and be televised over three days. "We really didn't know much of anything about pro football," Phyllis said. "We were told it was possible, but we didn't know for sure. Mick was thinking about teaching jobs. He probably would have wanted to be a high school coach, too, probably in Nebraska somewhere."

The draft came and went. Fourteen teams picked 280 players over 20 rounds. Twenty centers not named Tingelhoff were selected. "My degree was in science," Tingelhoff would say 53 years later when he joined the Pro Football Hall of Fame. "I probably would have been a science teacher."

Two NFL teams called him. The St. Louis Cardinals and a Vikings team coming off a 3–11 expansion season. The CFL also had interest. A guy named Jim Finks in Calgary and some other fella named Bud Grant in Winnipeg had a hunch that Tingelhoff wasn't too undersized to excel at center.

Tingelhoff chose the Vikings, who originally lined him up at linebacker, his other position at Nebraska. "On the second day of camp, we needed a center," quarterback Fran Tarkenton remembered. "Van Brocklin moved Mick to center, and the rest is history."

But it wasn't that smooth at first. "When Mick gets here, he misses an assignment or something," said former Vikings running back Dave Osborn, who would arrive in 1965 and become one of Tingelhoff's closest friends over the next 50-plus years. "Van Brocklin got mad and yelled, 'I gave you $500, and you come up here and do that?' Then Mick looks at him, says, 'You didn't give me $500.'"

Soon, Tingelhoff settled in at center and began proving he wouldn't be going anywhere for a very long time. "I do know," Tingelhoff said, "that Van Brocklin ended up giving me the $500."

# 54 Go to Mankato for Training Camp

Basking in the sun typically isn't associated with Mankato, Minnesota, but Vikings fans who want an up-close experience with their favorite players and coaches should make plans to visit training camp in late July to early August. Located 80 miles southwest of Minneapolis, Minnesota State University-Mankato, has been the late summer home of the Vikings since 1966. Every Hall of Famer who's played for the team has spent time sweating on these same grounds—except, of course, Brett Favre, the one-time enemy quarterback, who skipped training camp in 2009–10, when he switched sides of the Packers-Vikings rivalry.

During the three-week camp, fans typically can watch a morning walk-through followed by an afternoon practice. Autograph sessions usually follow the walk-throughs, and some players have been known to stop and sign as they leave the field, cross Stadium Road, and enter the locker room. Saturday night practices usually are held in Blakeslee Stadium and have been known to draw 10,000 fans. Fan Appreciation Night, which occurs near the end of camp, is held inside the stadium and ends with players throwing miniature footballs into the crowd as they're introduced before a booming fireworks show.

Vikings Village, located between the practice fields and Blakeslee Stadium, provides entertainment for fans, especially ones with young children. Walk up Stadium Road and one could run across former Vikings running back Chuck Foreman, who has operated a sports memorabilia tent for years during training camp.

Finding decent food within walking distance isn't difficult. Jake's Pizza has been a popular spot for years, while Pieology, a pizza place owned by Vikings left tackle Matt Kalil, joined the competition with its debut in 2015. A short drive across town is Tav on the Ave, a popular sports bar known for its wings. Other eateries are nearby as well.

Players typically aren't spotted out on the town at night nearly as often as they once were. In the early to mid-1970s, the two leaders in the enjoyment of a few public beverages were defensive linemen "Benchwarmer Bob" Lurtsema and Doug Southerland. Of course, it was a different time, a simpler time.

On gamedays when the Vikings had a home exhibition, coach Bud Grant allowed players to drive their own cars up to the game. Players were told to drive straight to Metropolitan Stadium in Bloomington for the game. They would have the night off and the next day as well.

Grant would release them around 1:30 PM, but no one dared to leave until defensive end Jim Marshall said so—or gave the signal. Marshall owned a big pistol that he brought with him to camp. Players would be sitting in revving cars waiting for their leader to exit the dorms and blast his pistol into the air. Tires were known to squeal not long after the shot was fired.

Players from the early days remember the inconveniences and all the fun they used to have in and around Gage Hall, the unair-conditioned dorm that housed the Vikings for years until it was torn down in 2013. And the rocket contests behind Gage Hall. Marshall, of course, is at the center of one of the more popular stories that have survived for decades. Marshall had a rocket that was about three feet long. Before launching it to see if it would go the highest, he tied a frog onto the rocket with a miniature parachute. He nicknamed the frog "Freddy" after then-head athletic trainer Fred Zamberletti. Marshall set off the rocket, which won the contest. But no one ever spotted Freddy or his parachute. "We never found Freddy the frog," Lurtsema said.

# 55 Jerry Reichow, a Scout's Life

Jerry Reichow was 27 years old when he scored the second touchdown in Vikings franchise history on September 17, 1961. He was 81 and still working for the Vikings when the 2016 NFL Scouting Combine arrived. "I guess you could say this is what I want to do with my life," Reichow joked.

As a player Reichow was a 6'2", 217-pound end/quarterback. The Detroit Lions drafted him in the fourth round in 1956. After three seasons in Detroit, he went to Philadelphia, where he met Eagles quarterback Norm Van Brocklin. When Van Brocklin retired after winning the 1960 NFL title to become head coach of the expansion Vikings, he brought Reichow with him.

Reichow never left the organization. In the first regular-season game in franchise history —a 37–13 upset of the Chicago Bears—he caught three passes for 103 yards and a touchdown. Bob Schnelker scored the Vikings' first touchdown on a 14-yard pass from Fran Tarkenton. Reichow had the next one, a 29-yarder from Tarkenton.

Reichow's best season was 1961, when he led the Vikings in catches (50), receiving yards (859), and touchdown receptions (11). He played 54 games as a Viking before his playing days ended in 1965. "The Vikings released me as a player that summer, and [general manager] Jim Finks hired me as a scout," Reichow said. "The draft was in December, and it started at 8:00 AM on a Saturday and went straight through to Sunday night. The only people in the draft room were me, Finks, and Norm Van Brocklin, and Van Brocklin had to leave Sunday morning because he had to go coach the team."

Reichow had a knack for spotting talent. He got a raise and, technically, a promotion. "I made $17,000 when I was named personnel director in 1966," Reichow said. "Of course, it wasn't hard directing since I was the only person in the department to direct."

In 1970 the Vikings added Frank Gilliam to their personnel department. He and Reichow worked together for the next 36 years. Gilliam is no longer with the team, but Reichow has remained as a personnel consultant, meaning he has been a part of the NFL for every season since leaving the University of Iowa to join the Lions in 1956.

Obviously, it was harder to gather information in the early days of scouting. Men like Reichow were the ones who made it happen with dogged determination and a lot of miles spent in the air and on the backroads across America. "Let's just say you wouldn't want to start figuring out what you made an hour," Reichow said. "Being a scout is hectic and tough. The job wears on you. It really does."

The evolution of the scouting process and the made-for-TV hoopla surrounding the draft amazes Reichow. Things were much simpler back in the day. "I remember I was just named director, and Finks had just hired Bud Grant," Reichow said. "Finks had to go to the hospital, so it's just Bud sitting with me in the draft room. And Bud had just come down from Canada, so it was the easiest draft day ever. There was nobody to argue with."

Reichow represented the team well that day. With three first-round picks, he selected Clinton Jones, Gene Washington, and Alan Page. "You get lucky sometimes," Reichow said. "Like the time we had the No. 1 pick overall in 1968. We went into draft day still undecided. We had five guys we could have picked. We ended up taking Ron Yary. Thank God."

# 56 Red and Randy Split

Billy Joe "Red" McCombs, the billionaire automobile magnate and sports team owner, whirled into the Twin Cities in 1998, buying the Vikings for $250 million and jump-starting a renewed love for the team with a first-round draft pick by the name of Randy Moss. Seven years later, in 2005, they left together when McCombs ordered Moss' trade to the Oakland Raiders two months before the $600 million sale of the team went through for the Wilf family.

Ten years after McCombs sold the team, the 87-year-old opened up on why he pulled the trigger on a trade that dispatched his favorite player. No, McCombs said, it wasn't a parting shot to Minnesota for seven years of denying him the new stadium he so coveted. "I didn't know that I wouldn't still be there [in 2005]," he said. "These people buying the team had been saying they were going to do something and then they didn't do it. I had two or three potential buyers on the string. But I didn't know if they were going to do it or not."

Reggie Fowler was the initial primary owner in the group that included the Wilfs. When Fowler's bid was rejected, the group reshuffled and presented Zygi Wilf as the lead. "If [then-governor Tim] Pawlenty would have helped me get a stadium, I never would have sold," McCombs said. "But he just told me straight out, 'I didn't intend to mislead you, but you're doing very well [financially], and we have a lot of problems in Minnesota. I'm not going to participate in that stadium.' So I said, 'I'm outta here.'"

McCombs said Moss had worn out his welcome and then some by the time the 2005 season rolled around. The moody receiver's enigmatic behavior likely hit its breaking point with McCombs when Moss walked off the field while teammates lined up for an onside kick with two seconds left in the loss at Washington in the 2004 regular-season finale. After the game center Matt Birk was livid and confronted him alone in the locker room. He told Moss that his behavior wasn't acceptable and that it couldn't happen again. Moss was, well, Moss—unaffected by Birk's comments. Later, with reporters watching, Birk approached Moss in the locker room and asked, "Do you have a minute?" Moss never said a word, put his headphones on, and walked out. Birk turned to the reporters and said, "Guess not."

"I called Randy myself the day we traded him," McCombs said. "He wasn't happy. He said, 'You've got to be kidding. I'll just retire.' I said, 'You're not going to retire. You still got another seven to 10 years in the league.' But you need to move on out of here. At that point, we came out pretty well in that trade, very well, I would say."

Raiders owner Al Davis had met McCombs' demand for a defensive starter (linebacker Napoleon Harris) and a first-round pick (No. 7 overall, used on receiver Troy Williamson, a draft bust). The Vikings also got Oakland's seventh-round pick (used on cornerback Adrian Ward, who didn't make the team). "The trade was 100 percent my call," McCombs said. "By the time the trade was made, there were very few supporters of Randy. There was a decided change in the locker room with Randy. Coaches said, 'Ah, that's the way it goes with Randy.' That's not the way it goes. I knew Randy was still very marketable, and it all boiled down to me saying, 'Hey, Randy's got to go.'"

Williamson, who was traded to Jacksonville for a sixth-round pick in 2008, had 87 career catches and has been out of football since 2009. The team's other first-round pick that year, Wisconsin defensive end Erasmus James, was selected at 18th overall and had five career sacks and has been out of the NFL since 2008. Meanwhile, the Green Bay Packers selected Aaron Rodgers No. 24 overall that year.

The Vikings hadn't even considered Rodgers because 2005 happened to be one of the few years they didn't need a franchise quarterback. Young Daunte Culpepper was coming off a career year, and it was seven months before he suffered a devastating knee injury in his final snap as a Viking. "It's too bad Daunte never got right again after that injury," McCombs said. "I never gave it any thought that the Moss trade could have turned into Aaron Rodgers. Obviously, that would have been something. But we did get a great pick for Randy. And it was time for him to go."

# 57 Keith Millard's Guns

Ah, training camp memories in Mankato, Minnesota: defensive tackle Chase Baker being duct-taped to a goal post and doused with Pepto-Bismol on the day coach Leslie Frazier denounced NFL hazing, fans oohing as Randy Moss catches deep ball after deep ball from Daunte Culpepper, Keith Millard throwing linebackers coach Monte Kiffin off the roof of Gage Hall...

*Wait, what?*

Apparently, the dogs days of August 1988 were particularly slow when head coach Jerry Burns decided to perk things up with a well-crafted prank involving Kiffin and Millard, the team's highly charged defensive tackle. After lunch one day, the three of them put the gameplan together. First, Kiffin would incite an argument while Millard was getting his ankles taped. Then Millard would pretend to get angry and tell teammates that Burns had better keep Kiffin away from him.

As the rest of the team headed out to the practice field, Kiffin and Millard snuck over to nearby Gage Hall, the 12-story dormitory that overlooked the practice fields and housed the players at the time. They went to the roof, where they began yelling and screaming to draw attention. "But because of the wind, we couldn't hear them," Burns told reporters afterward. "So I finally said, 'What the hell is happening up there?'"

Players watched from below as Kiffin and Millard started shoving each other and then disappeared from view. Then a stuffed mannequin dressed to look like Kiffin—including a $20 toupee that Burns purchased for the occasion—was flung off the roof to its demise. Millard was known to have a wild side. But apparently not wild enough to convince teammates that he'd actually throw a coach off the roof. Players reportedly laughed and clapped while one of them shook his head and told Burns, "Poor Monte."

Millard was the Vikings' first-round draft pick in 1984, but he spent one season with the Jacksonville Bulls of the United States Football League. He joined the Vikings in 1985 and was there through the 1991 season. When the Vikings switched to a 4-3 defense in 1986, Millard and Chris Doleman were paired on the line as one of the best pass-rushing tandems in league history.

In 1989 they were practically unstoppable. Doleman led the league with a franchise-record 21 sacks but lost NFL Defensive Player of the Year to Millard, who posted 18 sacks, a record for a Vikings defensive tackle.

Millard, of course, is also remembered for one of the more memorable quotes in franchise history. On the eve of training camp in 1986, he was arrested after a disturbance at the Radisson hotel in Bloomington, Minnesota. When hotel security called local police to help calm Millard, the 6'5", 270-pounder reportedly told an officer, "My arms are more powerful than your gun."

Millard ended up paying a $550 fine after pleading guilty to a disorderly conduct charge. He also sent a letter to the police apologizing for his behavior. In court Millard said he was having a phone conversation with a family member when hotel security came to his door. "I was pretty upset; I guess I was loud," he said in court. "I didn't realize it. Two security people told me to quiet down. I felt they were invading my privacy. I got out of line and said some things I shouldn't have said. Basically, I was rude."

# 58 Tony Dungy

Buddy Ryan, Pete Carroll, Tom Moore, Brian Billick, Mike Tomlin, Mike Singletary, Emmitt Thomas. The Vikings have had several big-name assistant coaches who were Hall of Fame players or went on to win Super Bowls with other teams. But Anthony Kevin "Tony" Dungy is the only one who became a Hall of Fame head coach, a Super Bowl winner, and a pioneer among black NFL coaches.

Born October 6, 1955, in Jackson, Michigan, Dungy was an all-state athlete who was drawn to the University of Minnesota because of Sandy Stephens, a national champion while helping break through college football's color barrier as a black quarterback. The man who recruited Dungy as a quarterback was Golden Gophers assistant Tom Moore, who would later become Dungy's most trusted assistant and confidante during a successful run that included the only Super Bowl victory by a black head coach. "Tony was very, very comparable in intelligence, passion, and work ethic to Peyton Manning," said Moore, who was offensive coordinator under Dungy when the two of them teamed up with Manning to help the Indianapolis Colts win Super Bowl XLI.

Dungy went undrafted but signed with the Pittsburgh Steelers, where he was a backup safety in 1977–78. He won a Super Bowl in 1978, but, more importantly, he was well-schooled in the Cover-2 scheme employed by defensive coordinator Bud Carson.

The Steelers released Dungy after the 1978 season, though fate would again be kind to Dungy, who ended up as a special teamer with the San Francisco 49ers. He lasted only one year, but, more importantly, he developed a special bond with Dennis Green, the 49ers' special teams coach. After spending the fall of 1980 as Gophers defensive backs coach, Dungy was hired for the same job with the Steelers. He became Pittsburgh's defensive coordinator from 1984–88 before moving on to become defensive backs coach for the Kansas City Chiefs in 1989.

In 1992 Green was hired to replace Jerry Burns in Minnesota. One of the first calls he made was to Dungy. "Going to Minnesota was special for me," Dungy said after being selected to the Pro Football Hall of Fame in 2016. "We had some great players, Chris Doleman, John Randle, just some perfect guys for what I wanted to do."

In 1993 Dungy had the No. 1-ranked defense. Seven head coaching openings came up after that season. Dungy was passed over for all of them. "That was a time that the Lord was testing my patience and my perseverance," Dungy said. "For me 1993 was a time when I wondered if it would happen."

In 1996 Tampa Bay hired him as head coach. He was 40. After losing his first five games, he turned the Bucs into winners with a defense that was so good, all future NFL Cover-2 schemes became known as a "Tampa-2" defense. Despite four playoff appearances over the next five seasons, Dungy was fired after the 2001 season. With Dungy in Indianapolis, Jon Gruden won Tampa Bay's only Super Bowl the following season.

Race, Dungy said, wasn't the only factor holding him down. His quiet demeanor and deep Christian faith worked against him, he said. When team executives would ask him during head coaching interviews if football would be the most important thing in his life, Dungy told them no. "There was a subconscious barrier," Dungy said. "I don't think it was directed at African Americans per se, but I think we had a vision of what a head coach looked like. The head coach of a successful team, to many people, looked like Vince Lombardi. It was a white, middle-aged coach, who screamed fire and brimstone."

Upon going into the Hall of Fame, Dungy credited Green for mentoring him in Minnesota. Even when Dungy was hired in Tampa Bay, he would call Green for advice, direction, or for a reminder on how they used to structure practice. "And he would tell me because he wanted me to be successful," Dungy said. "When I came into the league in 1977, I think there were only seven or eight African American assistant coaches in the entire league. So it wasn't a situation where you had a lot of role models. But I had a lot of people who believed in me and I'm very, very proud to represent those men in the Hall of Fame."

# 59 Jared Allen

The greatest game of Jared Allen's decorated career as an NFL pass rusher was upstaged by Brett Favre in a surreal *Monday Night Football* game against the Green Bay Packers at the Metrodome on October 5, 2009. "That's okay," Allen said after Favre's first meeting against his former team. "If it gets me five sacks a week, I'll shut up and not say a word."

Actually, it was a career-high 4.5 sacks in a 30–23 win. Favre got his revenge while his successor, Aaron Rodgers, got sacked eight times. Favre completed 77.4 percent of his passes with three touchdowns, no turnovers, and a 135.3 passer rating. But the win wasn't possible without Allen's energy that night. "It was a feeding frenzy kind of thing," coach Brad Childress said afterward.

In 2009 Favre completed 69.5 percent of his passes with seven touchdowns and no turnovers in two magical wins over the Packers. Rodgers also played well with passer ratings of 110.6 and 108.5. But the sack totals were the difference. Favre wasn't sacked once. Rodgers was sacked 14 times, and Allen had 7.5 of them.

All these years later, it's hard to believe Allen was considered a risky proposition when the Vikings traded for him before the 2008 draft. The reigning NFL sack king was considered the proverbial loose cannon. He had been arrested and charged with three DUIs and had served a two-game league suspension in 2007. The Kansas City Chiefs were so leery of Allen's behavior that they shopped him to the Vikings rather than give him a long-term deal. The Vikings gave up a first-round pick and two third rounders. Then they gave Allen a six-year, $73.5 million deal, a record for an NFL defender at the time.

People waited for Allen to get in trouble off the field. He never did. On the field, three of his four first-team All-Pro selections and four of his five Pro Bowls came with the Vikings.

In 2011 Allen had 22 sacks, breaking Chris Doleman's franchise record of 21 and coming within half a sack of Michael Strahan's NFL mark. Doleman was on the sideline at the Metrodome when Allen had 3.5 sacks in the season finale against the Bears.

When Allen left via free agency after six seasons, he hadn't missed a single start. In 100 games he had 89.5 sacks, including four in four playoff games. Not bad for a lean 265-pounder who got by mostly on sound fundamentals and sheer determination. "I'm a technique and leverage guy," said Allen, who was tied for

*Defensive end Jared Allen, who was raised on a horse ranch in California, celebrates his first-quarter sack against the Chicago Bears in 2012 with his signature calf roping move.*

ninth on the NFL's career sack list (136) at the end of the 2015 season.

Allen's non-stop motor was a factor in his prime. The clock in a quarterback's head tended to speed up when Allen was charging. Certainly, that was the case for Detroit Lions quarterback Dan Orlovsky when he made his NFL starting debut at the Metrodome in 2008.

Orlovsky was in his own end zone, running from an Allen sack when he accidently ran out of the back of the end zone for a safety, and it wasn't even close. "When the official started blowing the whistle, I was like, 'Did we false start, or was it an accidental whistle or something?'" Orlovsky said. "Then I looked down to see where I was and I was just like, 'You're an idiot.'"

One of Allen's career record-tying four safeties would cause the Lions to lose the game by two points (12–10) en route to the first 0–16 record in NFL history.

Raised on a horse ranch in Morgan Hill, California, Allen went from a fourth rounder out of Idaho State to celebrating sacks by dropping to a knee and pretending to rope an imaginary calf. He racked them up at a prodigious rate, recording 136 sacks while meticulously honing his craft. "When I first got to Kansas City, my line coach, Bob Karmelowicz, told me, 'If you get a sack one out of every 19 rushes, you end up with 17.5 sacks for the year,'" Allen said. "That's a great year, 17.5 sacks. But like Bob said, how do you handle those 18 other rushes that were failures? Using those 18 rushes to set up the move that gets the sack is key."

# 60 Robert Smith

The morning of February 7, 2001, brought one of the most abrupt—but not necessarily shocking—retirements in Vikings history. Running back Robert Smith was just 28 years old. He was coming off the best season of his eight-year career. He was about to start fielding offers for about $40 million over five years—with an $8 million signing bonus—as the NFL's prized free-agent running back. But it wasn't totally surprising.

Smith was an atypical NFL player. He marched to his own drumbeat and was quick to remind people of his many interests outside of sports. He talked more about astronomy, genetic research, and medicine. As a sophomore at Ohio State, he sat out the 1991 season, saying he wanted to focus on academics because his ultimate goal was to become a doctor.

Smith also wanted to leave the game before the game left him with debilitating injuries in middle age. He weighed that factor when surgery was needed on his right knee after setting what was then the franchise single-season rushing record of 1,521 yards in 2000. When more damage was discovered than anticipated, Smith didn't want to put himself through the difficult recovery process or risk his long-term health. So he sent an email to a reporter for *The Cleveland Plain Dealer* who had covered him growing up in Euclid, Ohio. He mostly thanked the fans for their support and called it a career. "And I also wanted to thank my teammates and coaches for believing in me throughout my career," Smith's statement read. "You know how much I appreciate all of you, but I could never express how much your presence through the highs and lows has meant to me. I wish the Vikings continued success under coach [Denny] Green and his staff."

The Vikings had reached the NFC Championship Game the month before Smith retired. In 2001, following Smith's retirement and the tragic training camp death of offensive tackle Korey Stringer due to heatstroke, the Vikings finished 5–11. Rookie first-round draft pick Michael Bennett led the Vikings in rushing that year with just 682 yards.

Smith was the 21$^{st}$ overall pick in the 1993 NFL draft. He missed 23 games in his first four seasons, never topping 692 yards rushing. But then he rattled off four straight 1,000-yard seasons to finish with what was then a franchise-record 6,818 yards. He also holds the record for average yards per touchdown run (27.2 yards on 32 touchdowns).

No other running back has run for as many yards as Smith did in 2000 and retired before the age of 29. Even Hall of Famer Jim Brown, who is remembered for hanging it up while still in his prime, was 29 when he ran for 1,544 yards in 1965 and then retired. "Robert had been talking about [2000] being his last year," teammate Chris Walsh told the *Minneapolis Star Tribune* in 2001. "I was perplexed at the time. After the season…he was pretty sure that's what he was going to do. He said, 'The thing that's sad to me is a guy who stays too long.'"

Ironically, 2000 was the only year Smith played in all 16 games. He also posted a career-high 295 carries. But months after his surgery and retirement, Smith told *The New York Times* that he was "looking for challenges." In 2005 Smith started an 11-year run as a college football analyst for ESPN before ending it in January of 2016 and joining Fox Sports and the Big Ten Network.

In 2011, as the national spotlight was brightening on the physical and neurological plight of former NFL players, Smith told the *Willoughby (Ohio) News-Herald* that he considered himself fortunate to have retired early. "I couldn't be happier [with my health] considering what I went through for eight years," Smith said. "My right knee gets sore for a while when the weather turns, and my right foot is sore every once in a while, but that's about it. I feel lucky."

# 61 Go to Adrian Peterson Day

If you find yourself about 110 miles southeast of Dallas in early to mid-June, head to Palestine, Texas, for "Adrian Peterson Day." The ninth annual party and parade celebrating the Vikings All-Pro running back's hometown roots was held June 13, 2015, in Reagan Park. The seven-hour festivity was open to the public per usual and was the first one held since Peterson's indictment and no-contest plea to reduced misdemeanor charges of recklessly assaulting his 4-year-old son while whipping him with a switch.

City leaders distanced themselves from the event, reminding people that the city of 18,000 doesn't sponsor the festivities and treats event organizers the same as they would those running any other rally that pays for a hosting permit. Carol Pegues, Peterson's cousin, organizes the event each year. She said she never considered canceling the 2015 event when Peterson missed the final 15 games of the 2014 season while banished from the NFL. "His indictment has nothing to do and no bearings on the day at all," Pegues told the *Palestine Herald-Press*. "In the first place, we all were raised with a switch. So it doesn't mean anything to us at all. We are just celebrating him because he does wonderful things for the community."

Peterson had just returned to the Vikings shortly before the ninth annual Adrian Peterson Day. When he arrived in Palestine

*During Adrian Peterson Day, the Palestine, Texas, hometown of the Vikings running back honors the player who has led the NFL in rushing three times.*

for the parade, the first thing he saw was a sign reading, "We Got Your Back!" "Yeah," he said, "it's a little different this year. The people who are out here are supporting you and never stopped supporting you."

Pegues estimates that 2,000 to 3,000 people show up each year for Adrian Peterson Day. The plan is to continue the event after Peterson's probable Hall of Fame career ends. "This day is special to me," Peterson was quoted as saying on Adrian-Peterson.com. "Growing up in Palestine, going through a lot at a young age, and thinking back to the stage that I'm at now, it's definitely an honor."

The first Adrian Peterson Day was in 2007 before Peterson's rookie season. It was a way to celebrate Peterson's past while looking to the future. As stated on Adrian-Peterson.com, "Long before he was the country's No. 1 high school recruit, Adrian dealt with heartache at a young age. A drunk driver took the life of his older brother, and as a teen, his father was sent to prison. Adrian said it all shaped him into the man he is now."

"It's been a long road," Peterson said on the website. "I had to clear a lot of obstacles along the way. But with all the support of my fans back home, my family, you know it makes it worth it, just knowing that they stood behind me, supporting me."

# 62 The Wilf's American Dream

Elizabeth "Suzie" Wilf remembers having to hide from the Germans. Aunts, uncles, cousins, a grandmother, friends she went to school with had been led away, never to be seen again. "When the Germans came, the Jews were put in the ghetto, an encircled barrier," she said. "From time to time, the Germans would come in and do a roundup. My parents decided it eventually would happen to us."

Suzie is the mother of Vikings owners Zygi and Mark Wilf. In 1943 she was a child living with parents Markus and Miriam Fisch and younger brother Erwin in Lvov, Poland.

Hitler's Nazi regime, which started World War II with the invasion of Poland in 1939, sent many of the Jews from the Lvov ghetto to the Belzec death camp about 55 miles away. More than 500,000 of the six million Jews killed during the Holocaust perished at Belzec from March 1942 to June 1943.

But fate and a brave, resourceful woman named Miriam would preserve the family's lineage. Because of Miriam, Zygi and Mark are billionaire businessmen and NFL owners. Because of Miriam, Zygi and Mark exist, period. "She really rescued the family," Mark said. "She had the strength and luck to do it. She lived a long life, and I was close to her. She is one of the heroes of my life."

With the help of a Jewish militiaman, Miriam obtained documents identifying her to the Gestapo as a Christian woman with two Christian children. "We wound up working for a woman who owned a farm, so we were able to hide my father in the barn under the floor boards," Suzie said. "Nearly two years we spent on that farm. That's where we were when we were liberated after the war."

Suzie's husband, Joe Wilf, became his sons' role model, providing their childhood head start on a bountiful life. It's the reason there's a Wilf Family Foundation that's donated more than $200 million to the Jewish community and Israel over the past 51 years. Joe and his late brother, Harry, also Holocaust survivors from Poland, founded Garden Homes, a New Jersey-based real estate development business that's been around since 1955 and now stretches to a third generation of Wilfs.

Before southern Poland was occupied by Hitler's Third Reich, the country was split up between Germany and the Soviet Union. The grandparents of Mark and Zygi, Oscar and Ella Wilf, were driven by the Soviets from their home in Jaroslaw to a Siberian labor camp. Sons Joe and Harry went with them, while their sister, Bella, stayed behind. The family believes Bella died in the Warsaw ghetto. "My father and Zygi's father survived the war sticking together," said Lenny Wilf, 68, Harry's son and Vikings part-owner/vice chairman. "I tell people my late father and my uncle didn't share a room. They shared a bed. They had nothing. And my mother's family, all were killed at Belzec, except for my mother and one sister. Her parents, three brothers, and two other sisters—all killed."

After the war Suzie and Joe met in the American-occupied zone in Germany. Zygi was born there before the family moved to America and settled in New Jersey. To help Americanize their sons, Harry and Joe became sports fans and New York Giants season-ticket holders in old Yankee Stadium. To this day Zygi still has a white football with signatures of Giants players he got while in the locker room with his father and uncle, who built homes for some of the players.

Joe Wilf had opportunities to buy NFL teams but turned them down. When his sons came to him for advice on the Vikings opportunity in 2005, Joe told them to follow their passion.

At the time the Wilfs were minority partners in a group of investors led by Reggie Fowler. When Fowler's bid fell through, the Wilfs stepped forward with Zygi as principal owner and chairman and Mark as owner and president. "I remember the Giants in the '60s and '70s lost lots of games," Zygi said. "I would be very distraught about the way we lost games. My father used to always go, 'Don't feel so bad. Think how the owner must feel.' Here I am now, and I know exactly how the owner feels."

Meanwhile, Suzie, now a great-grandmother, started to share more stories about the Holocaust and the family's history, stories she had kept from her sons when they were young. "It was not easy to go back to those times," she said. "We pushed away the memories of those life-threatening times and took to the good life of America. Americans should be more appreciative of America and be more tolerant. Even with all the things going on, it's still the best country in the world."

# 63 Boom Boom Brown

Bill Brown was into his second season with the Vikings before someone finally figured out the perfect nickname to describe how this 5'11", 230-pound fullback played the game of football. Some had referred to him as "Mr. Second Effort" or even the "Old Warrior," even though he had joined the league only three years earlier in 1961 as the second-round draft pick of George Halas' Chicago Bears.

Finally, a headline writer for a local newspaper tapped into the nickname that would last a lifetime for one of the toughest and more popular players in franchise history. "Boom Boom booms again!" the headline screamed alongside a photo of Brown plowing straight ahead in his muddied No. 30 jersey.

Brown didn't like the nickname at first. But there was nothing he could do but accept it, along with the groundswell following that it helped create. "My style of football brought that out in people," Brown told the *Minneapolis Star Tribune* years after his retirement. "My only way of doing it was straight ahead—knock people around."

Born June 29, 1938 in Mendota, Illinois, Brown was a multi-sport star before picking the University of Illinois over several other Big Ten schools. He ran over defenders, turned heads, and also won a Big Ten track title with a school-record distance of 54 feet, 10.5 inches in the shot put.

Halas lost interest in Brown after one season and traded him to the Vikings in 1962 for a fourth-round pick. Brown became one of the team's early stars, playing 13 seasons before retiring after the 1974 season. Brown played in four Pro Bowls and three Super Bowls. A powerful runner, a terrific blocker, and an excellent receiver, he became a regular in 1963 and led the Vikings in 1964 in rushing (866 yards), receiving (703), and touchdowns (seven rushing and nine receiving). He also led the Vikings in rushing four times in five seasons from 1964 to 1968 on his way to 9,237 combined yards (5,757 rushing, 3,177 receiving, 303 returning) and 76 touchdowns as a Viking.

Like all Vikings from that era, Brown is remembered for ignoring the thermometer when it crept near or below zero on game day at Met Stadium. Regardless of the temperature, Brown always played with those big, bare arms wrapped around the football. "I remember one game against the Rams," coach Bud Grant told the *Star Tribune* years later. "Brown had scabs all over his elbows. He was out there and he scraped them all off to get them bleeding before the game. Well, the Rams looked at that and thought, *This guy is crazy. How are we going to play against this guy?*"

# 64 Daunte Culpepper

Vikings owner Red McCombs was mingling with reporters on the day his team reported to Mankato, Minnesota, for training camp in 2003. Suddenly, he looked up, spotted quarterback Daunte Culpepper, and bolted. "Excuse me, fellas," McCombs said. "I'm going over to go say hello to my money."

A couple of months earlier Culpepper signed a 10-year, $102 million contract. It was the richest in Vikings history, though it turned out to be a heavily back-loaded deal that guaranteed only $15.1 million. Still, at the time it was considered a high-pressure situation for Culpepper. In Vikings history only four quarterbacks have been selected in the first round of the draft. Culpepper, the second of those four picks, is the highest one at No. 11 in 1999.

After sitting as a backup his rookie year, Culpepper helped the Vikings reach the NFC Championship Game in 2000. He had thrown a league-high 23 interceptions in 2002 but still was considered the long-term answer at the position. He was a powerful, massive (6'4", 264 pounds) runner with a big, accurate arm. "Without a doubt there's pressure on Daunte to lead us back to the playoffs," McCombs said in 2003. "Daunte knows I put pressure on him. Players should have pressure. We all have pressure. I put pressure on Daunte because I know he can handle it."

Culpepper would play only 49 more games for the Vikings. He'd go 7–7 while missing the playoffs in 2003, 9–9 with one playoff win at Lambeau Field in 2004, and 2–5 before a catastrophic right knee injury at Carolina changed the trajectory of his career and the Vikings' future in 2005. The Vikings faced third and 4 from the Panthers 33-yard line on October 30, 2005. They trailed 7–0 with 11 seconds left in the first quarter when the ball was snapped.

At that point 2005 had been tumultuous at best. Ownership changed hands from McCombs to Zygi Wilf; Randy Moss had been traded to Oakland; center Matt Birk was out for the season because of hip surgery; running back Onterrio Smith had been suspended after being caught going through airport security with "The Original Whizzinator," a gizmo designed to beat drug testing; coach Mike Tice had been fined $100,000 for scalping his Super Bowl tickets. And, oh yeah, the infamous "Love Boat" sex party scandal involving several players during the team's bye week was only a couple of weeks old.

Culpepper was 2–4 with six touchdown passes and 12 interceptions when he dropped back on that fateful snap. He saw no one open and took off running. He would barrel 18 yards downfield before Panthers cornerback Chris Gamble went low and safety Rick Minter went high, and Gamble took out the knee. The news was the worst possible. Culpepper had torn the medial collateral, anterior cruciate, and posterior cruciate ligaments.

He'd never play another down for the Vikings. And he'd never be the same player. After the season Culpepper never meshed with new coach Brad Childress and was traded to the Miami Dolphins for a second-round draft pick. He'd push himself too hard to return for the start of the 2006 season and further hinder his ability to ever return to full strength. He'd finish with a meandering, bizarre career path that finally ended with him and former Vikings coach Denny Green being reunited with the Sacramento Mountain Lions of the United Football League in 2010. Culpepper would throw 10 touchdown passes and 12 interceptions that season.

After the injury Culpepper started 20 of 24 NFL games over four seasons. He went 3–17 with Miami (1–3), the Detroit Lions (0–10), and Oakland Raiders (2–4). Before the injury Culpepper

*A dynamic quarterback before suffering a debilitating knee injury, Daunte Culpepper celebrates during a 2004 game against the Green Bay Packers.* (AP Images)

was a running force the size of which the league hadn't seen before at quarterback. He ran 454 times for 2,476 yards (5.5 yards per carry) and 29 touchdowns. After the injury he ran just 60 times for 176 yards (2.9) and five touchdowns.

It was a difficult end for Culpepper, who worked out for several teams as he tried to find starting jobs. The Green Bay Packers made him an offer to be their backup to Aaron Rodgers. Culpepper declined the offer and changed his mind only to discover that Green Bay had changed its mind, too. In September of 2008, Culpepper announced his retirement. A month later he announced he wanted to play again. A month after that, he was starting for Detroit, the only team to ever go 0–16.

The timing of Culpepper's injury couldn't have been much worse. In 2004 he was 27 years old and likely would have won NFL MVP honors had Peyton Manning not thrown a league-record 49 touchdown passes as part of his epic season for the 12–4 Indianapolis Colts.

Culpepper set a league record with 5,123 total yards. He completed 69.2 percent of his passes for 4,717 yards, 39 touchdowns, 11 interceptions, and a 110.9 passer rating while running for 406 yards and two touchdowns on 88 carries (4.6).

At that point, there was no guaranteed money left in the unfavorable 10-year extension Culpepper had signed just two years earlier. Months of negotiations with no results led to Culpepper skipping a day of training camp and returning with about $8 million more for the 2005 season.

He forced the Vikings' hand and won.

With the season he just had at 27, the pay bump was understandable—just like passing on Rodgers not once, but twice in the first round of the 2005 NFL Draft wasn't given a second thought. But with hindsight as a guide, it's painful for Vikings fans to reflect on the fact that their team took not one but two draft busts—Troy

Williamson at No. 7 and Erasmus James at No. 18—before the Packers nabbed Rodgers at No. 24. Culpepper would start only seven more games as a Viking.

# 65 Antoine Winfield

Nathan Winfield knew his grandson was born to tackle even before little Antoine turned eight years old and put on enough weight to become a 65-pounder for the Akron Firestone Pee Wee Rams. "He was real small but always tough," Nathan said. "I always knew he would be a good football player just by watching him play in the street out front."

Nathan and his wife, Velma, essentially raised their maternal grandson. Antoine's father, Anthony Finney, played an insignificant role in his son's life, which only fueled Antoine's desire to succeed and eventually become a better father to his three sons. "My dad was never around, and I definitely don't want to follow in his footsteps," Winfield said. "I always told myself that I was going to be better than him. So my kids come first."

Winfield was able to use his talent on the football field to give his sons the better life. He was a first-round draft pick of the Buffalo Bills in 1999. In 2004 he joined the Vikings, where he became perhaps the best free-agent acquisition in team history. The three-time Pro Bowler played nine seasons for the Vikings and 14 overall, finishing with 1,057 total tackles, 27 interceptions, 11 fumble recoveries, and four touchdowns. In his last season, 2012, he had 101 tackles at age 35.

All of this came from a man who never grew taller than 5'9" or got heavier than 180 pounds. Bill McGee, the former coach at

Akron Garfield High School, said a higher power should be credited for Winfield's impeccable tackling technique. "I guess I could say I developed it, but he was our best player the moment he came to us as a 137-pound freshman," McGee said. "Four years later I'd go to Ohio State to see him, and even then all the kickers were bigger than him. But that didn't matter."

Winfield played free safety and running back at Garfield. He was a 1,000-yard rusher who could catch and block. But the tackling is what stood out. "I put together sort of a training tape of Antoine's best plays," McGee said. "Everything he did was textbook. Teams just didn't throw to the middle of the field. Antoine either intercepted it, or they usually had to carry the receiver off the field."

Former Ohio State coach John Cooper said Winfield's football instincts were, "the best of any player I ever coached in 39 years." "I used to make Shawn Springs mad because I would say Antoine was the best cornerback I ever coached," said Cooper, referring to the No. 3 overall draft pick in 1997. "Springs would say, 'C'mon, coach, I'm the best corner you ever coached.' And I'd say, 'You're the best cover corner. Antoine is the best cornerback.' Antoine can do it all. Antoine plays better than you can coach."

In an era known for the slippage in tackling fundamentals, Winfield wasn't interested in following the herd in dismissing proper technique in favor of the all-or-nothing pursuit of the ESPN *SportsCenter* highlight hit. "That's not my game," Winfield said in 2006. "I try to find angles, grab, and hold on. I hit low, strike low before they see me, and try to wrap up. If you're talking about tacklers who just run through people, that's not me. But if you're talking about tacklers who get the guy on the ground, then I'm up there."

# 66 Les Steckel

Les Steckel stood at the front of the team meeting room in Mankato, Minnesota, with a pair of scissors in one hand and credit cards in the other. Players already leery of Bud Grant's overly gung-ho successor were looking on as their new leader prepared them for what was about to happen when the Vikings' 1984 training camp opened the next morning. "He took the credit cards and cut them in half," running back Teddy Brown told the *Minneapolis Star Tribune*. "He said the Bud Grant country club days were over."

Grant retired suddenly after 17 seasons and recommended Steckel, his receivers coach, as his replacement in part because offensive coordinator Jerry Burns was considered too old for the position. At 38 Steckel was the NFL's youngest head coach—and definitely the most wired.

Training camp opened, and Steckel had placed no footballs on the field. The former Marine combat leader in Vietnam decided instead to kick things off with an odd ironman competition designed to test players' will and endurance. Training camp, which was more relaxed under Grant the previous 17 seasons, became boot camp with players moving from station to station doing sit-ups, running sprints, leg pressing twice their weight, and climbing ropes. "Les went overboard, no question about it," said Scott Studwell, a linebacker and team leader who joined the team's scouting department after he retired. "It was a tremendous change, and Les tried to do things in almost the exact opposite way Bud had. Quite frankly, the players rejected it."

Steckel started the season 2–2 but then lost 11 of the last 12 for a franchise-record 13 losses. Steckel's one and only season ended with a six-game losing streak in which opponents outscored the Vikings 241–79. "I think everybody quit, I really do," tight end Joe Senser told the *Star Tribune*. "I think the guys who meant the most just said, 'Screw it.' They ain't playing for this guy."

There were legendary stories of players secretly laughing as Steckel gave bizarre motivational speeches in which he did things such as punch himself in the face and eat peanut butter from a diaper. Steckel also went way over the top comparing football to combat. When first-round draft pick Keith Millard defected to the Jacksonville Bulls of the USFL, Steckel said, "When I was in Vietnam, and the colonel told us to take the hill, we'd lose some guys. But by God, we'd take the hill. That's what we have to do now."

That helps explain why "Less Steckel" became one of the more popular bumper stickers around the Twin Cities in 1984. Players could have simply ignored the over-caffeinated rhetoric. What they couldn't avoid were the grueling practices that Steckel put them through up to five times a week. There were even times when the Vikings were in full pads and going through contact drills the day after games. "He tried to run a professional team with a high school attitude," Studwell said. "You can only take so much physical and mental pounding."

One day after the season mercifully ended, Steckel was fired. Grant, who had called the 1984 season "a joke," was coaxed out of retirement for one season. He went 7–9, restored a semblance of respectability, and stepped aside again. This time the Vikings did what they should have done in 1984. They promoted Burns to head coach.

# 67 Find a Community Tuesday Event

Brad Madson was a TV sportscaster for WQOW in Eau Claire, Wisconsin, when he stopped to reassess his earnest climb to the lower middle of his profession in 1992. "I lacked one key ingredient for the job," he said. "Talent."

Madson laughs. It's an infectious laugh familiar to those who love listening to the Vikings executive director of community relations tell stories that are heartwarming, funny, and not always fit for a PG platform because of the wide range of NFL characters and situations he has experienced while at his job since 1995. "It's a blessing," Madson said. "I got the best seat in the house."

Madson is the unseen engine that drives the team's Community Tuesdays program that sends players out to local schools, hospitals, and charity events on their only day off each week. Fans who want to get involved in the community and watch Vikings players do the same should try to find an event on the list of many causes that Madson pitches to players on a weekly basis. "I'm selling volunteerism," Madson said. "I keep a chart on all the players and I get to know their personalities. Our guys are great. I did have a player say one time, 'Brad, if you ask me again, I will set you on fire.' But I don't think that would have happened."

Madson said there have been too many "great guys" over the years to list them all. But one does stand out: former center Matt Birk, who holds the team record as a seven-time winner of the team's Man of the Year award for his community work. According to Madson, Birk got on board as soon as his hometown team drafted him in the sixth round in 1998. Birk's first charity event was both the beginning of a long relationship and a teaching moment for the relatively new community relations director. "He played in a charity flag football game at Canterbury Park [a horse racing track] against the jockeys on the Fourth of July," Madson said. "I was there. One of the jockeys broke his collarbone. So we didn't do that one anymore. Not all of my ideas go as well as predicted."

Meanwhile, former wide receiver Randy Moss is Madson's front-runner for most misunderstood player he has dealt with. In Madson's world Moss was ideal because he often came up with his own community outreach ideas and presented them to Madson with the same rule every time: "no TV cameras." Once in Mankato, Minnesota, Moss had an idea right in the middle of a training camp practice. So he yelled for Madson to come see him on the field. "When you're a pencil pusher like me, you don't just walk onto the practice field," Madson said. "Mike Tice was the coach and he heard Randy and gave me the nod."

Moss wanted to do a reading program at two schools. Between practice reps he worked out the details with Madson. When Madson suggested he buy some large pizzas and have a party to congratulate the kids for reading a book, Moss frowned. "Randy always thought things through to the smallest detail," Madson said. "He said, 'No, Brad. Buy personal pizzas. The kids will remember that Moss handed them their own pizza for reading the book.' Sure enough, I went to high schools in south Minneapolis 10 years later, and kids would say, 'Hey, you were there when Moss handed me a pizza for reading a book.'"

# 68 Brad Childress

Vikings right guard Anthony Herrera had three items on his to-do list when he woke up March 26, 2008: become a stronger NFL player, attend a meeting with coach Brad Childress, and become a U.S. citizen.

One of the NFL's 76 foreign-born players in 2007 and the only one from the southern Caribbean islands of Trinidad and Tobago, Herrera completed his first task with an early-morning workout at

## Childress vs. Williamson

Brad Childress was known to rub some players the wrong way. But his relationship with receiver Troy Williamson took on a certain WWE flavor on November 19, 2008. By then, Williamson was a former Viking playing in Jacksonville. The Vikings selected Williamson with the seventh overall draft pick that they received as part of the Randy Moss trade in 2005. Childress arrived a year later and never warmed up to Williamson. Then again, no one did since Williamson became a draft bust who was known for his many dropped passes before being dumped in Jacksonville for a sixth-round draft pick.

But the fractured relationship between Childress and Williamson went much deeper than dropped passes. Williamson never forgave Childress for the way he treated him following the death of his grandmother in the fall of 2007, when he was still with the Vikings. Williamson left the team for nine days when his grandmother, Celestine Williamson, died. He also spent time with his older brother, Carlton, who was in a coma in a Georgia hospital following a serious car crash the month before.

Childress, citing team policy and "business principle," docked Williamson a game check of $25,588.24 when he didn't show up for the game against the San Diego Chargers. Childress later returned the money following a national backlash of criticism and a meeting with a select group of Vikings veterans.

Winter Park. He was hoping to finish the second task early when he climbed the steps to Childress' office on the second floor of the Vikings complex. "He popped his head in the doorway and asked, 'Coach, can we do this now? I have to be somewhere at 12:30,'" Childress said. "I said, 'Oh yeah, where?' He said, 'I have to be in St. Paul for a ceremony. I'm becoming a U.S. citizen today.'"

Childress congratulated Herrera and asked who was accompanying him to the big event. Herrera said, "No one but me." His wife and young daughter were in Mississippi, his mother was in Florida, and Herrera hadn't even thought to bother his teammates by asking them to join. "I said, 'Anthony, you can't get sworn in as a U.S. citizen and not have anyone with you,'" Childress said. "I

A year later, the Vikings and Jaguars played in Jacksonville on November 23, 2008. On the Wednesday before, reporters in both cities went fishing for a juicy story and found a willing participant in Williamson, who not only criticized Childress from the locker room in Jacksonville, but also went on a conference call and did the same with reporters in the Twin Cities. Williamson also said multiple times that he and Childress should meet at midfield and "duke it out." Then he told reporters to pass it along to Childress.

A Jacksonville reporter did just that during a conference call. Childress played along when asked for his weight for a tale-of-the-tape comparison. "I'm 190 pounds of twisted steel and rompin', stompin' dynamite," Childress said. "Do you want my reach, too?"

When a Twin Cities reporter presumed that there would be no midfield hug between the two men, Williamson said, "You can truly say that. After my grandmother, I had no more respect for Childress. That's gone out the window, and I don't see that coming back ever. That bridge is burned."

There was no 50-yard line fight. Williamson, who went into the game with four catches in five games, was inactive because of a groin injury. He played 10 games in two seasons with the Jaguars, catching eight passes and scoring one touchdown before exiting the NFL for good.

said, 'Shoot, give me a minute. I'm going with you.'" Herrera took his spot with 244 other new U.S. citizens. Childress stood in the crowd and cheered.

Occurring in Childress' third season since going from Philadelphia Eagles offensive coordinator to Vikings head coach, this anecdote shows a side of Childress that goes against the narrative of that he had difficulty relating to his players. He had taken a 9–7 team from Mike Tice and went 6–10 and 8–8 while struggling with player relations. A strict demeanor and some notable missteps had caused him trouble in the locker room and contributed to his decision to form a leadership committee made up of veteran players.

In 2006 wide receiver Marcus Robinson was critical of Childress' leadership. Childress was livid when he saw the quotes in a local newspaper and released Robinson on the spot. It was Christmas Eve. Owner Zygi Wilf later criticized the transaction and its timing as not being in step with the team's family values. In 2007 wide receiver Troy Williamson's grandmother died. Williamson, who was raised by his grandmother, was excused for the funeral. When Williamson didn't return timely enough for Childress, the coach fined him one game check. Later, Childress refunded the game check after Wilf and the leadership group stepped in.

Childress did grow as a coach. He went 40–37, including 1–2 in the postseason, reached an NFC Championship Game, and oversaw perhaps the best regular season of Brett Favre's 20-year Hall of Fame career. But he would continue to struggle with player relations and a weakness for emotional knee-jerk decisions. On November 1, 2010, angry that Randy Moss had been wildly insubordinate in a loss at New England a day earlier, Childress broke specific team protocol by unilaterally releasing Moss. Twenty-one days later, following a 31–3 home loss to Green Bay, Wilf did the same thing to Childress.

# 69 Chuck Foreman

Imagine if Chuck Foreman had *never* played for the Minnesota Vikings. Well, it came within seconds of happening on draft day in 1973. "Normally, we don't have time to argue on draft day," Frank Gilliam, the longtime Vikings player personnel man, told the *Minneapolis Star Tribune* years later. "The exception was in 1973."

Gilliam and fellow player personnel guy Jerry Reichow wanted to pick Foreman. Coach Bud Grant and general manager Jim Finks wanted to trade the pick (the 12th overall) to the New England Patriots. "The trade offer was very tempting," Gilliam said. "We debated and debated. We were running out of time, and finally Jim Finks said, 'I think you better go with your guy Foreman.'"

With size, speed, and excellent hands, the 6'2", 210-pounder from the University of Miami was perfect for offensive coordinator Jerry Burns' pioneering system. Long before the West Coast Offense got its nickname from San Francisco, Burns was running a ball-control attack that utilized short passes to the running back.

Foreman's eight-year career began with five consecutive Pro Bowls. He won 1973 NFL Offensive Player of the Year while helping the Vikings to their first of three Super Bowls in four seasons. He rushed for 5,950 yards, caught 350 passes, and scored 76 touchdowns in 109 games. "For five years there wasn't a better back in football," Grant said of Foreman. A knee injury slowed his final two seasons in Minnesota and led to a trade to New England, where his career ended with 23 carries in 1980.

In 1975 Foreman led the NFL with 73 catches and the NFC with 22 touchdowns. He was second in the NFC in rushing with 1,070 yards. And those numbers could have been better if not for what happened in the regular-season finale at Buffalo on December 20, 1975.

Entering that game Foreman and Bills running back O.J. Simpson were pursuing the NFL record for touchdowns in a season. Gale Sayers had set the mark at 22 in 1965. Simpson had 21, while Foreman had 18. Simpson tied the record early, but Foreman roared back, scoring his fourth touchdown of the game in the third quarter. He was tied with Simpson and Sayers when Bills fans started throwing snowballs. One of the snowballs struck Foreman in the eye in the third quarter.

With the Vikings already in the playoffs and comfortably ahead, Grant decided to sit Foreman for the rest of the game. Simpson went on to score the record 23$^{rd}$ touchdown. And a day later, St. Louis Cardinals running back Jim Otis overtook Foreman's NFC rushing lead by six yards. That kept Foreman from leading the conference in receiving, rushing, and touchdowns. "I got hit in the eye in the last game and couldn't see," Foreman said. "I had to leave the game or I would have had the triple crown."

# 70 Warren Moon

Warren Moon refused to do it. He was a quarterback—period. And he wasn't going to switch to free safety, receiver, or running back simply because he was African American. "I'm pretty stubborn," Moon said in 2006. "That's the reason I was able to play the position one day."

And play it well. In 2006, 10 years after a 23-year professional career that weaved its way from the CFL to the NFL, Moon became the first black quarterback to enter the Pro Football Hall of Fame. Moon had spent 10 seasons with the Houston Oilers and was 38 when he joined the Vikings in 1994. His acquisition came during a stretch of years in which the Vikings essentially rented veteran quarterbacks at or near the end of their careers, including Jim McMahon (1993), Randall Cunningham (1998), Jeff George (1999), Brad Johnson (2005–06), Gus Frerotte (2008), and, of course, Brett Favre (2009–10).

Amazingly, from their first season in 1961 through the 2016 draft, the Vikings have selected only four quarterbacks in the first round of the draft. None has been a top 10 selection. Tommy Kramer was chosen 27th overall in 1977, Daunte Culpepper 11th in 1999, Christian Ponder 12th in 2011, and Teddy Bridgewater 32nd in 2014—hence the need for veteran quarterbacks to lead the team. Moon started 40 games for the Vikings from 1994 until being injured midway through the 1996 season. He went 21–19, including 0–1 in the playoffs, before moving on to start 25 more games for Seattle and Kansas City over the next four seasons. He played until he was 44.

Things were much different in the spring of 1978, when Moon, the reigning Rose Bowl MVP, got nary a nibble from the NFL. "Nobody in the NFL would have ever come right out and said African Americans can't play quarterback, but it was there," said Leigh Steinberg, Moon's agent. "Thirty years ago, if you viewed the interior positions on an NFL roster—quarterback, center, middle linebacker, safety—they were the so-called thinking positions. There were not a tremendous amount of African Americans in those positions."

Steinberg remembers finally asking Moon whether he would consider changing positions to satisfy the NFL. He quickly learned not to ask that again. "His response was rapid and dramatic," Steinberg said. "He said, 'Never.' He said, 'I was born to play this position, and nobody is going to force me to give up my dream.'"

As a Viking, Moon was still slinging the ball with that smooth, graceful, and powerful delivery. He threw a total of 58 touchdown passes, topped 4,200 yards twice, and led the league with 377 completions in 1995. Wide receiver Cris Carter set the NFL record for catches in a season with 122 in 1994 and matched that total the following season.

Moon's dilemma in the 1970s seems dated now. But it wasn't until Marlin Briscoe came along in Denver in 1968 that a black player started a professional game at quarterback. And he was switched to receiver the following year. James Harris was the first to play with distinction over a long period, beginning in the late 1960s. He was the first to start a playoff game and make the Pro Bowl, which occurred in 1974 with the Los Angeles Rams. "Growing up, I actually wanted to switch positions," Harris said upon hearing the news of Moon's Hall of Fame selection. "A young black kid wanting to be the next Johnny Unitas was only a fairy tale."

But then Harris met his college coach, the legendary Eddie Robinson of Grambling, who predicted the NFL would change its ways. "And then," Harris said, "I listened to Dr. Martin Luther King give a speech in 1963 about having a dream that one day we'd all be judged by our character, not the color of our skin. I decided to stay where I was."

# 71 Favre's Magical Metrodome Debut

Brett Favre's bag of tricks was about to runneth over on September 27, 2009. Trailing the San Francisco 49ers 24–20 with one minute, 29 seconds left in his first home game as a Minnesota Viking, Favre trotted onto the Metrodome field with no timeouts left and 80 yards to go to the end zone. "I figured we already blew our chances," said Favre, referring to the series before, when the Vikings turned the ball over on downs with 1:49 left.

But the defense held. With coach Brad Childress using all of his timeouts, the 49ers punted after dropping to 0-for-11 on third downs. "I was on the sidelines saying, 'Be Brett, be Brett, be Brett,'" defensive end Jared Allen said. "And the Silver Fox came through."

Just as he had all those times as a Packer. Just as he had in 42 previous fourth-quarter comebacks, eight of which had come against the Vikings. Favre completed 5-of-9 passes with two incompletions coming on spikes to stop the clock. He threw for 12 yards to tight end Visanthe Shiancoe, nine yards to receiver Sidney Rice, and five yards to receiver Percy Harvin on third and 1.

He spiked the ball at his own 46-yard line with 40 seconds left. He threw incomplete to Rice and then hit Harvin for 15 yards on third and 10. Then he spiked the ball at the San Francisco 39 with 16 seconds left before finding receiver Bernard Berrian near the sideline for seven more yards. Twelve seconds remained, and the ball was 32 yards from the end zone.

Favre had joined the Vikings on August 18 after the Mankato, Minnesota, portion of training camp had ended. On the field with him at that moment was receiver Greg Lewis, who had been with the team for only three weeks. "Brett came into the huddle and said, 'We're going to get this done,'" Lewis said.

Favre rolled right, avoided pressure, stepped up, and launched a laser to the back of the end zone. The play was designed to have four targets in the end zone, but Harvin, Berrian, and Shiancoe cut their routes short. Lewis, however, went to the last blade of plastic grass in the very back of the end zone.

Favre was knocked to the ground as he released the ball. He didn't see what happened, but he sure heard what 63,398 delirious fans had witnessed. With two defenders nearby, Lewis not only caught the rocket, but he also managed to tap 10 toes down just inbounds with two seconds left. "Still the most amazing play I've ever seen," running back Adrian Peterson would say six years later.

Favre didn't even know who he was throwing to when he released the ball. All he had seen was a flash of purple, the same color that had signified an archrival for 16 seasons. "I just saw one of our guys streaking across," Favre said.

The Vikings improved their record to 3–0 and set the prime-time stage for Favre's first game against the Green Bay Packers the following week at the Metrodome. "Just another day at the office," Childress said with a smile that suggested the 2009 season would be anything but ordinary.

# 72 The Williams Wall

Four days before playing the Vikings in 2006, Bill Belichick was asked why he would even consider running the ball against the vaunted "Williams Wall." The New England Patriots coach proceeded to explain the time-honored importance of establishing a balanced attack.

Four days later Patriots quarterback Tom Brady dropped back to pass 26 times in 32 first-half plays. Two of the first four runs were up the middle. The first was an eight-yard loss, and the second was a two-yard loss.

That's because they ran into the teeth—and bellies—of the 638-pound Williams Wall. "They call me 'Big Pat,' or 'Big Nasty,' or 'Big Duke,' or all kinds of crazy names," said Pat Williams, the nose tackle who looked much larger than his listed weight of 327 pounds. "I have fun, always. On the field I'll always be laughing when I whip your ass."

The under tackle was Kevin Williams, one of the best defensive linemen for a franchise known for its greatness at the position. Ironically, he also is one of the franchise's best first-round draft picks despite being associated with one of the worst draft-day gaffes in league history.

*The presence of Kevin (left) and Pat Williams (right) made for an impenetrable defensive interior for the Vikings from 2005 to 2010.* (AP Images)

In 2003 the Vikings had the seventh overall pick. When it was their turn to pick, they thought they had a trade agreement with the Baltimore Ravens to trade down to No. 10 and receive two late-round picks. The Ravens were believed to be coveting quarterback Byron Leftwich with the seventh pick. The Vikings called the trade into the league, the Ravens didn't, and the Vikings' allotted time expired. The Jacksonville Jaguars quickly jumped ahead of the Vikings and took Leftwich. Then, amid the confusion the Carolina Panthers also jumped ahead of the Vikings and selected offensive tackle Jordan Gross before the Vikings finally selected Williams ninth overall. "Yeah, I remember the fans getting all mad at the pick," Williams said years later when he was a six-time Pro Bowler and five-time first-team All-Pro selection. "But I think things worked out okay."

Coach Mike Tice faced a hostile crowd when he had to announce the selection at a draft day party hosted by the Vikings. After telling everyone to "calm down," the coach explained that Williams was the team's target all along. Over time, that was well proven. As for the Ravens, well, they ended up pulling the trigger on a trade with New England at No. 19. They took quarterback Kyle Boller, who became a bust, but they did get Terrell Suggs 10th overall.

Pat Williams signed with the Buffalo Bills as an undrafted rookie in 1997 and joined the Vikings via free agency in 2005. From 2006 to 2008, the Vikings became the first team since the 1970 AFL-NFL merger to lead the league in run defense three straight seasons. They were No. 2 in 2009. In 14 seasons Pat Williams' only Pro Bowl berths were alongside Kevin Williams from 2006 to 2008.

On December 2, 2008, the NFL announced that both pillars of the Williams Wall were being suspended for four games for violating the league's policy on banned substances. Both had taken StarCaps, an over-the-counter weight-loss product. One of the ingredients not listed on the product was a diuretic that was banned because of its effectiveness as a masking agent for steroid use. The league knew that StarCaps contained the diuretic but had not informed its players

The Williamses appealed the suspension in federal court in Minnesota. The case remained tied up through 2011. Pat Williams retired at age 38 after the 2010 season. Kevin Williams' suspension was reduced to two games in 2011.

The Vikings bid farewell to Kevin after the 2013 season. He went to his first Super Bowl with the Seattle Seahawks the next season and played a 13th season in 2015 with the New Orleans Saints. At that point he had 63 sacks (60 with the Vikings) and four touchdown returns (all with the Vikings). "How much longer do I want to play?" Williams said in his final days with the Vikings. "I'm not sure. I ain't too gray. But I'm ready for the end when it comes. It's been a good ride."

# 73 Tommy Mason and His Monkey

In 1961 the expansion Vikings paid Tommy Mason $12,000 as the first overall pick in the NFL draft. And they might have gotten him cheaper if not for the fact that he had offers from the Canadian Football League and from the Boston Patriots as the second overall draft pick in the American Football League. "I wasn't sure the AFL was going to last, and Canada seemed a long way away for a Louisiana boy," he told the *Minneapolis Star Tribune* in 2007. "There was some talk about an agent, but my dad, Bill, was a watchman at a chemical plant, and my mom, Mary, was a nurse, and they couldn't believe it, that this team from Minnesota was willing to pay their boy $12,000 to play football."

The running back from Tulane had a quiet rookie season on the field with only 60 carries in a backup role to 33-year-old veteran Hugh McElhenny, whom they got from the San Francisco 49ers via the expansion draft. Off the field, it didn't take long for the high-spirited 6'1", 195-pound Mason to become a fan favorite and an entertaining subject for the media. The flashy back made headlines for some of the purchases he made with his NFL riches. He loved to play the guitar, so he bought a nice one of those. He bought a silver Cadillac. And he acquired a monkey. Yes, a real monkey that he called "Dutch" in honor of head coach Norm Van Brocklin, whose nickname was "the Dutchman."

Van Brocklin had led the Philadelphia Eagles to the NFL championship as quarterback and NFL MVP in 1960. A year later he was Vikings head coach. As a player Van Brocklin had a Hall of Fame career. As a coach he's mostly remembered for having a caustic personality with which his players constantly struggled. When a Minneapolis newspaper did a big story on all of Mason's interests outside of football, Van Brocklin wasn't happy. It didn't help matters that the newspaper also ran a photo of "Dutch" the monkey.

When Mason missed a block that resulted in quarterback Fran Tarkenton being sacked on a hard hit, Van Brocklin pounced during the film session, which the offense and defense watched together. "Van Brocklin got to the play where I missed the block. He showed it, stopped the film, went back, and showed it again, then again…four, five times," he told the *Star Tribune* in 2007. "And then he turned off the projector, and in the darkness, all you heard was Norman's voice: 'Mason, take that Cadillac, that guitar, and that monkey and…'" Mason's quote ends there, but it's a safe bet that Van Brocklin had a colorful suggestion for where Mason could shove those items.

The following season was the finest of Mason's six seasons in Minnesota and 11 in the NFL. He posted career highs for rushing yards (740) and receiving yards (603). He had a 71-yard touchdown run, a 74-yard reception, and scored eight of the 39 touchdowns he'd score as a Viking.

After Pro Bowl seasons in 1962, 1963, and 1964, Mason injured his knee in 1965. He'd never be the same player and became expendable by 1967. In one of the best trades of general manager Jim Finks' Hall of Fame career, Mason was packaged, along with tight end Hal Bedsole and a second-round draft pick, to the Los Angeles Rams for the 15$^{th}$ overall pick in the 1967 draft. Finks used that pick to select defensive tackle Alan Page, who might be the best player in franchise history.

Mason lasted four seasons in Los Angeles before following coach George Allen to Washington for one season in 1971. He finished his career with 4,203 yards rushing, 2,324 yards receiving, 45 touchdowns, and a legendary monkey named "Dutch."

# 74 Jerry Burns

If the Vikings had won a couple of Super Bowls in the 1970s, their cutting-edge passing attack probably would have had an everlasting Upper Midwest moniker well before Bill Walsh, Joe Montana, and the San Francisco 49ers came along a decade later with what became known as the West Coast Offense. "We were doing the same things before they were," said Jerry Burns, Vikings offensive coordinator from 1968–85 and head coach from 1986–91. "It was just offensive football. Truthfully, I don't know what the hell the West Coast Offense is. I hear the TV analysts say a team is playing the West Coast Offense. If they are, then what kind of offense is the other team playing? East Coast?"

With four Super Bowl-winning seasons in the 1980s, Walsh trumped Burnsie and the Vikings, who lost four Super Bowls played in the '70s, but their offensive philosophy was similar. Walsh's goal was to gain at least 30 first downs a game with a high-percentage, ball-control passing attack. Short passes to running back Roger Craig essentially were long handoffs that lulled defenses forward and made them susceptible to medium-range slant passes and deep strikes to Jerry Rice and other receivers.

Burns' offensive experience went back to when he played quarterback at Michigan from 1947–50. He was head coach at Iowa from 1961–65 and helped win the first two Super Bowls by running the "Packer Sweep" for Vince Lombardi as an assistant coach in Green Bay. Bud Grant arrived in Minnesota in 1967. A year later Burns joined the Vikings as offensive coordinator. The two were together from 1968–83 and 1985 before Burns became head coach from 1986–91.

Burns was ahead of his time when it came to his belief that running backs could be used as underneath targets in a passing attack that meshed ball control with deeper strikes to receivers. His vision began to excel when the Vikings re-acquired quarterback Fran Tarkenton in 1972 and drafted running back Chuck Foreman 12th overall in 1973. Foreman led the team in receptions in 1974, '75, and '76. He had 73 catches in 1975. In 1978 another running back, Rickey Young, caught 88 passes, which remains the team record for a running back. "We threw the ball to Chuck Foreman and Bill Brown," Burns said. "We faked the ball to the back, pulled, and trapped with the guards. We had the short passes. We'd hit the receiver, Anthony Carter, on quick slants. We threw it deep. It was just offensive football, taking what the defense would give you. I never quite understood the whole 'West Coast' thing."

In 2006 the Vikings hired Brad Childress, who was a third-generation disciple of Walsh's West Coast Offense. Childress had learned it from Andy Reid, who had learned it from Mike Holmgren, who had coached with Walsh. During an interview in 2006, Walsh traced the origin of his offense to his study of Los Angeles Rams and San Diego Chargers Hall of Fame coach Sid Gillman and Blanton Collier, an assistant and successor to Cleveland Browns Hall of Fame coach Paul Brown. "Sid Gillman was the father of the passing game in football," Walsh said. "He really opened my eyes, though he was more wide open with the deep passing game than I was, and then Blanton was an absolute technician. I took ideas from both of them."

Though Walsh didn't mention Burnsie, those who watched the Vikings reach four Super Bowls have to wonder whether the "Northern Border Offense" would have had a lasting ring to it.

# Benchwarmer Bob's Place in History

Chances are the only perfect season in NFL history was made possible by a marginal roughing-the-passer penalty on one of the most lovable and gregarious players in Vikings history. "Benchwarmer Bob" Lurtsema played parts of six seasons with the Vikings (1971–76) before spending four decades as one of their most popular ambassadors. On October 1, 1972, in front of 47,900 fans at Metropolitan Stadium, Lurtsema was flagged for roughing Miami Dolphins quarterback Bob Griese on second and eight, giving the Dolphins a first down at the Vikings' 42-yard line while trailing 14–9 in the closing minutes.

Four plays later Griese threw a three-yard pass to tight end Jim Mandich for Miami's only touchdown and its first lead with only

1:28 left. The Dolphins' 16–14 win raised their record to 3–0 en route to winning Super Bowl VII and finishing 17–0. Every year since then, the surviving members of that team, including Hall of Fame coach Don Shula, celebrate by popping bottles of champagne when the NFL's last undefeated team loses. "And Don Shula still sends me a Christmas card every year thanking me," Lurtsema has joked frequently.

The Vikings led 14–6 with less than five minutes to play when Shula decided to let kicker Garo Yepremian attempt a career-long 51-yard field goal. On a sunny, beautifully calm fall day in Bloomington, the kick was good. Fran Tarkenton, who returned to the Vikings that season after spending five years with the New York Giants, took possession but went three-and-out. Miami had another chance, but the Vikings' defense had dominated.

The Purple People Eaters held running backs Larry Csonka and Mercury Morris to 66 and 28 yards rushing, respectively. Those two would go on that season to become the first NFL team-mates to rush for 1,000 yards each. Griese wasn't doing much better against the Vikings, though, completing only 16-of-33 passes for 127 yards and two interceptions.

Shula has called the Vikings game the toughest one the Dolphins had in 1972. It was one of only three in which Miami trailed in the fourth quarter. "I still get a lot of grief for that one," Lurtsema said in the book *Tales from the Minnesota Vikings Sideline*. "I could have prevented history—if only I knew."

At the time that game was viewed as a potential Super Bowl VII preview. "That was the game that really made us," Dolphins guard Bob Kuechenberg told reporters. "Those were the Vikings in the heyday of the Purple People Eaters. We didn't know how good we were yet, but we found out."

Lurtsema played defensive end for the Giants from 1967 until his trade to the Vikings. Tarkenton, who played with Lurtsema in

New York, has called him the best defensive lineman the Giants had at the time. In Minnesota, Lurtsema backed up the members of the famed Purple People Eaters. He started two of 55 games over parts of six seasons before being traded to the expansion Seattle Seahawks for receiver Ahmad Rashad in 1976. Overall, Lurtsema played 11 seasons, starting 46 of 144 NFL games, and actually was much better than he let on. Although sacks weren't an official stat when he played, Lurtsema has been credited with 63 of them.

But it was his self-deprecating humor and run as a hilarious TV commercial pitchman, including spots for TCF Bank, that warmed the hearts of Vikings fans and created a life-long persona as "Benchwarmer Bob."

# 76 Steve Hutchinson's Poison Pill

The Vikings typically are among the best teams in the league at managing the salary cap. If you're wondering why, look no further than Rob Brzezinski. Before joining the Vikings' front office in 1999, Brzezinski honed his creative contract negotiating skills during a six-season stint (1993–98) with the Miami Dolphins. A member of the Florida Bar with degrees from Nova Southeastern University in Fort Lauderdale, Brzezinski rose to staff counsel/ salary cap and gained notice around the league.

The Vikings hired him as director of football administration and promoted him to vice president of football administration in 2001. Before the Vikings changed their football operations to the more traditional general manager format in 2012, Brzezinski was one of the pillars in the team's "Triangle of Authority." Today he is executive vice president of football operations with his expertise being what it's always been: maneuvering the minefield that is the NFL's salary cap.

Brzezinski's most creative piece of work probably came in the spring of 2006 when he created the so-called "poison pill" provision that wrested Steve Hutchinson, a two-time All-Pro left guard still in his prime, from the defending NFC champion Seattle Seahawks. Hutchinson was tagged as a transition player, meaning the Seahawks had the right to match any offer. Brzezinski simply made them an offer they had no choice but to refuse.

Hutchinson was offered a seven-year, $49 million deal with a significant poison pill. If he wasn't the highest-paid offensive linemen on his team, all $49 million would be guaranteed. If he was, the guarantee was $18.5 million. Seattle would have had to guarantee all $49 million because left tackle Walter Jones had signed a more lucrative deal. In Minnesota the guarantee would be only $18.5 million for the best left guard in football.

Seattle declined to match and was livid. There were no rules against poison pills at the time, but they were frowned upon as violating the spirit of free-agency rules. Seattle countered later in the week. It targeted young Vikings wide receiver Nate Burleson, a restricted free agent. Seattle offered Burleson the same seven-year, $49 million deal with two significant poison pills. All $49 million would be guaranteed if Burleson played more than four games in Minnesota in one season or if Burleson was paid more on average per year than all of Minnesota's running backs combined. The latter poison pill was strange, but at the time Burleson's offer included an average that was higher than all of Minnesota's running backs combined.

The Vikings declined to match the offer, but unlike Seattle, which got nothing in return, the Vikings got a third-round draft pick. At the next league meetings, the Vikings and Seahawks were scolded for their actions. In 2011 the new Collective Bargaining Agreement banned the use of poison pills.

By that time Hutchinson was entering the sixth of his six seasons with the Vikings after playing his first five as Seattle's 2001 first-round draft pick. Hutchinson played one more season, his 12th in the NFL, for the Tennessee Titans in 2012. Four of his seven Pro Bowls and three of his five first-team All-Pro selections came as a Viking. Today his Twitter handle is @poisonpill76.

# 77 Enjoy Winterfest

More than $11 million had been raised for the Vikings Children's Fund from its inception in 1978 to the unveiling of the three-day Polaris Vikings Winterfest held in Duluth from February 19–21, 2016. The fan festival offers interactive family events, photo and autograph opportunities with current and former Vikings, ice skating, a Polar Plunge, a live concert, a youth football clinic conducted by former Vikings linebacker E.J. Henderson, and a $30,000 prize party giveaway.

Winterfest replaced the Arctic Blast Snowmobile Rally that took place mostly on Lake Mille Lacs for 20 years. There are nearby snowmobiling opportunities as well during Winterfest. If you don't mind the cold and the snow, join the party. And if you've never operated a snowmobile, well, don't worry. Henderson had never driven one either when he hit the trail in Thief River Falls in 2015. "It's almost like jet skis but a little heavier," Henderson told the *Grand Forks Herald* before noting that he hoped his next ride would be "a little smoother."

If you're one of those sunshine softies who shiver when the temperature dips below 70 above, come along. Even former Vikings who no longer brave the Upper Midwest winters have been known to fly back, seeking some frozen February fun. "It's drastically different from where I live," former running back Darrin Nelson, an Orange County, California, resident, told the *Grand Forks Herald*. "It was 77 degrees when I left [home]."

The Arctic Blast—and now Winterfest—is one of the largest events the Vikings hold to raise money for their children's fund. More than $6 million of the $11 million raised has been donated to children's medical research at the University of Minnesota. "We take great pride at the Minnesota Vikings in being able to give back to our community while focusing on the children of the Upper Midwest," said Vikings president/owner Mark Wilf.

Even ownership has braved the elements to partake in frozen fun of Minnesota in mid-February. The Wilf family has flown in from New Jersey to stretch the boundaries of their comfort zone. "I've been to the lakes," said Leonard Wilf, part owner, vice chairman and cousin of Mark and Zygi Wilf. "And, oh yeah, I spent one crazy night snowmobiling with the Vikings, which I never thought I'd ever do in my life."

# 78 Matt Birk

For a guy who was 36 years old and at the pinnacle of his playing career, Matt Birk spent an inordinate amount of his Super Bowl XLVII week talking about the day he will die. More specifically, what will become of his brain the day he dies. Birk will donate his brain to a Boston University medical school that studies chronic traumatic encephalopathy (CTE), a brain disease that can be caused by repetitive head trauma and has been discovered in several deceased NFL players. "Terrible pun, but it's a no-brainer," he said. "Once you're gone, you're gone. And if some of your organs or body parts can help somebody else or help further the understanding of the effects of football, then I'm all for it."

The St. Paul native had been banging helmets since the late 1980s. He played at Cretin-Derham Hall High School, Harvard, and then the Vikings for 11 seasons and the Baltimore Ravens for four more. Later that week he played in his first Super Bowl, helped the Ravens beat the San Francisco 49ers, and retired on top. But even as he was heading out of the league, he was, as usual, thinking beyond himself.

Born July 23, 1976, Birk didn't grow up picturing himself playing for the Vikings or any other NFL team. He told his parents he'd be an NBA player and was all-state in basketball as well as football. Always an excellent student, Birk chose Harvard over other Ivy League offers. No Ivy League offensive lineman had been drafted since 1985 when people started telling Birk during his senior year that he had a chance to be selected.

One of those people was Vikings offensive line coach Mike Tice. The Vikings drafted Birk in the sixth round in 1998. He was a backup offensive tackle his first two seasons. In 2000 he stepped in for Jeff Christy, even though he had never played center. It wasn't long before it was obvious that Birk would join the likes of Mick Tingelhoff, Dennis Swilley, Kirk Lowdermilk, and Christy as standouts to play center for the Vikings. Of Birk's 210 regular-season games played and 187 starts, 146 games and 123 starts came as a Viking. With six Pro Bowls, he shares the franchise record for a center with Tingelhoff, a Hall of Famer.

Birk's tireless community service also won him a record six straight Vikings Man of the Year awards. In 2011 he added the Walter Payton NFL Man of the Year award. Birk never was afraid to take a stand. He took on Gene Upshaw when Upshaw was head of the players union, challenging the NFL to take better care of former players in need. When Minnesotans were about to vote on marriage rights, he argued that marriage should be defined as between one man and one woman.

Birk also took on Vikings management. After missing four games of the 2004 season because of surgery to repair a sports hernia, Birk needed more surgery to repair a hip injury before the 2005 season. Tice, who was head coach by that time, suggested publicly that Birk's ability to play was only a matter of pain tolerance. Birk responded by saying he would play through the injury, but only if the Vikings guaranteed the remainder of his contract.

They declined the offer, Birk had the surgery, and he missed the entire season. "Probably rightfully so from the Vikings' perspective, they couldn't do it," Birk, who became the NFL's director of football development in 2014, said before Super Bowl XLVII. "Thankfully, they didn't, and I had that surgery. Since then, I've played seven years and haven't missed a game. I don't think that would have happened had I tried to play through that stuff. My career never would have lasted to where I am right now."

# 79 Matt Blair's Scary Journey

U.S. district judge Anita Brody was giving final approval of a class-action settlement of NFL concussion claims in early February of 2015, about the same time former Vikings linebacker Matt Blair was in a Twin Cities doctor's office with his wife, his neurologist, and, sadly, more bad news. "Well," Blair said at the time, "it's coming. It's going deeper for me."

With that revelation the still-chiseled 64-year-old broke down in tears in a scene that has become all too familiar for NFL retirees and spouses coming to grips with early signs of dementia. Over 50 former Vikings, including Blair and Hall of Famers Carl Eller, Mick Tingelhoff, and Paul Krause, were part of more than 200 lawsuits that were condensed into the consolidated suit. At the time of Brody's ruling, Blair wasn't sure what impact the ruling would have because of anticipated challenges to the decision and uncertainty over who would determine the eligibility for financial restitution.

But, mainly, Blair was just scared. Fred McNeill, his best friend, former Vikings teammate, and fellow linebacker was in a nursing home suffering from advanced dementia and amyotrophic lateral sclerosis (Lou Gehrig's disease). And now Blair was struggling with memory loss and being told by his doctor that things were getting worse.

In November of 2015, McNeill died. His brain was examined and was found to have chronic traumatic encephalopathy (CTE) caused by repeated head trauma from playing football.

According to Blair, McNeill never had a diagnosed concussion. Blair had two, one of which hospitalized him between consecutive starts in the Vikings' playoff run to Super Bowl IX in 1976. "I'm in a better position than most players," Blair said in February of 2015. "But I know it's going to come at me big time. I just don't know what all is going to happen to me. All the players I've talked to and seen and heard about and what they've gone through, if I ever go through that, man, my life is gone."

The Vikings made Blair the 51st overall draft pick in 1974. The former Iowa State standout played 12 seasons in Minnesota, went to six consecutive Pro Bowls, and played in two Super Bowls. He still ranks No. 2 in franchise history in tackles (1,452) and first in blocked kicks (20). The only starter who played on all special teams, Blair became known as an expert when it came to the timing and leaping ability needed to knock down punts, field goals, and extra points. Blair's blocked punt against the Pittsburgh Steelers in Super Bowl IX was recovered in Pittsburgh's end zone for Minnesota's only points in a 16–6 loss.

Back in that small room in the Twin Cities in February of 2015, results of Blair's six-hour psychological testing from December confirmed an earlier brain scan that suggested signs of dementia. Medicine hadn't worked. His dose was doubled, and he was told to return in eight weeks for further examination and the possibility of being switched to much stronger medicine geared for people who likely have developed CTE. "Spouses get stronger because we have to be," his wife, Mary Beth, said. "I realize I can't get emotional because two of us emotional together would be a mess. At the appointment when the doctor was talking, I could see Matt's eyes welling up with tears. I'm thinking, *breathe, breathe* because inside I want to cry, too."

At first, Mary Beth figured her husband, like his peers, was just getting older and forgetful. "But then it became things like, 'Really? You've known this guy for how long? And you seriously can't remember his name?'" Mary Beth said. "There's someone he golfs with and has done business with and has been a friend of Matt's since he played football. He's been to our house about five times in the last six months. Every time he comes, Matt can't remember his name and keeps calling him by a different name. It's frightening."

# 80 Grady Alderman Was No Stiff

The inaugural American Football League draft for the 1960 season was held in Minneapolis on November 22, 1959. A group of Minnesota businessmen had been accepted as owners of an original AFL team, so they joined seven other teams in selecting 33 players. One of those players was future Pro Football Hall of Fame center Jim Otto, but Otto never was a Viking. That's because two months after the draft, the Vikings left the upstart league to join the NFL as its 14th team beginning in 1961. The Vikings didn't take those 33 players with them. The Oakland Raiders stepped into the AFL void and inherited the picks.

Meanwhile, the Vikings still had no players when the NFL's 1961 draft arrived. So an expansion draft was held beforehand. Every team, except the 1960 expansion Dallas Cowboys, exposed eight players to the Vikings, who picked three per team. Acerbic first-year coach Norm Van Brocklin, the former quarterback and league MVP for the NFL champion Philadelphia Eagles, wasn't impressed. He looked at the list and complained publicly. "They gave me 36 stiffs for a football team," he said.

Sixteen of them never made the team, 13 more were gone before the start of the second season, and all but one was gone by 1964. But the last man standing certainly was no stiff.

Left tackle Grady Alderman lasted 14 seasons. He played in six Pro Bowls, three Super Bowls, and was named first-team All-Pro once before being released after the 1974 season. Alderman was a Detroit kid who grew up in the inner city. He didn't play organized sports until he was in 10th grade, but the 6'2", 245-pounder became a gritty, self-made football standout.

He turned down Michigan State to play at the University of Detroit. The Detroit Lions noticed and drafted him in the 10th round in 1960. After 11 games with no starts, he went on the expansion draft list. As a Viking, Alderman helped the Vikings transition from the discombobulated early days under Van Brocklin to perennial Super Bowl contenders under Bud Grant. He started 184 of 205 games as a Viking, including playoffs. And though he didn't start in 1974, he did play in Super Bowl IX.

Alderman signed with the Chicago Bears in 1975 but was released before the regular season. Having become a certified public accountant early on in his playing career, Alderman moved into the Vikings front office as a financial expert. "I knew that playing wasn't going to last forever and I expected to live a lot longer than I played," he told the Vikings' website in 2011. "I figured I needed something to do later in life. And there wasn't a lot of money in those early years. We all needed to work in the offseason as well."

Alderman made $8,000 in his first season with the Vikings. He also remembers liking preseason games because players were paid $50 per preseason game. Those six games per year put an extra 300 bucks in his pocket every summer. Alderman spent 1981 and most of 1982 as Denver Broncos general manager. He also spent four years as color commentator on Vikings radio broadcasts. While he sat in judgment of players in those roles, he no doubt thought twice before deeming anyone a "stiff."

# 81 Go to U.S. Bank Stadium and Join Club Purple

U.S. Bank Stadium was built with the modern fan in mind. Case in point: check out Club Purple. It's a premium seating area, but it's not your father's premium seating area. "It has different seating, more couch and lounge seating to watch the game," said Lester Bagley, the Vikings' executive vice president of stadium development and public affairs, during a tour of the $1.1 billion stadium in February 2016, six months before its scheduled opening. "But if you go up behind the seating, there's a lounge and a bar with TVs and a ticker where you'll be able to follow your fantasy team."

The largest public/private project in state history was carefully planned to attract and sustain the growing number of fans, particularly younger ones, who prefer watching games at home on HD big screen TVs while scrolling for NFL news on their phones. Club Purple, which costs between $250 and $800 (as of press time) but did not require a personal seat license, aims to provide that feeling. But it also allows fans to turn around and see the action in the stadium with the Minneapolis skyline visible beyond five 95-foot high pivoting glass doors that open to a nearly three-acre plaza. "We've gotten a lot of feedback from folks and fans that care about fantasy football," Bagley said. "It's all about the fan experience. We have to get people off their couches and get them into the stadium. The fan experience is paramount."

If the Vikings have a late kickoff, fans will be able to enter Club Purple to watch the early games on TV. The Vikings are even providing fantasy football experts that will give weekly lineup advice. "Fantasy football has become dominant on gameday,"

Bagley said. "So we've tried to roll with that and listen to the experts."

The public is responsible for $498 million of the cost of the 66,000-seat stadium. The Wilf family ownership group originally was responsible for about $477 million through the sale of personal seat licenses, naming rights—including an 11-year, $220 million contract with U.S. Bank to put its name on the building—and some out-of-pocket expenses. The Wilf's portion of the costs rose by about $100 million as upgrades to the fan experience were added early on during the building process.

The stadium has other state-of-the-art features such as LED lighting, the largest transparent ethylene tetraflouroethylene (ETFE) roof in the nation, a record 30,000-square-foot Hyundai Club for premium seating, and about 1,300 Wi-Fi access points strategically located throughout the building. "It's designed so 66,000 people can all get on their phones at the same time—both the Internet and otherwise," Bagley said. "Connectivity is extremely important as we go forward."

With 60 percent of the roof transparent and 220,000 square feet of windows throughout the building, the aim was to provide an outdoor look in a climate-controlled setting that in some spots, such a Club Purple, feels like your living room.

# 82 "Two-Minute" Tommy

Thomas Francis Kramer was born March 7, 1955, on a dusty, 100-acre farm in San Antonio, Texas. "Two-Minute" Tommy was born December 4, 1977, on a frozen, 100-yard field in Bloomington, Minnesota.

Kramer, the Vikings' first-round draft pick in 1977, was on the sideline as the San Francisco 49ers led 24–0 midway through the third quarter. Starter Fran Tarkenton was out, having broken his leg against the Cincinnati Bengals. Veteran Bob Lee was in and struggling. "I remember it was so cold I couldn't feel my feet," Kramer said years later.

But things began to heat up when coach Bud Grant turned to Kramer with the Vikings trailing 24–7 in the fourth quarter, even though Kramer had thrown only 10 passes in three NFL games. The Vikings won 28–27 in what is still tied for the fifth largest comeback in league history. Kramer completed 9-of-13 passes for 188 yards and three touchdowns to three different targets. The game-winner was a 69-yarder to Sammy White with 1:38 left.

Kramer was a Texas legend at Robert E. Lee High School and Rice. At the former he won a state title one year and threw 54 touchdown passes the next. At Rice the All-American led the nation in passing and clinched his spot in the Texas Sports Hall of Fame. The Vikings hadn't drafted a quarterback in the first round until taking Kramer 27th. Tarkenton wasn't happy or willing to mentor, telling reporters, "I don't train quarterbacks."

Kramer had a solid 13-year stint in Minnesota. But his career also symbolizes how the Vikings tend to tease their loyal followers. Euphoric highs are so often followed by crushing lows. After Kramer's brilliance as a rookie against the 49ers, he started the following week and threw three interceptions in a 35–13 loss at Oakland, allowing Lee to regain the job.

Kramer had 20 game-winning drives and 16 fourth-quarter comeback victories. Yet he won 56 games and lost 58, going 2–2 in the playoffs. Yes, he threw the famous "Miracle at the Met" Hail Mary to Ahmad Rashad to beat the Cleveland Browns and clinch a playoff spot in 1980. But three weeks later, he threw five second-half interceptions in a 31–16 playoff loss to the Philadelphia Eagles.

Kramer was the NFL Comeback Player of the Year, a Pro Bowler, and the league's passing leader in 1986. Yet it was Wade Wilson who took the Vikings on their unexpected playoff run through the New Orleans Saints and a takedown of the top-seeded San Francisco 49ers in 1987. Kramer spent his last three years as a Viking locked in a love-hate relationship with Jerry Burns, who went from offensive coordinator to head coach in 1986. Injuries and inconsistent play caused Burns to flip-flop between Kramer and Wilson from 1987 to 1989.

Off the field, Kramer liked to have fun. But he also waged a very public battle with alcoholism with stints in rehab. In fact the 1987 training camp began with Kramer and cornerback Issiac Holt in rehab. Kramer had been arrested for drunken driving a month earlier in Bloomington.

But overall Kramer is remembered for the excitement and success he could bring late in games, and it all started on December 4, 1977. "My ankles were so frozen I could barely move them, so it wasn't my favorite time to enter a game," Kramer said. "But after I got on the field, the juices started flowing."

On the winning touchdown, Kramer saw its potential unfold as soon as the offense broke the huddle. "Burnsie had been saving that play for me, and he said, 'Okay, run '73' if you think it's there,'" Kramer said. "Somehow, I knew Sammy was going to be open, and he was."

# 83 Randall McDaniel, Student-Athlete

The toughest job of Randall McDaniel's life wasn't playing left guard at a Hall of Fame level for 14 NFL seasons. "I worked in a slaughterhouse growing up," he said. "They brought the cows in one door, slaughtered them, froze them, and we loaded them in the trucks out the back door."

McDaniel did this as a teenager working a summer job at the Sun Land Beef Company processing plant near Avondale, Arizona, his hometown. Each of those slabs of meat weighed between 200 and 400 pounds. McDaniel's shifts started at 4:00 AM and lasted until the trucks were full some 10 to 12 hours later. He'd leave with an aching back, raw shoulders, and his white coat soaked in blood. "That's the job that told me I knew my attitude would never be a problem," said McDaniel, who played his first 12 seasons (1988–99) with the Vikings. "If I could do that, I knew that if someone gave me a job to do, I was going to do it."

O.K. Fulton, McDaniel's Hall of Fame presenter in 2009, can attest to that. Fulton was McDaniel's mentor and the athletic director when McDaniel attended Agua Fria High School. "In 12 years that kid never missed a day of school—not one," Fulton said. "Only three kids did that while I was there. And I was there 41 years."

McDaniel had working-class role models in parents, Lela and Robert. Lela worked as a cashier at the local A.J. Bayless supermarket. Robert drove a school bus for 25 years and cleared tables at the Ramada Inn. Their four kids chipped in with odd jobs to help pay the family bills.

Education was a priority, no matter what the athletic calendar said. Because of that, years later, when his NFL career ended, McDaniel transitioned seamlessly into his next career in elementary education.

McDaniel had been working with children's education since his playing days at Arizona State. He would read regularly to a third-grade classroom. "The boys said only women and sissies read," McDaniel said. "They saw me reading, and it changed their

*A 12-time Pro Bowler at left guard, Randall McDaniel now teaches basic skills to elementary school students in the Twin Cities.*

perception. And after I was done playing, I knew I could do whatever I want or live wherever I want. But when I saw the difference I could make in just that one hour reading to those kids, that's when I realized that this is what I was going to do."

The day he announced his retirement was the same day he got his license to work full time in elementary education. He took a job in the special education department at Hilltop Primary School in the Westonka Public School District in the Twin Cities. He helps teach basic skills to children in grades K-5. By the time McDaniel had reached the Hall of Fame eight years after his last season, his students were way too young to have seen him play. They didn't even know he had played until enough parents told enough kids that McDaniel was a former Viking. "I'd say, 'Yeah, I used to play a little football,'" McDaniel said. "By the time they figured out I was pretty good at it, they already knew me as Mr. McDaniel—just a guy out there doing my job."

# 84 Roy Winston

While growing up in Baton Rouge, Louisiana, Roy Winston was the kind of athlete who could play anything from halfback to offensive tackle. He was rugged and strong enough at 218 pounds to play guard and defensive tackle at Louisiana State University. But it didn't take long for Vikings coach Norm Van Brocklin to see that Winston had the mind of a linebacker.

Of course, Winston had never played linebacker before in his life. That didn't matter.

The Vikings were heading into their second season in 1962 when they selected Winston in the fourth round of the draft. He lasted 15 seasons and was one of 11 Vikings to play in all four Super Bowls.

But first the Vikings had to outbid the AFL's Buffalo Bills, who had acquired Winston's AFL rights in a trade with the San Diego Chargers, the team that had selected Winston in the sixth round. "I signed with the Vikings for $12,000 per year with a $4,000 signing bonus," Winston told the team's website in 2011. "I thought I was rich. I think my dad was making about $5,000 or $6,000 at the time. It was real good money."

Winston backed up middle linebacker Rip Hawkins in 1962 before becoming a starter at left outside linebacker in 1963. In time he would team with his two best friends and hunting/fishing partners to fill out the starting linebacker spots. Wally Hilgenberg wore No. 58 and lined up at right outside linebacker. Lonnie Warwick wore No. 59 and was at middle linebacker. And, naturally, Winston wore No. 60 and was at left outside linebacker.

For years, anytime they were together—on the field, the sideline, or in a duck blind after they had retired—these three men lined up in the same order: Wally on the right, Lonnie in the middle, Roy on the left. All three were instinctive and tough. Winston was the only one teammates called "the Computer." It was a nod to his mind's ability to quickly decipher what the offense was going to do and relay that information.

Center Mick Tingelhoff started calling Winston "Moonie" after the comic strip *Moon Mullins*, whose main character was a tough, good-natured lug who could take and deliver his share of punches. Winston played in 190 games, starting 160—the same total as Hall of Fame defensive tackle Alan Page—before retiring after the team's fourth Super Bowl.

On October 25, 1964, Winston had three of his 12 career interceptions in a 27–22 win against the San Francisco 49ers at Kezar Stadium. That's three reasons the Vikings overcame Jim Marshall's infamous wrong way run.

One of Winston's two career touchdowns came in the emotional 1970 season-opening win over the Kansas City Chiefs at the Met. Marshall recovered a fumble and headed for the correct goal line. As he was being tackled at the Chiefs' 14-yard line, he lateralled to Winston, who gave the Vikings a 10–0 lead in a 27–10 win. Coach Bud Grant had been stewing over not only the humiliating Super Bowl IV loss to the Chiefs, but also how Kansas City head coach Hank Stram had belittled the Vikings during giddy sideline banter that was captured for eternity on NFL Films. Among other things, Stram mocked the Vikings for having an outdated defense. "They've been shoving it down our throats for eight months," Grant said after the game. "Today we proved that the defense of the 1960s can beat the offense of the 1970s."

# 85 Super Bowl LII

Super Bowl celebrations aren't something that's generally associated with Minnesota. But the state technically has won a couple of Super Bowls—as in winning the right to host the big game.

On May 20, 2014, Minnesota beat out popular Super Bowl venue New Orleans and successful 2012 host Indianapolis to join Detroit as the only northern cities to host the game twice. U.S. Bank Stadium, the $1.1 billion Vikings home set to open in downtown Minneapolis in August of 2016, will play host to the 52nd Super Bowl—Super Bowl LII—on February 4, 2018. "We did it," screamed members of the Minnesota host committee as they danced about in celebration after owners were forced to cast three tiebreaker ballots inside the Ritz-Carlton Hotel in Atlanta's upscale Buckhead neighborhood.

The vote was considered an upset. Ten-time host New Orleans was counting on an 11th Super Bowl to showcase as part of the city's 300th anniversary. Hence, it took four ballots to pick a winner. "The way they jumped for joy was the way I felt inside," Vikings owner Zygi Wilf said during a news conference that day.

The Minnesota bid was titled, "Built for the Bold," a nod to the stadium that took years of dogged lobbying efforts by two owners and community leaders. The Wilf family finally prevailed with a public/private deal that cost taxpayers $498 million. "That's what swayed most of the owners," New York Giants owner John Mara told the *Minneapolis Star Tribune*.

The last time Minneapolis won the right to host a Super Bowl was 1989. Three years later Super Bowl XXVI was held at the Metrodome. The Metrodome, which was demolished to make room for U.S. Bank Stadium, was built for $55 million in 1982. That is $179 million in 2016 dollars.

Yes, it will be cold when the national spotlight is shown on Minneapolis as waves of out-of-towners pump millions of their dollars into the local economy. But the Minnesota host committee embraced the obvious concern head-on with a theme titled, "The Bold North." An outdoor Super Bowl boulevard theme similar to the one in New York City in 2014 is being planned.

# 86 Dirty Jobs

August in Mankato, Minnesota, is the annual reminder that preparing for an NFL season is a long, sweaty, stinky, exhausting, and painful proposition. But it's also nowhere near being the worst working experiences that most of the men in purple have had in their lifetimes.

Once upon a time, these were working stiffs making meager wages while only dreaming of NFL stardom. "You think this is hot?" Vikings quarterback Christian Ponder said in 2012. "Try replacing sewage pipes while standing on blacktop during the summer in Florida. Now that's hot."

Way too many of Ponder's teammates dealt with manure. Lots and lots of manure. The kind of manure that smelled even worse than the Vikings 3–13 record in 2011. "Worst job?" asked defensive end Jared Allen. "Cleaning stalls for my dad on the ranch in [Los Gatos,] California." How much did Pops pay? "Just the right to live in his house another day," Allen said.

Linebacker Chad Greenway grew up working on his parents' farm in Mount Vernon, South Dakota. Even on a day when he practiced in full pads in a 96-degree heat index, he said he still prefers taking on fullbacks than loading pigs for market at 4:30 AM. "Who's tougher: an NFL player or a farmer?" Greenway asked. "A farmer—any day of the week."

Neither Greenway nor Allen—nor any other Viking with manure management on his resume—could top the tale told by their general manager, Rick Spielman, who worked on a pig farm in Carbondale, Illinois, during the summers that he played football at Southern Illinois University. "I did everything no one else wanted to do," Spielman said. "In the mornings the pigs that were inside the barn, I had to go in there when it was over 100 degrees and shovel all the…" um, well, you know. "They'd put 10 pigs in a pen. They were the ones that weighed about 220 pounds right before they were shipped to market. They don't move. All they do is lay in that pen and sleep and…" um, well, you know. The, um, stuff, "would be three feet deep," Spielman said. "And I had to scrape it into a gulley and then shovel it out to a tractor so they could use it as manure."

Spielman's first day on the job came with a warning. "You think you're this big, tough football player, that nothing fazes you," Spielman said. "They tell you you're not going to be used to the ammonia smell. Well, my first time in, I get my shovel and take my first swoop. That ammonia went right up into my nose. I went down, fell right into all that pig …" um, well, you know. "I could tell you my pig breeding story, too," Spielman said. "But that's not one for [print]."

Leslie Frazier, the Vikings coach in 2012, said his worst job was cleaning up the local graveyard in Columbus, Mississippi, when he was 14 years old. "I'm 14 and in the graveyard, man," Frazier said. "That's an eerie job for a young man, real eerie."

Center John Sullivan worked for a mason in Old Greenwich, Connecticut. "I was running the wheelbarrow, mixing concrete," Sullivan said, "just being miserable in general. So, yeah, I'm very happy I'm in the NFL."

# 87 Joey Browner and Family

Legend has it that Ross Browner, the oldest of Jimmy Sr. and Geraldine Browner's eight children, was acting up and not giving his full effort in school while growing up in Warren, Ohio, in the early 1970s. So Jimmy Sr., who had spent his entire adult life working in the steel mill, decided to give young Ross a glimpse of a future without the kind of education afforded to a top football recruit. He took him to the steel mill and made him put in a full day's work. "Dad worked 30 years in the steel mill," Keith Browner, one of Ross' younger brothers, told the *San Francisco Chronicle* years later. "He took Ross there and said, 'Do you want to work here?' He worked there for one day. He straightened up [in school], became a great athlete, and we all followed his example."

Boy, did they ever.

There were six Browner sons. All six played Division I college football. Four of them played in the NFL, including fourth son Joey, a hard-hitting playmaker at safety for the Vikings from 1983 to 1991. Jimmy Sr. didn't live to see it. He died of lung cancer in 1976. He was 49. "Before he died he told us to look out for one another," Joey told the Associated Press in 1982. "When he died, Ross was the one left in charge. Ross really takes care of us. And I think he and my brother Jimmy [Jr.] graduating from Notre Dame showed the rest of us it could be done."

Ross, a defensive lineman, won the 1976 Outland Trophy and the 1977 Lombardi Award before going on to a standout career with the Cincinnati Bengals and Green Bay Packers. Jimmy Jr., a defensive back, also played for the Bengals.

Joey and Keith, a linebacker, chose Notre Dame rival Southern Cal. Keith went on to play in the NFL with the Tampa Bay

Buccaneers, San Diego Chargers, San Francisco 49ers, and Oakland Raiders. Keith's son, Keith Jr., played defensive end for the Houston Texans and Chicago Bears. And Ross' son, Max Starks, played offensive tackle for the Pittsburgh Steelers.

Joey went to high school in Warren through his sophomore year before moving to Atlanta. He was an all-state defensive end, a track standout, and a high school basketball teammate of Dominique Wilkins. At USC he switched from corner to safety and was team MVP in 1982. The Vikings drafted him 19th overall.

At 6'2", 220 pounds, he was an intimidating hitter who racked up 1,110 tackles. He also had 37 interceptions, 18 forced fumbles, 16 fumble recoveries, and a Pro Bowl-record three fumble returns for touchdowns. With six Pro Bowls, three first-team All-Pro selections, and a spot on the NFL's Team of the Decade for the 1980s, Browner is routinely nominated for consideration for the Pro Football Hall of Fame but has not garnered enough support to make it further in the reduction process.

Browner, though, can't complain too much. He learned to appreciate a household whose mantra was: "No grades, no football." "I got to thank my mom and dad," Browner said years after Geraldine passed away in 1990. "They instilled in us the things we needed to succeed."

# 88 Studwell, Greenway, and the Art of the Tackle

Chad Greenway had a career-high 191 tackles to choose from when asked to pick the one he remembered most from the surprising 2012 playoff season. He chose a first-quarter sack of then-San Francisco 49ers quarterback Alex Smith in Week 3. No, you won't find that hit in the ESPN *SportsCenter* archives. Smith was rolling out on third down. Greenway was shadowing him when he charged and caught Smith by surprise. At the point of contact, Greenway's head was up and to the side of Smith. His eyes were open. His legs were driving Smith to the ground.

It was the kind of tackle that made Scott Studwell nod his approval from the press box as the team's record-shattering tackler and, at the time, its director of college scouting. "Too many players today are out of control," Studwell said. "Some players are always looking for the big hit. Chad's a sound tackler because he's a good athlete. He's not out of position, not out of control."

From 1977 to 1990, Studwell, a ninth-round draft pick out of Illinois, set franchise records for tackles in a career (1,928), a season (230), and a game (24). "Stud was something else," said Greenway, who ranks second in most tackles in a game (22). "His statistics are ridiculous. That career record most likely is out the window."

After his 10th season in 2015, Greenway, also a linebacker but a first-round pick out of Iowa, had 1,289 career tackles. No. 2 behind Studwell is former linebacker Matt Blair, who had 1,404 stops from 1974–85. Greenway tied Studwell's record of consecutive seasons of leading the team in tackles (six). Studwell did it from 1980–85; Greenway did it from 2008–13. In 2014 Greenway fell five tackles shy of the team lead despite missing four games because of injuries. Greenway missed his rookie season after tearing an

ACL covering a kickoff in the first quarter of the preseason opener. He returned in 2007 and didn't miss a game over the next seven seasons. "Chad's gotten better and more productive every year since he injured his knee as a rookie," Studwell said. "He knows how to get the guy on the ground."

According to Studwell, the modern tackler has a harder time perfecting his craft than he did. College and pro practices are more limited with less contact. Forcing turnovers is more of an emphasis than sound tackling. And defenders are more gun-shy because they're punished more with penalties and fines designed to promote player safety. "They're over-regulating a very physical game," Studwell said. "Guys are probably pulling up a little bit more than they used to just because they don't want to get fined or flagged. That's hard to do as a tackler."

But one thing hasn't changed, at least according to Studwell. "Tackling," he said, "is about 10 percent technique and 90 percent effort and heart."

# 89 Big Play Bobby Bryant

A poor kid from Macon, Georgia, goes to the University of South Carolina as a 6'0", 140-pound halfback and, well, he's going to be called "Bones." But soon they start calling him "Big Play" Bobby Bryant. He went to South Carolina for football and track. By springtime he decided he'd give baseball a twirl instead of track. The left-hander would go on to become the first Gamecock to strike out 100 batters in a season on his way to being drafted by the New York Yankees in 1966 and the Boston Red Sox in 1967. On the football field, Bryant was even better.

Old-timers still talk about his 98-yard kickoff return for a touchdown against North Carolina State. The 1967 Atlantic Coast Conference Athlete of the Year became the Vikings' seventh-round draft pick as a 170-pound cornerback. The team had no contact with him before the draft and had its equipment manager call him to let him know he was a Viking. A serious knee injury left over from college wiped out Bryant's rookie season. But he returned in 1968 and put together a 14-year career before retiring after the 1980 season.

Because of his size, or lack thereof, Bryant often played with injuries or missed time because of them, but his 175-game career included four Super Bowls, 11 division titles, and a franchise-record six playoff interceptions. His 51 regular-season interceptions rank second behind Pro Football Hall of Fame safety Paul Krause, who had 53 of his NFL-record 81 picks as a Viking. Bryant had a flamboyant side that made him a fan favorite, especially when he was blowing kisses to the crowd after making yet another big play.

He also wasn't afraid to speak up or out against something controversial either. When coach Bud Grant released defensive tackle Alan Page in the middle of the 1978 season, it was Bryant who was among the leaders who criticized the move and suggested it had more to do with Page's deteriorating relationship with Grant.

Page was 33 when he was cut on October 10, a couple of days after a loss to the Seattle Seahawks. Stoic as ever, Grant told reporters, "Nobody has meant more to the Vikings, but he just can't make the plays anymore." But Grant also didn't care for Page's work with the players' union or how much weight he had lost while committing to a long-distance running regimen. Bryant, who often helped Page in union matters, told reporters that Grant's decision, "showed a lack of class by the Viking organization."

Mainly, though, Bryant is remembered for making big plays in big games. His 63-yard interception return for a touchdown helped secure the 27–10 win at Dallas in the 1973 NFC Championship

Game. Three years later, he had an even bigger game in the 1976 NFC Championship Game against the visiting Los Angeles Rams. In that contest he scored the game's first points when he returned a blocked field goal 90 yards for a touchdown. He also intercepted Pat Haden twice. With the Rams trailing 17–13 and driving late in the game, Haden launched a ball for Ron Jessie, who was wide open deep—or so everyone thought. "Haden never looked to my side," Bryant told the Vikings website years later.

Bryant was on the other side of the field in man coverage against Harold Jackson. "Both Jackson and Jessie ran post patterns so they went down the field for about 10 yards and cut into the middle," Bryant said. "Jessie had [Vikings cornerback] Nate Wright beat by about four or five yards. When Haden let the pass go, I just left my guy. Jessie had his eyes on the ball with his hands up ready to catch it, and I just plucked it out of his hands."

# 90 Lynn Loathed Replacement Players

Unlike many of his peers, Vikings general manager Mike Lynn stubbornly refused to spend any time preparing for the possibility of having to play replacement games in the event of a players' strike in 1987. "I really didn't think the league would go through with it," Lynn said in 2011. "I always thought there would be some breakthrough at the last second."

There wasn't. The Vikings were 2–0 when NFL players voted to strike on September 22, 1987. The NFL responded by canceling one week of the schedule and announcing they would play with replacement players for however long they had to after that. Lynn had less than two weeks to field an entire team from scratch. "I had connections to Memphis, so we just made an announcement in the papers down there that we were having tryouts," Lynn said. "Whoever showed up, showed up, as far as I was concerned."

The strike ended up lasting 24 days and three games before the players surrendered. "It was the damnedest mess I ever saw in the 40 years I coached," said Jerry Burns, the Vikings coach at the time. "Just a nightmarish operation start to finish. I recommend they never try it again."

Replacement games are remembered for small crowds and an amateurish, blooper-quality level of play. They are also remembered for the unbelievable stories that belonged to hundreds of ragtag players who had to be scrounged up from all walks of life. The Vikings quarterback didn't come from the 300 hopefuls who showed up for the Memphis tryout. He came in fresh off a flag football league playoff game in Kansas City. Tony Adams was with the Chiefs from 1975 to '78 but hadn't played a down of pro football since leaving the CFL seven years earlier. He was a happily retired 37-year-old financial planner, but he also had connections to the Vikings coaching staff. Paul Wiggin, the defensive line coach, was his head coach with the Chiefs. And Bob Schnelker, the offensive coordinator, was Adams' offensive coordinator with Kansas City and the San Diego Chargers. "My flag football team won the league tournament on a Sunday, and Paul called me that night," Adams said. "I talked to Mike Lynn on Monday, flew to Minnesota on Tuesday, practiced on Wednesday, and started for the Vikings that Sunday."

Replacement players with no NFL experience made about $5,000 a game and half a share of any playoff money. Vested veterans such as Adams made much more. "I figured I could take a beating or two for what they were paying," Adams said. "I made as much in those three games as I ever made in a single year with the Chiefs and Chargers. Of course, it took me six months to recover. I never thought it would last three weeks."

The Vikings lost all three replacement games. They lost 27–7 at the Chicago Bears, 20–10 at the Tampa Bay Buccaneers, and 23–16 to the Green Bay Packers in front of 13,911 fans at the Metrodome. "We had guys from everywhere just thrown together," said Kurt Ploeger, a defensive end from Gustavus Adolphus who was brought in because he had played in four NFL games in 1986. "We had a defensive lineman who was an engineer. He had to leave the team one week because he had already used up all his time off from work. We had a guard I went against in practice who told me, 'I've never played guard in my life.'"

"It was sick," Burns said. "The guys we had on our strike team, they couldn't have made Eden Prairie's high school team."

The real Vikings rebounded to finish 8–7 and advance to the NFC Championship Game. Many people involved in those games looked back on the experience over the years and laughed. Lynn never did. "I didn't think any part of it was fun or funny or hilarious," Lynn said. "It was embarrassing. It was a bad, bad part of the history of the National Football League."

# 91 Feisty Prankster Wally Hilgenberg

Only Wally Hilgenberg would have had the courage and craziness to dump a wastebasket full of water onto the toupee-covered head of sportscasting legend Howard Cosell two days before the Super Bowl. And only Wally Hilgenberg would have had the ability to recruit someone of Alan Page's stature to assist him.

The Vikings were staying at the Hilton Hotel in New Orleans. Cosell had secured a one-on-one interview with Vikings quarterback Fran Tarkenton on the Friday before the Vikings played the Pittsburgh Steelers in Super Bowl IX. Cosell's only oversight was setting up below an overhanging balcony. On the count of three, Hilgenberg and Page bombarded Cosell from a couple stories up. Hilgenberg ran. Page leaned over the railing and smiled. More than a tad upset and his toupee shifted considerably, Cosell canceled the interview and never allowed the incident to air. Teammates say Hilgenberg typically was in the middle of any such prank.

In every other situation, one could find old No. 58 lined up to the right, No. 59 Lonnie Warwick in the middle, and No. 60 Roy Winston to the left. Lifelong friends and hunting partners—to the dismay of ducks throughout the Upper Midwest—they were the starting linebackers in Super Bowl IV. Winston and Hilgenberg started two more Super Bowls together, while Hilgenberg started in all four.

Who would have thought that was possible in 1967–68? Certainly not Hilgenberg. Newly married to his wife Mary, Hilgenberg thought a torn knee ligament before the 1967 season had ended his career. In reality, it was only the beginning.

Hilgenberg was born September 19, 1942 in Marshalltown, Iowa. His family soon moved to Wilton Junction, Iowa, where Wally became a multi-sport star. He ended up at the University of Iowa, where he played for Jerry Burns. Hilgenberg was drafted in the fourth round by the Detroit Lions in 1964. Over the next three seasons, he started only nine games until suffering a serious knee injury before the 1967 season. Hilgenberg said years later that he almost died from that injury because of blood clots that formed after the surgery. After sitting out the 1967 season, Hilgenberg was traded to the Pittsburgh Steelers, who cut him.

By that time, Burns was in Minnesota as Bud Grant's offensive coordinator. He went to general manager Jim Finks to vouch for Hilgenberg. Finks paid the $100 waiver wire fee.

Over the next 12 seasons, Hilgenberg started 117 of 158 games. One of his greatest highlights was his interception of a tipped pass in the end zone to thwart a 98-yard drive by the Los Angeles Rams in the 1974 NFC Championship Game at Metropolitan Stadium. The play and the 14–10 victory that sent the Vikings to Super Bowl IX prompted Rams defensive end Jack Youngblood to tell reporters in the losing locker room, "The Big Man upstairs did not want us to win this one."

The "Purple People Eaters" who made up the defensive line were the identity of the Vikings at the time. But Hilgenberg's toughness and feisty attitude was just as important and fit the era perfectly. His signature tackle was the clothesline, which no longer is legal. In 1971 the Vikings shut out three teams and led the league in scoring defense, allowing just 9.9 points per game. Their leading tackler was Hilgenberg with 110.

In late 2006 Hilgenberg's body began to twitch. He was diagnosed with amyotrophic lateral sclerosis, Lou Gehrig's disease. He died on September 23, 2008, at age 66. Hilgenberg's brain was examined after death by doctors at the Center for the Study of Traumatic Enchephelopathy at Boston University. Two years later they determined that the cause of Hilgenberg's death was the result of repetitive brain trauma from playing football.

Late in his career, Hilgenberg became a devout Christian and often spoke publicly about his faith. He and his wife, Mary, stayed in Minnesota, where Wally and former teammate Stu Voigt were longtime business partners in real estate and banking. In Hilgenberg's last days, many teammates visited with their old friend, who by then was unable to communicate except for a look in the eye that they all remembered. Mary said Wally never complained. In the book *Vikings 50: All-time Greatest Players in Franchise History*, Mary shared Wally's words when he knew ALS was about to consume his body: "I have had a great life and I have no regrets."

# 92 Anthony Carter

The 1987 Vikings were an exceptional team that struggled to gain any traction.

They were 2–0 when the 24-day players strike began and 2–3 when it ended after three weeks of replacement games. The real Vikings won five of their next six but then finished the regular season 1–3. "We had a talented football team that maybe wasn't playing up to its ability," said Scott Studwell, the starting middle linebacker on that team. "When you're going along like that, the team needs one positive thing to happen to it. You can believe you can win and you can prepare as if you're going to win, but it's that shadow of a doubt that gets erased when that one big positive thing finally happens."

Meet Anthony Carter, that one big positive thing in 1987.

Carter grew up in Riviera Beach, Florida, with four brothers and seven sisters. He was a multi-sport star known as the "Little Gnat" before becoming a record-setting receiver at the University of Michigan. After three seasons in the United States Football League, he signed with the Miami Dolphins but was traded to Minnesota, where he played from 1985 to 1993.

In 1987 the Vikings backed into the playoffs at 8–7 when the Dallas Cowboys beat the St. Louis Cardinals on the final week of the regular season. From there, an improbable postseason run became an everlasting highlight reel for the dynamic 5'11", 168-pound Carter.

The Vikings traveled to New Orleans to play the 12–3 Saints in a wild-card game. The favored Saints were leading 7–3 late in the first quarter when Carter fielded a punt and returned it 84 yards for a touchdown. "That's the one positive thing we needed," Studwell said. "After that it became one of those days when we couldn't do anything wrong, and New Orleans couldn't do anything right."

The Vikings won 44–10 to earn a trip to San Francisco to play the NFC's top-seeded 49ers (13–2) in the divisional round. San Francisco was favored by 11 points and had outscored their last three opponents 124–7.

*Wide receiver Anthony Carter runs away from San Francisco 49ers defenders for a chunk of his 227 receiving yards during the Vikings' 1988 playoff victory at Candlestick Park.*

It was no contest. But it was the Vikings who rolled 36–24.

Defensively, they harassed Joe Montana to the point where he fell behind 20–3, got booed, and was benched in favor of the more mobile Steve Young. Offensively, it was Carter who stole the show right in Jerry Rice's own backyard. On a day when the greatest receiver in NFL history caught three passes for 28 yards, Carter grabbed 10 for 227 yards with an electric array of slants, deep routes, and gravity-defying catches. "I never saw a guy completely dominate a game the way Anthony Carter did in that game," said Jerry Burns, the Vikings coach at the time. "[Quarterback] Wade Wilson was hot, but he just threw the ball down there, and Anthony went and caught it, whether it was single coverage, double coverage, whatever. When Anthony began to take over, it was a lift for the whole team."

The Vikings lost the following week in Washington in the NFC Championship Game. But Carter's 1988 postseason run remains one of the best in NFL history. Carter's 227 yards receiving was a postseason single-game record at the time and still ranks second all time. Meanwhile, his three-game totals of 642 all-purpose yards and 221 punt return yards still stand as postseason records. "Anthony got us started," Studwell said. "He was exactly what we needed."

# 93 Gene Washington

Long before Randy Moss was even born, there was a purple-clad No. 84 racing past defenders and stretching the field as a receiver for the Minnesota Vikings. Gene Washington, of course, didn't have the prolific numbers that Moss would post in a much different era. But on January 4, 1970, when the Vikings were one win from their first Super Bowl berth, it was the slippery 6'3", 208-pound Washington who was most responsible for staggering the visiting Cleveland Browns with the kind of skills that Moss would display decades later.

On an 8-degree afternoon that felt like 16-below with the windchill, it was Washington who kept his feet and his speed against an overmatched Cleveland secondary that struggled with Metropolitan Stadium's frozen field. Observers of that final NFL title game before the merger suggested the Browns appeared to accept defeat once Washington stunned them with two huge plays in a 14–0 start.

When defensive back Walt Sumner slipped, Washington caught a 33-yard pass from quarterback Joe Kapp to set up the first touchdown. Moments later, Washington shifted to the other side of the field. When defensive back Erich Barnes fell, Washington was able to adjust to an underthrown ball, make the grab, and finish off a 75-yard touchdown. The Vikings won 27–7 to reach Super Bowl IV. Washington finished with 120 yards on three catches. The Browns weren't exactly surprised, having given up seven catches for 119 yards and three touchdowns to Washington in a 51–3 loss at Metropolitan Stadium earlier that season.

Born January 25, 1944, Gene Washington grew up in the segregated south in LaPorte, Texas, a small town of about 6,500. His mother was a maid, and his father worked for an electric company. They worked long hours to make ends meet, so Gene often relied on coaches for rides home after practice. Washington became better known as one of the top high school hurdlers before his talents transferred to the football field. He wanted to stay in Texas for college, but only the all-black schools showed any interest.

Then Michigan State made its pitch, and Washington boarded an airplane for East Lansing, Michigan. Until that visit he had never flown or even eaten in a restaurant. Washington would become a two-time first-team All-American on a team that would win back-to-back national titles in 1965 and 1966. In 1967 four Spartans would be taken in the top eight spots in the draft. The Vikings would get two of them in running back Clinton Jones at No. 2 and Washington at No. 8. Both would play for the Vikings through 1972. Washington, who would go on to play two more years with the Denver Broncos, was a two-time Pro Bowler who was most explosive as a first-team All-Pro during the Vikings' first Super Bowl season.

Yes, the 1969 Vikings were known more for a defense that allowed a league-low 9.5 points per game. But Washington averaged 21.1 yards per catch (while recording 821 receiving yards) and nine touchdowns for an offense that led the league with an average of 27.1 points per game. Washington then opened the playoffs with four catches for 90 yards to help the Vikings beat the Los Angeles Rams 23–20 for the first postseason win in franchise history.

Super Bowl IV, of course, was a different story. The Vikings did a lot of things wrong in that 23–7 loss to the Kansas City Chiefs. Getting Washington only one catch for nine yards ranks right up there.

# 94 Ed White

CBS was looking for ways to keep NFL viewers from switching channels during halftime breaks in 1975. The winning idea was something the network called the National Football League Players Association Arm Wrestling Championship. The first step was identifying a representative from each of the league's 26 teams. In Minnesota it was a no-brainer.

Edward Alvin White was a bear of a man with big mitts, a killer grip, and brute strength honed early on from helping his father work construction as a kid growing up in Southern California. "Arm wrestling is something that I always did," White told Viking Update in 2011. "I would arm wrestle for hamburgers in high school. In college we would arm wrestle for beer on Friday nights, so I took it pretty serious. It requires quickness and initial strength more than anything."

Legend has it the only time White ever lost was as a teenager when he took on a man who weighed 200 pounds more than he did. Legend became television reality when White continued to pummel his NFC opponents on CBS every week in 1975. Buffalo Bills guard Joe DeLamielleure kept doing the same in the AFC. In the conference finals, White beat Derland Moore of the New Orleans Saints to set up the $10,000 championship bout with DeLamielleure. (All these years later, it does seem ironic that a Buffalo Bill and a Minnesota Viking—representatives of franchises that each have lost four Super Sunday contests—would meet in the Super Bowl of arm wrestling.) White, who had beaten six of his opponents in a total of 14 seconds, won the title. It aired on January 4, 1976, during halftime of the NFC Championship Game.

White's strength and speed came in handy in his day job as well. The 6'1", 269-pounder was a second-round pick of the Vikings in 1969. He played nine seasons for the Vikings before a contract squabble got him traded to San Diego, where he played another eight seasons for the Chargers. "The one guy I truly think belongs in the Hall of Fame who isn't in is Ed White," said former Vikings right tackle Ron Yary, a teammate of White's for nine seasons. "He was one of the strongest players I ever played with."

White was a four-time Pro Bowler while playing in 241 games with 210 starts. He blocked for Fran Tarkenton and Dan Fouts, played in four Super Bowls with the Vikings, and played in two

AFC title games with the Chargers. He's a member of the Chargers Hall of Fame and on the list of 50 greatest Vikings, which was put together for the team's 50th season in 2010.

As natural as White was at guard, it's hard now to believe that he was an All-American noseguard who didn't play offense at the University of California. He didn't want to play offensive line at the next level either, but the Vikings were pretty well stocked on the defensive line with the Purple People Eaters.

It was Vikings longtime personnel man Jerry Reichow who scouted White and saw his potential as an offensive lineman. White had the quick feet and hands, but mainly he had extraordinary strength. The kind of strength he often displayed when non-believers challenged him to tear phone books in half with his bare hands. Those big hands now belong to an accomplished painter and sculptor living in Julian, California. (Don't believe it? Check out edwhiteart.com.)

# 95 Isiah Thomas vs. Cris Carter

Successful NFL players have a competitive drive that won't back down. Legendary Detroit Pistons point guard Isiah Thomas got an early look into that side of Cris Carter during the spring of 1980. Thomas was a freshman at Indiana. Carter was an eighth-grader in Middletown, Ohio. Butch Carter, Cris' older brother, was a senior at Indiana.

Butch would go on to be drafted by the Los Angeles Lakers later that year. He'd play seven NBA seasons for four teams before becoming a head coach. Thomas, as you may recall, also played some mean basketball. Cris was a confident young teenager who figured he could beat anyone on the basketball court or the football field—even the prized point guard on Bob Knight's powerhouse Hoosiers team.

Butch, the oldest of seven Carter kids, was as much a father figure to Cris as an older brother. To help his single mother, Butch would take in some of the younger siblings during spring breaks. "My senior year at Indiana, I remember running around campus trying to find Cris because he wandered off," Butch said. "Finally, I find him at 1:30 in the morning."

There in a quiet corner of campus was Cris, Isiah, and a basketball court. "They had car lights on, and the lights are pointed at the basketball court," Butch said. "And Cris is playing Isiah Thomas one on one."

And losing repeatedly. "I mean Isiah is a college freshman, and Cris is 12 or 13 [actually 14]," Butch says. "Isiah is beating the crap out of Cris. Isiah sees me and comes up to me and says, 'Butch, I'm sorry, but I can't get him to quit.'"

Cris scored 1,600 points in his high school basketball career. He was named all-state and came close to quitting football before his junior season. He would have, too, if Bill Conley hadn't been hired to coach the Middletown football team before Carter's junior season. "People told me we had this one kid, Cris Carter, but he probably won't play because his brother is in the NBA, and he wants to focus on basketball," Conley said. "But Cris did come to a football camp we had. The second day of camp, I said, 'This guy is going to be something special.' Then all of a sudden, I see him do a 40-inch vertical and I said, 'This is not a normal human being.'"

It was Conley who convinced Carter he could play both sports and not hurt his chances of going far in either. Carter became all-state in both. When it came time to pick a college, his decisions came down to Michigan, Ohio State, and Notre Dame in football and Louisville in basketball. Decades later he and Isiah both ended up in their own Halls of Fame.

# 96 The Tragic Case of Orlando Thomas

Orlando Thomas never had a bad day. Oh sure, life would knock him down sometimes. But friends, former teammates, and relatives say their beloved "OT" always got back up with a smile and five words that will forever define the former Vikings free safety: "Every day is a holiday," said former Vikings strong safety Robert Griffith, repeating his friend's favorite mantra and chuckling at so many memories of playing next to Thomas from 1995 to 2001. "He'd say it probably once a day, sometimes three or four times. Even when he'd be hurt and standing on the sideline, you'd hear him yelling, 'C'mon, Griff. You gotta make that play. Get your name in the paper. Remember, *every day is a holiday!*'"

Thomas still was saying those five words into his mid-30s. But by then they were barely a whisper and mumbled by a bedridden man to his wife, Demetra, in words only a soulmate could decipher. Married February 27, 1998, only two months after their first date and five months after first meeting at Cheese Car Wash in north Minneapolis, he and Demetra spent about a decade side by side coping with the fact that Orlando, a father of three, was dying of amyotrophic lateral sclerosis (ALS), more commonly known as Lou Gehrig's disease.

Once an imposing 6'1", 225-pound presence on the football field, Thomas died on November 9, 2014, in his hometown of Crowley, Louisiana. He was 42 and one of many former NFL players to be told by medical experts that his condition likely resulted from the repetitive head trauma he suffered while playing the game he loved so much. Lou Gehrig's disease is a "progressive neurodegenerative disease that attacks nerve cells in the brain and spinal cord resulting in muscle weakness and atrophy," according to the ALS Association's website. Eventually the condition destroys the motor neurons necessary for voluntary movements and causes total paralysis, including the ability to swallow and breathe.

Only 30,000 Americans will have the incurable disease at one time. But that's in part because the average life expectancy, following diagnosis, is two to five years, according to Dr. Lucie Bruijn, chief scientist at the ALS Association. Thomas lived 10 years after his diagnosis.

By the summer of 2007, the 34-year-old Thomas was paralyzed above the waist and had only limited movement in his legs. He couldn't sit up on his own and was unable to chew or swallow. He was fed through a tube and needed his throat cleared regularly by suctioning, but Demetra said he never once asked, "Why me?" "I used to think that Orlando was just real carefree," Demetra said in 2007. "But I'm learning so much from him now. He can't walk into a room and bring on the excitement or bring out his favorite quote—'Every day is a holiday!'— like he used to. But he's showing that, regardless of what's going on in your life, if you live from the heart and you have love, joy, and peace, there's nothing greater than living from that place within."

In 1995 Thomas was named first-team All-Pro after leading the NFL in interceptions with nine. Twelve years later his mind was as sharp as ever, but he couldn't move or speak clearly or loudly enough to be understood by anyone but Demetra. But through her, he was able to manage a message from his bed to Vikings fans everywhere: "Tell all of them that I said, 'Thank you!'"

# 97 Visit Lambeau Field, the Site of Moss' Moonshot

As soon as Randy Moss beat Al Harris for a 34-yard touchdown catch, he jogged to the back of the end zone, bent over, and pretended to pull his pants down and moon the fans in Lambeau Field. Then he bumped his butt against the goal post as a fourth-quarter exclamation point on a 31–17 NFC wild-card rout of the Green Bay Packers on January 9, 2005.

The reaction in the Fox television booth that day is almost as memorable as what Moss did on the field. "That is a disgusting act by Randy Moss," play-by-play announcer Joe Buck said. "And it's unfortunate that we had that on our air live. That is just disgusting by Randy Moss."

Perhaps a little more context would have lightened the mood and lowered Buck from his high horse. Granted, the act in question was performed by Moss. And it was the enigmatic Moss who was still embroiled in controversy from having left the field as the Vikings were lining up for an onside kick in the closing seconds of their loss at the Washington Redskins the week before.

But there was an underlying story involving a tradition of Packers fans mooning the opposing team buses. Even Jim Marshall, whose Vikings career began with the team's expansion season in 1961, remembers seeing an awful lot of cheesehead-sized moons back in the day. "They have the tradition of mooning us from the time we get off the plane," Marshall said. "Going into the city, virtually every window you would pass, every car you passed, somebody's showing you their rear end. And that was during the years when they sold glass bottles in stadiums. The fans would throw the bottles at us, so you'd be going down the concrete tunnel, and bottles would be bouncing off and breaking all over the place."

Moss explained his action by saying, "Just having a little fun with the boys a little bit." The league office didn't laugh. Moss was fined $10,000.

It was just another memorable, albeit odd, moment inside the football shrine that all fans, including purple-clad ones, should visit. To visit Lambeau Field is to experience a modern museum of NFL football woven into a 59-year-old stadium. Take the 280-mile trek east of Minneapolis to soak in the history of the NFL's smallest city.

Originally dedicated as City Stadium on September 29, 1957, and renamed on September 11, 1965, this grass playing field is old enough to have carried Bud Grant and his Purple People Eaters of the late '60s. You can't get that in Minnesota, where the land that housed old Metropolitan Stadium is now an amusement park inside the Mall of America.

Tailgating in the quaint neighborhood surrounding Lambeau Field and then heading inside to watch a game is the ideal visit. But if tickets are too hard to come by, there are stadium tours lasting from 60 to 90 minutes with a top price tag of $21 for adults. For details on the tour and everything the stadium has to offer, check out packers.com.

The stadium also houses a fun sports bar called the "1919 Kitchen & Tap" and a two-story, 15,000-square-foot Packers Hall of Fame. One also can pick up a map that lays out the "Packers Heritage Trail" around town. The "Lambeau-Lombardi Spur"—designed as a 12.5-mile bike trail—leads to several sites, including Curly Lambeau's gravesite in Allouez Catholic Cemetery and Vince Lombardi's former home on Sunset Circle in Allouez. "It's a great rivalry," Marshall said. "And I think it all started with the Packer fans. They really didn't like us much when we first started. So it got pretty heated."

# 98 Rick Spielman

Rick Spielman was working in the Columbus State Community College athletic department in Ohio in 1989 when the Detroit Lions called him about a job with the BLESTO scouting service. If he chose to, Spielman could hop in his old Jeep, drive down to Cincinnati, and write scouting reports from Bengals home games, so that the Lions and BLESTO scouting network would have data on all the Bengals players. The pay was $50 a game.

Spielman wanted a life inside the NFL. The original plan, of course, was to make it as an undersized linebacker out of Southern Illinois. But that ended quickly when he failed to make the final roster with the San Diego Chargers in 1987 and Lions a year later.

A reluctant Spielman gave those scouting reports a shot, and, well, that was that. He was hooked on a life in NFL personnel evaluation. "It was the perfect fit because Rick loves football, and he's a detail guy who leaves no stone unturned," said younger brother Chris Spielman, a former Pro Bowl linebacker for the Lions. "When he was in school, he had endless piles of binders filled with notes. And he wrote so small. I'd ask him, 'Why do you write so small?' And he'd say, 'Because I got a lot to write.'"

After 15 seasons with the Lions, Chicago Bears, and Miami Dolphins, Spielman joined the Vikings after the 2006 draft. He replaced vice president of player personnel Fran Foley, who was fired after three turbulent months in which he alienated key members of the organization and was caught with fabrications on his resume.

Over the next six seasons, Spielman was part of the "Triangle of Authority," a three-pronged system, in which the head coach, Spielman, and salary cap expert Rob Brzezinski would make all football decisions by consensus and each report directly to ownership. Eventually, owners Zygi and Mark Wilf saw the pitfalls in that system when they found themselves in the unqualified position of having to make final football decisions when there was no consensus. So in 2012 Spielman was promoted to general manager. The team hadn't had a general manager with final say on all football matters since Jim Finks in 1974. "It's very tough to be a Monday morning quarterback in figuring out what we should have done differently," Zygi said in 2015. "Learning from experience is the only way you can get better, and we were learning."

In his first three years as general manager, Spielman made 15 trades involving 39 picks and five veteran players. He earned his "Trader Rick" moniker by making seven first-round picks, an NFL record over a three-year span. But his most significant decision was taking a chance on 57-year-old Bengals defensive coordinator Mike Zimmer as the franchise's ninth head coach on January 17, 2014.

Zimmer had never been a head coach but had built a stellar 35-year coaching reputation on excellent defenses, strong teaching techniques, and an honest, outspoken personality that's as blunt as a sledgehammer between the eyes. "I know that type of person," Spielman said. "I took quite a few of those hammers to the forehead from my dad. I'm used to it. I think it will be good for us when it comes time to discuss the roster."

Spielman's late father, Sonny, was a blue-collar high school coach whose honesty often came wrapped in a verbal punch to the nose. Rick and Chris both played for Sonny when he was an assistant at Massillon (Ohio) Washington High School.

Zimmer's father, Bill, was the same way—only he coached his son at Lockport (Illinois) Township High School. "My father was the quarterback, and my granddad was the coach," said Adam Zimmer, Mike's linebackers coach with the Vikings. "My father tells the story of how he threw an interception and came over to the sideline, and my granddad punched him in the stomach. So, yeah, my granddad was a hard-nosed guy, too."

It's that kindred spirit that Spielman and Zimmer drew comfort from during an initial interview that lasted 10 hours and a second interview that lasted almost as long. Spielman had interviewed six other candidates during a three-week search. But it was Zimmer, the man who had gone 0-for-5 in five previous head coaching interviews, who stole the show before any other candidate gained a second interview. "It's like when I met my wife," Spielman said, "you just know."

In two years they turned a 5–10–1 team into an 11–5 division champion. "We will be fine," Zimmer said. "I'm direct and can get mad at people. He's direct, and I'm sure he can get mad at people. But we understand that both of our butts are responsible for each other."

# 99 Mike Zimmer

He swaggered into Winter Park, calling himself "the Fixer" during an introductory press conference on January 17, 2014. Skeptics snickered, but Mike Zimmer went to work fixing things. The 58-year-old first-time head coach inherited a 5–10–1 team that ranked last in the league in points allowed (30) in 2013. A year later it was a 7–9 team that ranked 11th in points allowed (21.4). A year after that, it was an 11–5 division champion with a defense that ranked fifth in points allowed (18.9).

So much for the skeptics.

From 2006, when Brad Childress hired Mike Tomlin as his defensive coordinator, until Leslie Frazier was fired after the 2013

*Head coach Mike Zimmer stands on the sideline during the 2015 season, during which he led the Vikings to their first divisional title since 2009.*
(AP Images)

season, the Vikings ran the same Cover-2-based defense. That's eight seasons with a read-and-react scheme that didn't feature much in terms of deception and exotic blitz packages. "I don't think our defense got outdated," defensive end Brian Robison said. "I just think sometimes you get schemed against, and it doesn't work in your favor. We play Green Bay and Chicago and Detroit twice a year. When they see your defense over and over and over again, heck, there were times when we'd line up, and [Packers quarterback] Aaron Rodgers was calling out our defenses."

In 12 regular-season games against the Vikings' Cover-2 scheme, Rodgers posted a 116.8 passer rating, the highest by any quarterback against a single team since the AFL-NFL merger in 1970. He completed 71.4 percent of his passes with 27 touchdowns and four interceptions.

Rodgers and the Packers were 3–0 against Zimmer's Vikings heading into the 2015 regular season finale. But with the NFC North title on the line at Lambeau Field, the Vikings won 20–13. Rodgers' 80.8 passer rating was his worst against the Vikings since 2008, his first year as a starter. "The thing with Zimmer's defense is he's going to definitely keep teams off-balance," Robison said. "There are so many disguise looks and so many ways we line up even with different fronts. It's all over the board." Or, as linebacker Chad Greenway put it, "It's like playing offense on defense. A lot of times, we make the offense have to adjust to what we're doing."

Zimmer built his coaching reputation on being a strong, no-nonsense teacher and a creative defensive strategist known for aggressive blitz packages that include his many Double A-gap looks. He won a Super Bowl with the Dallas Cowboys as a defensive backs coach and was later mentored by Hall of Famer Bill Parcells on a subsequent Cowboys team before moving on and eventually turning the Cincinnati Bengals from laughingstock to an elite defensive squad.

In 18 seasons before Zimmer's arrival in 2008, the Bengals had one top 10 ranking on defense. With Zimmer on board, they did it four times in his final five seasons in Cincinnati. "If you were to say, 'What are Zim's superpowers?' I would tell you his superpowers are finding flaws," then-Bengals defensive back Chris Crocker said in 2014. "He knows when something doesn't look right and he knows how to fix it."

# 100 The 2015 Season and Beyond

Eventually, air returns to the body of every Vikings fan who has felt the inevitable sucker punch that comes with being a Vikings fan. The pain and purple pessimism that flowed after Blair Walsh duck-hooked his 27-yard field goal with 22 seconds left in the 10–9 playoff loss to the Seattle Seahawks did subside in early 2016. It was replaced by the usual optimism for the following season, as was the case after four Super Bowl losses, "The Push-off," the 1998 NFC Championship Game, the 41–0 loss to the New York Giants in the 2000 NFC title game, and, well, you get the idea. "I'm proud of these guys," coach Mike Zimmer said. "They work hard and they never give up. We'll never know how far we could have gone. But we did a lot of things that a lot of people didn't think we could get done."

The Vikings won 11 games—four more than 2014. They ended Green Bay's four-year stranglehold on the NFC North with a 20–13 victory in a winner-take-all regular-season finale at Lambeau Field. For the first time since 2009, they celebrated a division title and hosted a playoff game.

It was a rocky start that began with the season-opening stinker at San Francisco against a 49ers team that would go 5–11. "Maybe we're just not ready for primetime yet," Zimmer said after the 20–3 loss. "In 17 ballgames here, that did not look like the football team that I know."

The Vikings would lose only four more times as Adrian Peterson won his third NFL rushing title, and Zimmer's rebuilt defense continued its upward surge to No. 5 in points allowed (18.9 per game). That was up from 11th the year before and last (30 per game) in 2013, the year before Zimmer arrived.

The Vikings won at Chicago for the first time since 2007 when Walsh kicked a 36-yard field goal as time expired. A week later, Walsh kicked a 40-yarder in overtime to beat the St. Louis Rams after Zimmer won the coin toss and deferred because of wind conditions, a concussed starting quarterback, and a well-founded belief in his defense. "I'd much rather have some big wins, but hey, a win is a win," Zimmer said. "The last three or four ballgames, this kind of shows what kind of team we are as far as how we are on offense, how we are defensively, and how we are on special teams. We're probably not going to go up and down the field like the 'Greatest Show on Turf.' This is how we're built to win right now."

The Vikings had two similar 23–20 losses on the road to the eventual Super Bowl-champion Denver Broncos in Week 4 and an 11–2 Arizona Cardinals team 10 weeks later. In both games the offensive line was beaten badly in the closing seconds with the Vikings driving near midfield. Both times, Teddy Bridgewater was sacked and fumbled the ball away.

However, the Vikings found inspiration in how they played in both games and bounced back admirably. They won five straight after losing to Denver and closed with three wins after losing to the Cardinals with a beat-up roster that was starting a franchise-record six rookies.

Overconfidence was a factor in at least one loss. The Vikings had won five straight when they faced the Packers at home on November 22. Zimmer had "Beat Green Bay!" T-shirts made and distributed on the Monday before. Players wore them proudly until the Packers came to town and snapped a three-game losing streak with a 30–13 win.

The Vikings led the league in fewest penalties (88) in 2015. But in the loss to the Packers, they would amass eight penalties for a season-high 110 yards. Left tackle Matt Kalil tackled a pass rusher on the first snap. Kick returner Cordarrelle Patterson topped that by head-butting kicker Mason Crosby later on. As the rematch neared, the Vikings pounded the Bears 38–17 and the New York Giants 49–17. All the while Zimmer was playing up the underdog role, once declaring, "We're still the guys from the low-rent district."

The nation watched as Zimmer's defense protected a 20–3 fourth-quarter lead to overtake Aaron Rodgers' penthouse suite in the division. A week later the defending NFC champion Seahawks returned to Minnesota for the third-coldest game—minus-6 with a wind chill of minus-25—in NFL history. As honorary captain for the NFC wild-card playoff game, 88-year-old Bud Grant kicked things off in style by walking to midfield in a short-sleeve shirt as the crowd roared. Unfortunately, after a sluggish offensive effort and a Peterson fumble to set up Seattle's winning field goal, Walsh couldn't close the deal in the waning seconds of the 10–9 loss.

A day after that, Zimmer already was focused on 2016. Making the team's offseason priority perfectly clear, he fired offensive line coach Jeff Davidson and put all of his linemen on notice that no one's job was safe. Asked why he didn't renew Davidson's contract, Zimmer didn't even attempt to sugarcoat his dissatisfaction with a unit that was mostly responsible for the team's 31st-ranked passing attack and Bridgewater facing pressure on a league-high 46.9 percent of his drops. "I didn't want to," Zimmer said.

Zimmer hired former Miami Dolphins head coach Tony Sparano as line coach. Sparano, who had been working as 49ers tight ends coach, brought a different scheme and a more fiery coaching style. Then, on the first day of free agency, the Vikings landed their top target, 49ers guard Alex Boone.

Perhaps Zimmer is the man to win that elusive Super Bowl, to take the franchise one step further than Bud Grant, another no-nonsense coach whose words and actions were delivered straight between the eyes. "I like Zimmer and I think he can do it," said Vikings Hall of Fame left guard Randall McDaniel. "It's going to happen at some point. The Vikings are going to win a Super Bowl. I just hope I'm around to see it."

# Acknowledgments

First of all, thanks to all the NFL players, ex-players, coaches, scouts, front-office executives, and owners who have taken the time to be interviewed for the many Vikings stories I've done over the past 13 years. Without your access and patience, many of these stories could never have been told. Thanks also to many of the families of these people, including one particularly special woman, Phyllis Tingelhoff, Mick's wife, whose help in 2015 was instrumental in assembling a story that hopefully was worthy of Mick's great career and long overdue enshrinement in the Pro Football Hall of Fame.

Another special thanks to another Hall of Famer, Randall McDaniel, who has shared many Vikings stories with me and agreed to do the foreword for this book. Other Hall of Famers, future Hall of Famers, and a notable should-be Hall of Famer named Jim Marshall have helped me understand the Vikings' rich heritage over the years. Cris Carter even invited me to spend "Cris Carter Day" with him and his family in Middletown, Ohio, three months before he was enshrined in Canton.

Thanks to Triumph Books for the opportunity to do this project, and to my editor, Jeff Fedotin, for being patient, extending a deadline or two and for sparking some ideas with his attentive editing.

With 100 chapters covering a franchise that began in 1961, I wasn't able to draw on direct knowledge and coverage for each chapter. Thanks to my employer, the *Minneapolis Star Tribune*, for having a fantastic filing system to help me refer to events that have been covered so well by the paper for decades.

# Sources

In addition to the many personal interviews conducted, the author gratefully acknowledges the following sources used in researching Vikings history for this book. A special nod goes to a must-read book for all Vikings fans who want to take the complete journey through their favorite team's history. In *Minnesota Vikings: The Complete Illustrated History*, Patrick Reusse, a *Star Tribune* columnist, gives readers all the information they need in his typically entertaining style.

### Books
Reusse, Patrick. *Minnesota Vikings: The Complete Illustrated History.* MVP Books. 2010.
Bruton, Jim. *Vikings 50: All-Time Greatest Players in Franchise History.* Triumph Books LLC. 2012.
Williamson, Bill. *Tales From the Minnesota Vikings Sideline.* Sports Publishing. 2012.

### Newspapers, Magazines, and Websites
*Minneapolis Star Tribune*
*Sports Illustrated*
*Green Bay Press-Gazette*
*The New York Times*
*The Washington Post*
*Sioux Falls Argus Leader*
Redskins.com
Yahoo! Sports
*The Willoughby (Ohio) News-Herald*
*Palestine (Texas) Herald-Press*

Adrian-Peterson.com
*Grand Forks Herald*
Vikings.com
*San Francisco Chronicle*
Associated Press
VikingUpdate.com
Packers.com
*Rocky Mountain News*